Under
restor

CRIME AND JUSTICE
Series editor: Mike Maguire
Cardiff University

Crime and Justice is a series of short introductory texts on central topics in criminology. The books in this series are written for students by internationally renowned authors. Each book tackles a key area within criminology, providing a concise and up-to-date overview of the principal concepts, theories, methods and findings relating to the area. Taken as a whole, the *Crime and Justice* series will cover all the core components of an undergraduate criminology course.

Understanding victims and restorative justice

James Dignan

Open University Press

Open University Press
McGraw-Hill Education
McGraw-Hill House
Shoppenhangers Road
Maidenhead
Berkshire
England
SL6 2QL

email: enquiries@openup.co.uk
world wide web: www.openup.co.uk

and Two Penn Plaza, New York, NY 10121–2289, USA

First published 2005

A catalogue record of this book is available from the British Library

ISBN 0 335 20979 3 (pb) 0 335 20980 7 (hb)

Library of Congress Cataloging-in-Publication Data
CIP data applied for

Typeset by RefineCatch Ltd, Bungay, Suffolk
Printed in the UK by Bell & Bain Ltd, Glasgow

Contents

Series editor's foreword

James Dignan's book is the twelfth in the successful *Crime and Justice* series published by Open University Press. The series is now established as a key resource in universities teaching criminology or criminal justice, especially in the UK but increasingly also overseas. The aim from the outset has been to give undergraduates and graduates both a solid grounding in the relevant area and a taste to explore it further. Although aimed primarily at students new to the field, and written as far as possible in plain language, the books are not oversimplified. On the contrary, the authors set out to 'stretch' readers and to encourage them to approach criminological knowledge and theory in a critical and questioning frame of mind.

James Dignan is a well-known and experienced writer in the criminal justice field, who combines expert knowledge with the ability to put over complex ideas in accessible language and a lively style. His book draws together in an original way ideas and arguments from two areas of criminology and criminal justice which have grown enormously in importance in recent years. The idea of basing responses to crime around the principle of 'restorative justice' has attracted huge levels of interest among criminologists and policy-makers around the world, especially in the wake of innovative contributions on the topic by the influential Australian writer, John Braithwaite. Dignan explores the key theoretical ideas behind restorative justice, and presents a wide range of empirical data illustrating how it has been used in practice, how it is perceived by victims and offenders, and the extent to which it is 'effective' in reducing reconviction (though this is not necessarily its main purpose). The second key set of ideas he explores is that arising from the somewhat older (but still growing) literature on 'victimology', the broad term often used to describe the study of victims, and of social and criminal justice responses to victimization. This includes questions about the relationships between victims and offenders, about the 'welfare' of victims (for example, what special services – if any – should they receive, over and above those open to victims of accident or illness?) and about their role in the criminal justice system (for example, to what extent should their views be taken into account by sentencers or in parole decisions?). Generally speaking, writers on restorative justice have paid rather less attention than one might have expected to academic writing on victimology, and while first and foremost a textbook to help students understand the debates in both areas, Dignan's book also provides an original, synthesizing contribution to both literatures.

Other books previously published in the *Crime and Justice* series – all of whose titles begin with the word 'Understanding' – have covered criminological theory (Sandra Walklate, penal theory (Barbara Hudson), crime data and statistics (Clive Coleman and Jenny Moynihan), youth and crime (Sheila Brown), crime prevention (Gordon Hughes), violent crime (Stephen Jones), community penalties (Peter Raynor and Maurice Vanstone), white collar crime (Hazel Croall), risk and crime (Hazel Kemshall), social control (Martin Innes) and psychology and crime (James McGuire). Two are already in second editions and other second editions are planned. Other new books in the pipeline include texts on prisons, policing, social attitudes to crime, criminological research methods, drugs and crime, race and crime, 'cybercrime' and political violence. All are topics which are either already widely taught or are growing in prominence in university degree courses on crime and criminal justice, and each book should make an ideal foundation text for a relevant module. As an aid to understanding, clear summaries are provided at regular intervals, and a glossary of key terms and concepts is a feature of every book. In addition, to help students expand their knowledge, recommendations for further reading are given at the end of each chapter.

Mike Maguire
August 2004

Acknowledgements

Many people have contributed – wittingly or unwittingly – to the production of this book: far too many to mention all of them individually. Special thanks are due, however, to colleagues (past and present) at the Sheffield University Centre for Criminological Research including Paul Wiles, Tony Bottoms, Mick Cavadino and Iain Crow. I am particularly indebted to the following team of colleagues, who are responsible for evaluating the Home Office funded evaluation of adult-based restorative justice initiatives, and whose discussions have proved enormously helpful at critical points in the writing of this book: Joanna Shapland, Anne Atkinson, Helen Atkinson, Becca Chapman, Emily Colledge, Marie Howes, Jenny Johnstone, Rachel Pennant, Gwen Robinson and Angela Sorsby.

Thanks are also due to colleagues in the wider academic community, particularly Andrew Ashworth, Adam Crawford, Tony Peters, Andrew Sanders, Dan Van Ness, Lode Walgrave and Richard Young. And also to a number of restorative justice practitioners, including in particular Stephanie Braithwaite (from Mediation and Reparation, Southampton), Chris Stevens (Crime Concern), Barbara Tudor (West Midlands Probation Service) and Adrian Wright (former director of the Kettering Adult Reparation Bureau).

I am especially grateful to Justin Vaughan for initially inviting me to write this book, to Miriam Selwyn and Mark Barrett (past and present members of the editorial team at the Open University Press/McGraw Hill), and also to series editor Mike Maguire, all of whom have provided constructive support and encouragement but, above all, endless reserves of patience. Special thanks also to Gwen Robinson and Kirsty Welsh for their helpful comments on the draft manuscript. Last, but not least, thanks are also due to several generations of MA students whose contributions to the course I teach on Restorative Justice, Mediation and Victimology have helped to shape the form and content of the book.

The final and biggest debt of gratitude is owed to Angela and Corinne, without whose love and support it would have been impossible to complete the book.

Introduction

Attempts to define restorative justice
An analytical framework
Structure of the book
Notes

This book focuses on two related sets of developments whose influence on criminological theory and the direction of criminal justice policymaking and practice in recent years has been unparalleled. The first development is associated with the emergence and gradual unfolding of a specifically victim-focused agenda over the last half century. The second relates to the more recent, but equally impressive, growth of a distinctive restorative justice agenda that has taken just a quarter of a century to leap from a position of virtual obscurity to one of increasing international influence.

Although these two sets of developments are clearly related, there have been surprisingly few attempts to consider the nature of this relationship, or to clearly differentiate between the various sets of initiatives that are associated with each of them. An obvious casualty of this neglect has been a lack of engagement on the part of most restorative justice advocates with many of the issues and concerns that have previously been raised by victimologists. They include some of the issues dealt with in chapter one, concerning our understanding of who victims are, how they come to be so defined and the extent to which victims and offenders form mutually exclusive categories.

There has also been a reluctance on the part of some restorative justice advocates to acknowledge the extent to which the 'regular' criminal justice system has been overhauled in recent years by a succession of victim-focused reforms, and its capacity for further reform in the future. Indeed there has been a tendency within much of the restorative justice literature to contrast the emerging restorative justice approach and the regular criminal justice system in highly dichotomous terms as being 'polar opposites' in almost every respect. Although this tendency is understandable when seeking to explain new concepts to people who are unfamiliar with them, it runs the risk of caricaturing the two positions, by exaggerating the differences – and at the same time playing down the similarities – between them.

One important aim of the book will therefore be to explore these two related sets of developments, and to take a fresh look at the theory and practice of restorative justice in the light of questions and insights that may be derived from this earlier victimological tradition. A second aim will be to assess the strengths and weaknesses of various restorative justice initiatives without making any presuppositions about the nature of the conventional criminal justice system.

Attempts to define restorative justice

Another casualty of the failure to elucidate the unfolding relationship between restorative justice and other victim-focused initiatives has been a degree of conceptual confusion with regard to the term 'restorative justice'[1] itself, which also extends to the principles and practices that it encompasses. While most people would accept that the term applies to practices such as victim–offender mediation, various forms of conferencing and circle sentencing, it has also been applied (by both supporters and detractors) to a variety of other practices. They include the provision of services by victim support organizations, the development of victim compensation schemes, the introduction of procedural reforms such as the use of victim impact statements and the extension of rights of audience to victims in criminal trials. The term has also been applied to a variety of court-imposed sanctions including community service, reparation and financial compensation orders imposed on offenders.

The scope for, and likelihood of, serious conceptual confusion with regard to the meaning of restorative justice is compounded by the fact that what is sometimes referred to as the 'restorative justice movement' is far from being monolithic. Just as, within the field of victimology, various tendencies and schools of thought have developed over the years so also, as we shall see, there are a number of actual or potential fault lines within restorative justice thinking. Some of these have generated tensions that are not always acknowledged, and may be difficult to resolve (Dignan, 2002a).

Against such a background, the task of defining restorative justice presents a seemingly intractable challenge since many attempts have been made in the past, none of which have proved to be universally acceptable. The most widely accepted definition[2] was formulated by an early advocate of restorative justice, Tony Marshall (1999: 5) in the following terms:

Restorative justice is a process whereby parties with a stake in a specific offence collectively resolve how to deal with the aftermath of that offence and its implications for the future.

Despite its widespread (though by no means universal) appeal, however, Marshall's formulation is of relatively limited value as an aid to conceptual clarification (see also Daly, 2002a: 58; Roche, 2001; Walgrave, 2000a: 418). First, it restricts the scope of restorative justice to the criminal justice arena and thereby overlooks the undeniable fact that restorative justice values and processes have also been applied in a variety of other contexts that may have little or nothing to do with the resolution of specific criminal offences. These other contexts include conflict in schools, decisions relating to child care and protection matters, and also neighbour and community disputes, none of which necessarily involve the resolution of specific criminal offences. Another context in which restorative justice values and practices have been applied relates to the resolution of intercommunal and group conflict. Such conflict frequently results in the commission of extremely serious offences including various crimes against humanity, some of which may be committed by agents and institutions of the state itself.[3] In some parts of the world restorative justice initiatives have been developed that seek to go beyond the resolution of the specific offences themselves and attempt to address the underlying conflict that gave rise to them.[4] Even though this book is itself mainly concerned with restorative justice issues within a criminal justice context, it is important to acknowledge at the outset that these developments do form part of a much broader constellation of restorative justice policies and practices.

A second weakness with Marshall's definition is that it characterizes restorative justice as a particular type of *process*, and even though this is flexible enough to accommodate variants such as mediation, different forms of conferencing and circle sentencing, it contains no explicit reference to *outcomes*. The need to take account of outcomes as well as processes is important for two main reasons. First, some restorative justice processes often result in negotiated outcomes that are not only purely symbolic, or even simply 'reparative', but may also include the imposition of additional obligations for offenders. Some such outcomes may be every bit as onerous – and indeed punitive – as the sentencing outcomes that may be imposed at the end of a conventional criminal trial. As such, they raise well-founded concerns relating both to the fairness of restorative justice processes themselves and also the outcomes to which they give rise (see Roche, 2001: 344; Dignan 2003). At the very least, they highlight the need for adequate safeguards for both offenders and victims. They also underline the need for restorative justice advocates to acknowledge that concerns raised by sceptics with regard to issues such as proportionality and fairness are well founded and do need to be addressed. To argue that such concerns can simply be sidestepped because they are not key values of restorative justice as some have suggested (McEvoy et al, 2002: 469) is to miss this important point.

Second, the absence of any reference to outcomes in Marshall's definition is also problematic in the eyes of critics (e.g. Bazemore and Walgrave, 1999: 48; Dignan, 2002a: 175), who point out that there are always likely to be cases for which restorative justice processes may not be applicable or appropriate.[5] In cases such as these, it may be felt preferable, if only in the interests of consistency, to adapt the sentencing powers of the courts so that, as far as possible, they also seek to secure outcomes that attempt to repair the harm that has been caused by the offence; and to do so in a way that as far as possible is consistent with restorative justice goals and values. Otherwise there is a danger of creating a twin-track system that applies two completely different sets of standards and principles depending on whether a case is referred to some form of restorative justice process or is dealt with in a more conventional manner. Thus, the distinction between restorative justice processes and restorative or reparative outcomes is an important one and will feature prominently throughout this book.

A third problematic feature with Marshall's definition of restorative justice is that opinions may differ as to the identity of the parties who have a stake in a specific offence. Who are these 'stakeholders'? Here again there are tensions within the restorative justice movement.[6] For one strand – the so-called 'civilian tendency'[7] – only the parties who are most directly affected by an offence – offenders and victims – are counted as stakeholders (see also Dignan, 2002a: 176). Others within the civilian camp are prepared to extend the term to include those who may have been less directly affected by the offence, such as the families and friends of either offenders or victims: the so-called 'offence community'. Some would extend it even further to include all those who are 'concerned' in some way about the offence. This broader 'community of interest' (Young and Morris, 1998: 10) could include those who are concerned for the well-being of either the victim or the offender, and others who might be concerned about the offence and its consequences, or who might be able to contribute towards its resolution. Another strand within the restorative justice movement – the so-called communitarian tendency – would include representatives of the wider community as stakeholders, whether or not they had been affected by the offence or had any direct concerns relating to it. But even this does not exhaust the range of possibilities since the state itself, or rather its authorized agents and institutions comprising the criminal justice system, furnishes another group of potential stakeholders. Once again there are differences of opinion among restorative justice advocates: first, with regard to the relationship between restorative justice processes and conventional criminal justice processes; second, concerning the role – if any – that criminal justice agencies and officials should play within the former.

A fourth problematic feature with Marshall's definition is that it not only fails to specify which of these various potential stakeholders should be invited or expected to participate in the restorative justice process, but is also silent with regard to the level or type of participation that might be required in order for it to 'count' as restorative justice. How important is it, for example, for victims to take part in such processes? And is there a minimum acceptable participation rate on the part of victims? Are there any restrictions on the type or degree of victim participation? Does it have to involve a 'face-to-face' encounter? Or are other forms of dialogue acceptable, by enabling views, questions or answers to be communicated indirectly, for example? Is it important for the victim's actual views to be communicated to the offender, or is it acceptable for 'surrogate' victims[8] to take their place, or for the offender to be required to take part in generalized 'victim awareness' exercises? Do letters of apology that are written by the offender count as a form of communication and, if so, do they still count if they are not actually requested, sent to and received by the victim?

Finally, Marshall's definition says nothing about the aim of the process. Is it an end in itself, irrespective of any outcome, as some restorative justice advocates would contend; or is it a means to some other end? Even those advocates who believe that restorative justice processes may be intrinsically beneficial because of their supposed 'cathartic' potential are likely to have in mind some implicit 'ends', though they might disagree over what these ends consist of. For some they may relate to the satisfaction of the parties themselves. For others they may relate to the potentially 'transformative' effects that the process might have, either with regard to the attitudes or behaviour of participants or, possibly, on wider social processes such as the rejuvenation of 'communities' or the operation of the criminal justice system.

An analytical framework

The difficulties that have been identified are not unique to Marshall's definition.[9] Indeed, it is hard to imagine how the concept of restorative justice could be redefined in a non-problematic and universally acceptable way. And yet there is a clear need for conceptual clarification, particularly when seeking to explore the relationship between restorative justice approaches and other victim-focused approaches that arguably do not form part of this tradition, and some of which may be fundamentally incompatible with restorative justice values. Rather than attempting to define the term restorative justice, therefore, it may be more helpful to think in terms of an analytical framework.[10] Such a framework will need to be capable of accommodating the full range of philosophical, practical, procedural and political differences within the restorative justice movement while still enabling distinctions to be drawn between approaches that could be said to form part of a coherent restorative justice tradition and other victim-focused approaches that arguably do not.

Table I.1 sets out an analytical framework of this kind in the form of a typology of victim-focused approaches to policymaking.[11] Readers

Table 1.1 Typology of victim-focused reforms

Name of model variants	Welfare model	Criminal justice model	Restorative justice models			
			Victim–offender mediation	Family group conferencing	Police-led conferencing	Reparation board
Goals	Help for victims	Punishment of offender 'Right of acknowledgement' for victims	Accountability Reparation Empowerment of victims/offenders Reconciliation	Accountability Reparation Empowerment of 'offence community'	Accountability Reparation Empowerment of 'community of interest' Reintegrative shaming	Accountability for offenders Reparation for victims or community Community empowerment
Focus	Exclusively victim focused	Mostly offender orientated Some concessions for victims	Direct victims and offenders only	'Offence community' or 'community of care'	Community representation	Offender, victim and also the wider community
Process	Administrative (CICA) Personal counselling (VS)	Adversarial trial procedure	Face-to-face or indirect mediation (optional)	Family group conferencing (court oversight)	Restorative cautioning or conferencing Scripted format	Citizen panel or reparation board
Institutional framework	CICA Victim Support Detached from CJS	Police, public prosecutor and court acting in 'public interest'	Statutory or voluntary agency Stand-alone in UK and USA Semi-integrated in Europe	Integrated into juvenile justice system in NZ and parts of Australia Stand-alone elsewhere	Partially integrated into pre-trial procedure at police force level in parts of USA, UK and Canberra	Partially integrated into criminal justice system in England and Wales, Vermont, etc.

Name of model variants	Welfare model	Criminal justice model	Restorative justice models			
			Victim–offender mediation	Family group conferencing	Police-led conferencing	Reparation board
Victim definition	Restricted to victims of violent crime	Stereotypical victim Direct victim only	Restricted to direct victim and offender	Direct and indirect victims	'Multiple victim perspective'	Victim and supporters or representatives
Victim measures	State-funded compensation Practical/emotional help General welfare	VIS Victim allocution Compensation from offender Community service	Apology Compensation Reparation	Apology Compensation Reparation	Apology Compensation Reparation	Apology Compensation Reparation
Role of victim	Supplicant or claimant Client in need	Witness if needed Provision of information	Dialogue with offender or 'shuttle diplomacy'	Scope for active participation where present Veto but no say over outcome	Scope for active participation where present including some say over outcome	May be restricted to 'having a say' but often no input into outcome

may find it helpful to refer back to this framework when reading about the different types of victim-focused initiatives that are dealt with in later chapters. One aim of the typology is to explicate the philosophical foundations of the various recent victim-based reforms. Another aim is to clarify the operational context in which various sets of victim-focused initiatives – including restorative justice measures – have developed, and also to differentiate between them so that they are not confused with one another.

As with all typologies, however, this one is deliberately framed in somewhat abstract terms in order to highlight significant variations between three distinct sets of victim-oriented initiatives that are derived from and associated with three very different philosophical and policy-oriented traditions: first, those associated with a 'welfare' approach (featured in Chapter 2); second, those associated with a more conventional 'criminal justice' approach (dealt with in Chapter 3); third, those associated with a 'restorative justice' approach. This third approach, which encompasses a number of distinct variants,[12] is introduced in Chapter 4 and then assessed in more detail in Chapters 5 and 6. The reason for adopting this typology is purely as an aid to conceptual clarification, and in order to draw attention to important differences between these three main sets of victim-focused initiatives.

These differences relate to their aspirations (*goals*) and orientation (*focus*), the way they operate (*process*) and also their practical consequences for, and impact upon, victims. With regard to their operational context, the framework also sets out the institutional setting within which each set of measures operates, one important aspect of which includes its relationship, if any, to the conventional criminal justice system. The framework also seeks to encapsulate the way victims are defined within that particular approach, the victim-focused measures with which it is associated and also the role that is allocated to the victim. However, again as with all typologies, it is important to remember that it *is* based on a simplification of a very complex set of initiatives and that, in reality, these are rarely as simple, straightforward or logical as they are portrayed here for the purposes of explanation and analysis.[13]

The term 'restorative justice' has come to be applied to a variety of practices that share three principal features. One relates to the goal of putting right the harm that is caused by an offence. The second relates to a balanced focus on the offender's personal accountability to those who may have been harmed or affected by an offence – which could include individual victims and, possibly, the wider community – and on the latter's entitlement to some form of reparative redress. The third relates to an inclusive and non-coercive decision-making process that encourages participation by key participants in determining how an offence should be dealt with (see also Van Ness, 1996: 23). These three elements – *goals*, *focus* and *process* – form the basis of the analytical framework that I will be using to map out the relationship between restorative justice and other victim-focused approaches.

This three-dimensional analytical framework suggests that the term 'restorative justice' should be restricted solely to those initiatives that combine all three elements. Because restorative justice approaches vary considerably in the way the three elements are combined, however, it may be more helpful to think in terms of a continuum of approaches. This allows for the fact that – at one end of the restorative justice spectrum – all three elements may be defined rather narrowly, as is the case with most victim–offender mediation programmes. Here, the goal may be limited to repairing (whether materially or symbolically) the specific harm that has been caused by an offence; the focus may be restricted to the offender's accountability towards the immediate victim and the latter's entitlement to redress; and they are likely to be the only parties who are invited to participate in the decision-making process. At the other end of the restorative justice spectrum all three elements may be given a broader interpretation, as is the case with many forms of 'conferencing'. Here, the goals may extend beyond the repair of any specific harm that may have experienced by the victim and could also include the reintegration of offenders back into the community and, possibly, the re-empowerment of communities themselves. The focus is also likely to extend beyond the parties who are directly (or even indirectly) affected by an offence, and this may be reflected in the range of people who are invited to participate in the process. With some forms of conferencing this might also include not only the parties and their 'supporters' but also representatives from the wider community who may have an interest in the outcome. With some forms of restorative justice processes, such as circle sentencing or healing circles (dealt with in Chapter 4), the focus may be wider still. Here, it often encompasses the whole community, or at least very significant sections of it, extending far beyond those who may have been directly affected by the offence itself.

Another advantage to be gained by adopting an analytical framework of this kind is that it might help to resolve some of the doubts referred to earlier as to whether particular kinds of interventions should 'count' as restorative justice interventions or not.[14] Thus, it could be argued that 'participation' in a restorative justice process might take a number of different forms, some of which are likely to be more 'fully restorative' than others. It would thus include both face-to-face and indirect mediation (sometimes referred to as shuttle mediation). Other more limited forms of participation such as the mere 'exchange of information' between the parties – even if the exchange does not contribute materially to the decision-making process that determines the outcome of the offence – might also be included provided they are consulted and agree to this. However, it has to be conceded that this does require a more flexible interpretation of what is meant by 'a decision-making process'. Similar considerations would apply to the use of 'surrogate victims'. Although such encounters are likely to prove 'less restorative' for the actual victim, the latter might agree to 'their' offender meeting a surrogate victim, who could explain how they were affected, particularly if the actual victim does not wish to participate directly.[15] Finally, some interventions do not involve any form of dialogue, exchange of information or even consultation between parties. They include general victim awareness sessions for offenders and also letters of apology that offenders may be asked to write even though there is no intention of sending them to the victim (who may or may not even have been consulted on the matter). Such interventions are likely to be minimally restorative at best, and then only with regard to one of the parties.

The reason why it is important to be able to elucidate the concept of restorative justice at the outset in this way is that it would otherwise be impossible to differentiate between it and the extensive array of other recent victim-focused measures. An ability to distinguish between different types of victim-focused approaches is also important when assessing the extent to which they may each be capable of addressing those concerns that have been raised in the victimological literature. Even when the focus shifts from conceptual analysis and empirical evaluation to policy prescription, it is equally important to be able to specify how compatible or incompatible these different approaches might be; for example, when formulating proposals that will best meet the needs of victims while also taking into account the interests of offenders and the wider society.

Structure of the book

Chapter 1 focuses on what we know about victims and the process of victimization, including its effects on victims. It also looks at the different ways in which victims might respond to this process, and briefly reviews some of the main concerns that have been addressed within the victimological literature. An important consideration throughout the chapter is to identify issues that may prove challenging for victim-oriented approaches in general.

Chapter 2 switches the focus to victim-oriented policymaking and begins by examining two *welfare-based* measures that operate for the most part alongside and independently of the criminal justice system. The first concerns the provision of state-funded compensation for crime victims who are injured in the course of a criminal offence; the second consists of victim assistance schemes. Victim-focused responses such as these share the same 'harm redressing' goal as restorative justice and, to that extent, are *compatible with* restorative justice ideals, though they lack the latter's focus on the offender's personal accountability to those who have been harmed. Nor do they involve an inclusive decision-making process, which is why they are depicted in Table I.1 as constituting a separate 'welfare model'.

Chapter 3 examines some of the main victim-oriented reforms that have been adopted within the *conventional criminal justice system*. They include measures that are intended to minimize the impact of secondary victimization; to enhance the ability of victims to participate in the process; or to provide redress in the form of financial compensation for victims. With regard to the various victim participation measures that have been adopted within common law jurisdictions they generally provide at best a one-way channel for communication between victims and criminal justice decision-makers including sentencers, but lack the possibility of facilitating dialogue *between* the principal parties. Thus, they fail to satisfy the principle of inclusive participation and make little attempt to maintain a 'balanced focus', both of which are hallmarks of a restorative justice approach.

In Chapter 4 the focus switches from welfare-based and criminal justice measures to *restorative justice approaches* and their potential relevance for victims. Various restorative justice critiques of the criminal justice system are identified and related to different possible 'reform agendas' together with their implications for victims. Recent policy initiatives relating to the development of restorative justice are identified and their impact on victims is assessed. Chapter 5 assesses the extent to which restorative justice processes may be capable of meeting the needs of victims in the light of available empirical evidence from a variety of jurisdictions. Finally, Chapter 6 assesses restorative justice from a more critical victim-focused perspective that is informed by the issues raised in Chapter 1. It assesses the limits of restorative justice, examines the extent to which restorative justice may be capable of addressing some of the concerns raised by the broader victimological literature and appraises its claim to strike an appropriate balance between the interests of various sets of stakeholders.

Notes

1 Albert Eglash (1977) is usually credited as the original progenitor of the term, though extensive usage since then has extended its meaning considerably beyond the notion of mere 'restitution' that lay at the heart of Eglash's initial formulation.

2 It has also been adopted by the British government (see Goggins, 2004: 10).

3 See, for example, Ingram and Harkin (2004), which contains evidence relating to allegations of complicity and collusion on the part of British security services in scores of murders in Northern Ireland that were carried out by loyalist paramilitaries against their political opponents.

4 The South African Truth and Reconciliation Commission (1998) is the best known but by no means the only example of such initiatives (see also Huyse 1998).

5 Bazemore and Walgrave favour the adoption of what they call a 'maximalist' approach, whereby the term restorative justice is used to cover 'every action that is primarily oriented towards doing justice by repairing the harm that has been caused by crime' (Bazemore and Walgrave, 1999: 48). The problem with

this formulation, however, is that it is too all-encompassing, since it embraces such diverse measures as welfare-oriented, state-funded compensation initiatives and victim support schemes together with various criminal justice initiatives in addition to those covered by Marshall's more restrictive definition.

6 These tensions are discussed more fully in Chapter 4.

7 The category would include, for example, Cantor (1976) and Wright (1991).

8 'Surrogate' victims in this context are those who have been victimized by an offender other than the one with whom they participate in a restorative justice process.

9 See, for example, Roche (2001), who seeks to supplement Marshall's process definition by the inclusion of additional restorative values in pursuit of a multidimensional definition.

10 A different form of analytical framework has been proposed by Paul McCold (2000: 401), who has devised a Venn diagram to differentiate between various different sets of ostensibly restorative practices on the basis of the scope they provide for participation by the three principal sets of direct stakeholders: victim, offender and community.

11 The typology is a somewhat modified version of one that originally appeared in Dignan and Cavadino (1996).

12 The typology is not exhaustive, and omits one additional restorative justice approach – circle sentencing – that is described in Chapters 4 and 5. It does so partly on the grounds of simplicity and lack of space, but also because the latter approach has so far mainly been associated with aboriginal communities in Canada.

13 As will become apparent in Chapter 4, which introduces a range of court-based restitutive and reparative measures that combine certain elements of a restorative justice approach within a conventional criminal justice context.

14 In practice it has to be acknowledged that the application of such a framework will not always be straightforward. For example, some forms of conferencing incorporate an 'inclusive' decision-making process that allows for participation by a variety of stakeholders even though victims may not always (and in some instances may not frequently) be involved. As we shall see, it cannot simply be assumed that all forms of restorative justice are necessarily 'victim oriented' in practice even though in principle they appear to incorporate the three main features that are associated with such an approach.

15 The process would be less restorative still, from the victim's perspective, if such an encounter went ahead without the consent of the victim or without the victim even being asked, though there could still be restorative benefits for the offender and, conceivably, for the surrogate victim.

Victims, victimization and victimology

Who or what are victims, and what do we know about them? Such questions are disarmingly and misleadingly simple, appearing as they do to invite a straightforward factual response. In reality, however, questions relating to the concept and identity of victims are highly problematic, often controversial and generally call for highly nuanced answers. It is important to stress this at the outset because our attitudes towards victims and how they should be dealt with are likely to be shaped by the assumptions we make about them, which may not always be well founded. This applies just as much to those who advocate restorative justice approaches as the most appropriate way of dealing with victims as it does to those who are responsible for formulating other aspects of criminal justice policy, or indeed to criminal justice practitioners, those working in the media or the public at large.

We may start by observing that, contrary to contemporary popular perceptions, the apparently inextricable connection in the public mind between 'victims' and 'crime' is a relatively recent phenomenon. Formerly, the term 'victim' was as likely to be associated with general misfortune as it was with crime. This point is reinforced by the *New Shorter Oxford English Dictionary*, whose definition starts by referring to 'a person killed or tortured by another', but then continues: 'a person subjected to cruelty, oppression, or other harsh, or unfair treatment, or suffering death, injury, ruin, etc., as a result of an event, circumstance or oppressive or adverse impersonal agency'.

Thus, when post-war social policymakers began to lay the foundations of the welfare state, the 'victims of misfortune' for whom they sought to make provision were those oppressed by the five 'giant evils of society' – want, disease, ignorance, squalor and idleness – but not crime[1] (Mawby and Gill, 1987: 38). During the early post-war period, crime victims were for the most part invisible, not only to public policymakers[2] but also to criminal justice agencies and practitioners, the media, the general public and indeed to most criminologists. Several decades were to elapse before crime victims were recognized as a distinct social category in their own right, and the first co-ordinated responses were formulated to address their concerns also.

Factors contributing to the increase in victim 'visibility'

The much higher public profile that is currently accorded to victims is the result of a lengthy process to which various factors have contributed. First, and somewhat ironically, the interests of victims were initially championed by penal reformers who are usually better known for their campaigns on behalf of offenders. The most notable example is Margery Fry (1951, 1959), who campaigned tirelessly to promote the idea of victim compensation as something to which they should be entitled both from the state and also, by way of reparation, from their offender (Jones, 1966). Although their motives may not have been entirely disinterested – since the provision of additional assistance to victims was seen as the key to reforming the penal system for the benefit of offenders[3] (Priestly, 1974) – their impact was nevertheless profound. At the penal policy level they helped to shape some of the first victim-focused reforms of the criminal justice system. But also at an ideological level, their arguments that the law should not just 'take it out of the offender' but ought rather to 'do justice to the offended' (Fry, 1951: 125) helped to pave the way for a later generation of restorative justice advocates. For they were among the first to argue for a reconceptualization of crime, suggesting that we should view it not (simply) as a 'violation of the legal order' but (also) as a 'violation of the rights of the individual victim'.

A second important and much more obvious factor in the process of increasing the visibility of victims relates to the role of the media and is exemplified by the continuing prominence given to the families of murder victims in such notorious cases as the 'Moors Murders' during the 1960s. The convictions of Ian Brady and Myra Hindley in May 1966 for a series of gruesome child murders that were committed in the early 1960s coincided with the dawn of the television age. Both the original convictions and the further confessions that followed in 1987 resulted in intense media

USE TO LINK WITH MEDIA

.posure not only for the killers themselves but also the families of their victims. In subsequent high profile murder cases the media have again not only continued to ensure the much greater visibility of victims but have also frequently accorded to victims' families a prominent voice in public debates about the way 'their' offenders should be dealt with.[4] Indeed, in some cases, they have provided them with a public platform from which to campaign for wider criminal justice reforms.[5]

A third factor contributing to the higher public profile that is now accorded to victims in general was a growing sensitization during the 1960s and 1970s towards the existence and needs of particular groups of 'vulnerable' victims: notably women who experienced domestic violence at the hands of abusive partners; women who had been sexually assaulted or raped; and children who were the victims of incest or other forms of abuse. The women's movement, comprising political and practical activists who were inspired and often radicalized by feminist ideals, played a major role in this process. Campaigning activists responded by not only setting up support networks such as the Women's Refuge Movement[6] and 'Rape Crisis Centres',[7] but also by drawing attention to the manifest inadequacies of the criminal justice system in dealing with such offences. Initiatives such as these helped to fuel broader concerns about the way victims in general are dealt with,[8] and these now form part of the agenda of the so-called 'victims' movement', though the aptness of this term is belied by its ideological diversity, as we shall see in Chapter 2.

A fourth factor contributing towards the higher public profile for victims of crime in recent years relates to the spate of well-publicized incidents both at home and abroad involving serious acts of politically inspired criminal violence. They include acts of terrorism that are directed against innocent civilians, political assassinations, violent outbursts resulting from ethnic or intercommunal tensions and even, on occasion, violent acts carried out by state agencies. At a more mundane but equally significant level – not least because its effects have had a more immediate personal impact – the period between the early 1950s and mid-1990s witnessed a dramatic escalation in the level of recorded crime in most modern industrial countries.[9] Both sets of phenomena have received extensive media coverage, much of which has focused on their impact on victims.

The fifth factor relates to the introduction and increasingly widespread use of victim surveys on the part of both central and local government agencies. The first such survey was conducted on behalf of the American President's Crime Commission in 1967, which was established in the wake of serious urban rioting in over 150 US cities earlier in the year (Ennis, 1967; President's Commission on Law Enforcement and the Administration of Justice, 1967). The motive for conducting the survey was partly in response to concerns about the impact of the increasing level of crime on ordinary Americans. But it was also prompted in part[10] by a desire to devise more accurate ways of measuring crime that might avoid some of the known defects associated with traditional methods based on police records. This ulterior motive was reflected in the widespread use of the term *crime survey*, both initially in the United States,[11] and also in the many other jurisdictions that have subsequently adopted the same technique. They include Canada (since 1981), England and Wales (since 1982), Scotland (since 1983), Australia, the Netherlands and Switzerland. In addition to these national crime surveys, a series of international crime victim surveys has also been conducted,[12] which provides a range of comparable data relating to victims and victimization in different countries.

The sixth and final factor that may have contributed, albeit marginally, to the much higher public profile that is now accorded to crime victims relates to the often belated and sometimes grudging response made by academic criminologists to these various phenomena. Much early post-war criminology could be described without exaggeration as comprising a victim-free zone, though some feminist criminologists of the 1970s and early 1980s[13] deserve an honourable mention for bucking the trend (Rock, 2002a: 3). However, even the ground-breaking furrows they ploughed were prompted by the work of other feminist political activists. For other radical criminologists (for example, Lea and Young, 1984) it took the incontrovertible data provided by the first British Crime Survey (BCS) to drive home the message that much crime impacts most heavily on the poorest and least privileged urban sectors of the community. Or, as Downes (1983) had rather more pithily put it, much crime operates as a 'regressive tax on the poor'.[14] More recently, the growing prominence accorded to victims has not only been acknowledged by growing numbers of academic criminologists but, as we shall see, has helped to carve out a new agenda for the discipline. Some police studies, for example, have engendered a much more realistic – and modest – appreciation of the extent to which the police depend upon victims' readiness to report crime and provide relevant information rather than their own unaided powers of detection (see Reiss, 1970; Shapland and Vagg, 1988). Others (for example, Shapland and Vagg, 1988: 136ff; Bucke, 1995; Sims and Myhill, 2000) have documented widespread dissatisfaction on the part of victims at the quality of service they receive from the police and other criminal justice agencies, which is further compounded by declining detection rates. Still others, as we shall see, have supplemented the information imparted by victimization surveys by undertaking more detailed investigations of the impact of crime on different categories of victims (for example, Maguire, 1980 on the victims of burglary and Morgan and Zedner, 1992 on child victims).

Despite the increased prominence that is now accorded to victims, there are still many unanswered questions, for example; relating to:

- the identity of victims and their attributes
- the way they are affected by crime and the way they respond to it
- the way they are represented in academic criminological discourse
- the extent to which they are acknowledged and provided for by criminal justice policymakers.

The first three sets of issues are addressed in the rest of this chapter; the final set of issues is addressed in subsequent chapters.

Victims: identities and attributes

The most obvious category of victims encompasses those who have been personally affected by 'conventional crimes', which are the kind of predatory offences involving assaults or property loss or damage that are most likely to be recorded by the police. What we 'know' about even these victims is both contingent and contested, however, depending as it does on the type of discourse – academic, administrative, legal, media, political – from which it is derived, the purpose for which has been compiled and the methodology on which it is based.

One helpful starting point in exploring 'what we know' about the identity and attributes of victims is Nils Christie's (1986) celebrated stereotype of 'the ideal victim'. Christie perceptively identified six attributes that – at the level of social policy – are most likely to result in the conferring of complete, legitimate and unambiguous victim status on someone who has had a crime committed against them. Paraphrasing Christie, the six attributes are:

1 The victim is weak in relation to the offender – the 'ideal victim' is likely to be either female, sick, very old or very young (or a combination of these).
2 The victim is, if not acting virtuously, then at least going about their legitimate, ordinary everyday business.
3 The victim is blameless for what happened.
4 The victim is unrelated to and does not know the 'stranger' who has committed the offence (which also implies that the offender is a person rather than a corporation; and that the offence is a single 'one-off' incident).
5 The offender is unambiguously big and bad.
6 The victim has the right combination of power, influence or sympathy to successfully elicit victim status without threatening (and thus risking opposition from) strong countervailing vested interests.

It seems probable that assumptions based on this stereotypical image of the 'ideal victim' may help to generate criteria by which those in the media assess the 'newsworthiness' of specific crime stories.[15] Such images may also be invoked, consciously or unconsciously, by 'moral entrepreneurs',[16] single issue campaigners and also politicians when seeking to promote the interests of victims or influence the way their offenders are dealt with. It is possible (though difficult to prove) that they may influence the specific content of reforms that are devised by social and criminal justice policymakers. An interesting though, as yet, largely unexplored question,[17] is whether such assumptions derived from Christie's image of the 'ideal victim' may also have influenced restorative justice theorists, advocates and practitioners. This is an issue to which we will return in the final chapter of the book.

Idealized 'images' and empirical 'realities'

Meanwhile, another obvious question concerns the extent to which Christie's stereotypical 'ideal victim' image is confirmed or confounded by empirical data, and the possibly contrasting light that these may shed on the 'actual' identity of victims and their attributes. Most of the demographic information relating to victims is derived from victim surveys, and therefore needs to be treated with considerable caution. This is partly, as we have seen, because despite their name they are largely compiled for administrative purposes; to supplement and improve the accuracy of the existing criminal justice database for example. They also suffer from methodological shortcomings since they omit significant populations at risk of victimization.[18] The British Crime Survey,[19] which is typical, for instance, concentrates mainly on certain types of conventional crime, particularly the so-called 'household' offences such as assaults, burglary or vehicle theft, but excludes many others. So-called 'victimless' offences (such as motoring and many regulatory offences) and those in which victims are complicit (such as prostitution and those involving drug or alcohol abuse) are excluded. So are newer types of crime (including those involving fraud or use of the internet), and even other forms of personal crime such as stalking and sexual abuse[20] (Kershaw et al., 2001: i, 3). Moreover, even with regard to the limited range of offences that it does cover, certain whole categories of victims are missing from the BCS. They include victims under the age of 16,[21] victims of whatever age who live in institutions[22] or who have no home[23] and non-personal victims including commercial and public sector enterprises and establishments.[24]

These are all significant omissions but, with these important caveats in mind, such victim surveys can nevertheless shed some useful light on the susceptibility of different groups of personal victims to particular types of crime. The pattern they illuminate contrasts sharply in several important respects with Christie's 'ideal victim' stereotype. Thus, with regard to violent crime, men are twice as likely to be victimized as women,[25] and those most at risk are young men aged 16 to 24 (Simmons and Dodd, 2003: 84). Men are also the victims of 83 per cent of assaults by strangers, and of 59 per cent of muggings, though women are the victims in 73 per cent of assaults involving domestic violence: statistics that graphically illustrate the gendered nature of much personal violence.[26] Conversely, the extremely elderly of both sexes are among the least likely to be involved in violent assaults of any kind, notwithstanding the fact that they may approximate much more closely to the 'ideal victim' stereotype on the statistically rare occasions on which this does happen.

Victim surveys also reveal that certain individuals and groups run a disproportionately high risk of being victimized compared with others. For example, it is known that people living in certain kinds of neighbour-hoods[27] are far more likely to be victimized than those living elsewhere. In the case of violent offences, the level of victimization reported by those living in council estates that are characterized by multi-ethnic occupation and low income levels is more than three times the level reported by those living in affluent suburban, rural or retirement areas. In the case of burgl-aries, the rate of victimization reported by those living in areas of council housing experiencing greatest hardship is nearly seven times as high as it is for those living in affluent rural communities. In general, it may be said that victims are likely to live in the same kind of impoverished communities as offenders are likely to be found in. To the extent that Christie's 'ideal victim' stereotype implies that victims and offenders form entirely separate categories, inhabiting completely different geographical and social milieux, therefore, it is again at odds with the 'real world', at least insofar as this is accurately captured by victim survey data.

Moreover, it is also known that the burden of victimization falls unevenly on individuals even within those populations that are known to be most at risk (Genn, 1988; Trickett et al., 1995; van Dijk, 2000). Thus, while the overall 'victimization rate' for adults living in private house-holds in respect of conventional personal crimes was 26.8 per cent in 2000,[28] a significant proportion of this subset was repeatedly victimized (Kershaw et al., 2001: 21, Table A2.9). Indeed, approximately one in seven adults who had been the victim of at least one violent offence during the previous 12 months reported three or more such incidents (rising to one in four of those whose victimization involved acts of domestic violence); and one in ten who had been the victim of a burglary reported three or more such incidents. Even so, there are strong grounds for believing that the incidence of 'multiple victimization' is likely to be significantly *under-reported* in victim surveys (Genn, 1988: 90). In part this is because victim surveys tend to adopt a rigid 'counting' frame of reference, which requires respondents to be able to specify fairly precisely when each incident occurred, and partly because an arbitrary upper limit is generally imposed on the number of incidents that any one victim will be deemed to have suffered. This approach causes problems in the case of those victims for whom victimization is not so much a series of discrete and relatively infrequent events, but is more of a process, or even a way of life. This methodological weakness is confirmed by other studies which have shown not only that such 'chronic' victims do exist, but that they also tend to be concentrated – in both Britain and America – in poor, run-down residential districts (Sparks et al., 1977; Skogan, 1981; Hough, 1986). Once again, victims' experiences in the 'real world', where a sig-nificant minority are liable to be repeatedly victimized by those who live alongside or even with them is markedly at odds with the pervasive 'ideal victim' stereotype.

Furthermore, there is also evidence to suggest that not only are victims and offenders drawn from the same populations, but they may sometimes form overlapping categories (see e.g. Fattah, 1994; Peelo et al., 1992). In the case of violent offences it is known, for example, that both men and women who themselves admit to having committed violent offences or being aggressive in the recent past are very much more likely to be victimized in this way than those who have never offended (Hough, 1986: 126; Pedersen, 2001). As Hough (1986: 126) laconically remarks, this may 'reflect the fact that some people who start fights lose them, ending up as "victims" '. It is also known that violence-related victimization patterns are to some extent related to lifestyles, including the frequency of visits to pubs and clubs and, presumably therefore, the consumption of alcohol. This also invokes a victim image that contrasts sharply with Christie's ideal type. In reality it seems that victims of violence are often young men who hang around bars and become involved in altercations – in respect of which they may not be entirely blameless – with other young men, with whom they may already be acquainted. In many such instances, it may be more or less fortuitous who is labelled 'the victim' and who 'the offender' assuming the incident comes to the attention of the authorities.

A recent study in Sheffield has shown that a similar blurring of categories may also be found with regard to a wide range of recorded property offences,[29] in respect of which prevalence rates were statistically significantly higher for offender households than they were for non-offender households (Bottoms and Costello, 2001). Yet again such findings are at odds with the stereotypical 'ideal victim' image, which is predicated on an empirically false assumption that victims and offenders are invariably polar opposites of one another in almost every respect. To the extent that much legal, media and political discourse represents vulnerable and innocent victims as the very antithesis of dangerous and wicked offenders, it is failing to engage with a far less predictable world in which much crime is committed in the context of highly complex social interactions between victims, offenders and possibly others. Real victims and offenders – like most human beings – rarely conform to such stereotypes.

Expanding the category of victims

So far we have been concentrating on personal victims who have been directly affected by 'conventional' predatory crimes that have been committed by personal offenders, since they are the ones who are most likely to be fully and unambiguously identified and acknowledged as victims. The range of people who are affected even by these crimes often extends beyond those who are directly harmed by them, however, which raises a further set of questions about the 'identity' of victims and how this is constructed. Does it include secondary or indirect victims, such as the immediate relatives of murder victims (see Rock, 1998)?[30] Does it also extend to those who witness such events, or whose professional duties require them to assist and deal with the possibly traumatic aftermath?[31] And what about those who may be indirectly but possibly deeply affected by less serious offences, such as the children of households that have been burgled (Morgan and Zedner, 1992)? Should we also include among this category of indirect or secondary victims, the families of offenders who have been convicted and imprisoned, some of whom may also suffer as a result of the crime committed by the offender?[32] And what about the families of those who may have been killed while in police custody or in prison?[33]

Once we move beyond the realms of conventional predatory offences, further questions abound relating to the identity of victims. Should it include the victims of those killed or injured in road crashes, for example, at least where these are caused by a culpable motoring offence? Or what if the 'offender' is a corporation or business entity and thus falls outside the scope of Christie's implicit 'ideal offender' stereotype? In many cases of corporate malfeasance involving so-called 'regulatory offences',[34] the issue of 'victim identity' is especially problematic because the wrongdoing may not be unambiguously recognized – either legally or in the popular imagination – as criminal (Sanders, 2002: 198). Recent examples abound in which lives have been lost and horrific injuries sustained as a result of recklessness or gross negligence on the part of organizations that would have resulted in criminal convictions if the failing had been attributable to a single individual.[35] In 2000 the Corporate Homicide Bill was introduced which would have introduced the offence of corporate killing where management failure by a corporation was the cause, or one of the causes, of a person's death. However, the Bill appears to have been dropped in somewhat mysterious circumstances, prompting accusations that the government was reluctant to expose large corporations to the threat of criminal sanctions for fear of antagonizing them (Mansfield, 2002). If true, such accusations testify to the veracity of Christie's observation that victim status is unlikely to be accorded to victims who pose a threat to strong countervailing vested interests, however closely they might conform to the 'ideal victim' stereotype in other respects. A similar point could also be made in respect of crimes that are committed by or on behalf of agents of a state, for example, those involving unlawful acts of violence resulting in the deaths of those detained in police custody or in prison. Neither those who die in such circumstances nor their relatives are likely to be acknowledged or dealt with as victims (Ruggiero, 1999: 27).[36]

Even where corporate wrongdoing is acknowledged to constitute a criminal offence, as in the case of corporate fraud, victims may not always be aware that they have been victimized, or may be unwilling to admit that they have been cheated (Box, 1983: 17). It is still fairly unusual for the plight of such victims to be acknowledged and when this does happen it is normally only in exceptional circumstances. Recent examples include cases where either the scale of the fraud is exceptionally notorious, as in the Barings Bank affair, or the victims conform more closely to Christie's stereotype, as was the case with the beneficiaries of the pension funds that were embezzled by Robert Maxwell (Levi and Pithouse, 1992, 2005 forthcoming).

Finally, it needs to be acknowledged that business corporations and other public bodies, as well as individuals, can also be *victimized* in a variety of ways.[37] Such cases may also represent a departure from the stereotypical image of victim and offender attributes, at least where they involve offences that are committed by relatively weak offenders, sometimes in extenuating circumstances, against ostensibly very powerful and wealthy organizations. Legally, however, the identity and status of the corporate victim is not usually in doubt in such cases, notwithstanding this departure.

This review of our current state of knowledge concerning the identity and attributes of victims has confirmed its often highly contested and contingent nature.[38] It has also thrown up a number of challenging questions relating to the way victims (and offenders) are conceptualized by and within the conventional criminal justice system. However, the questions that are summarized below also pose a major challenge for those who favour the adoption of a restorative justice approach, whether as theorists, advocates or practitioners.

1 To what extent has restorative justice theory, ideology and practice been influenced by stereotypical assumptions about the identities of both victims and offenders and their respective attributes?
2 Are there any types of victims (or offenders) for whom restorative justice initiatives are inappropriate or potentially harmful?
3 How suitable are restorative justice initiatives for (and how sensitive are they towards) victims and offenders who do not conform to the 'ideal victim/offender' stereotypes?
   - e.g. victims who know their offenders as opposed to offenders who are strangers
   - e.g. victims who inhabit the same social milieu as their offender(s)
   - e.g. victims (or offenders) who are inarticulate, lacking in social skills etc., and who may consequently find it more difficult to actively engage in any offence-related dialogue
   - e.g. victims who have been victimized not just once but repeatedly (whether by the present offender, or by various offenders) as is often the case with offences involving domestic violence
   - e.g. victims who may be capable of posing a threat to the physical safety, economic well-being or emotional stability of the offender (or conversely, who may be threatened, physically, economically or emotionally by the offender)
   - e.g. victims who may not be entirely blameless with regard to this particular offence
   - e.g. victims who may also have offended against this offender or against others in the past
   - e.g. victims who may have had prior dealings with criminal justice agencies in the past (either as victims or as offenders)

- e.g. corporate victims.
4 How suitable are restorative justice initiatives for dealing with cases in which the 'identity' or 'status' of the victim is in some way problematic?
    - e.g. cases involving indirect or secondary victims
    - e.g. cases involving victims of corporate wrongdoing
    - e.g. cases involving wrongdoing by agents of the state (or other forms of wrongdoing that are not universally acknowledged as crimes).
5 How suitable are restorative justice initiatives for dealing with so-called 'victimless' or 'victim complicit' offences (see above)?
6 To what extent are restorative justice initiatives capable of striking an appropriate and fair balance between the interests of victims, offenders and other interested parties including the wider community?

The above questions present an alternative set of *victim sensitive* criteria against which it should in principle be possible to assess the various restorative justice initiatives and compare them with conventional criminal justice (and other) approaches. This is a task to which we will return in the final chapter of the book. In the meantime it is important to consider what we know about the way victims are affected by crime and the manner in which they respond to it.

Victimization and its effects

Victimization is a highly complex process encompassing a number of possible elements. The first element (often referred to as 'primary victimization') comprises whatever interaction may have taken place between offender and 'victim' during the commission of the offence, plus any after effects arising from this interaction or from the offence itself. The second element encompasses 'the victim's' reaction to the offence, including any change in self-perception that may result from it, plus any formal response that s/he may choose to make to it. The third element consists of any further interactions that may take place between 'the victim' and others, including the various criminal justice agencies with whom s/he may come into contact as a result of this response. Where this interaction has a further negative impact on the victim, it is often referred to as 'secondary victimization'.

Primary victimization and its consequences

We will consider each of these elements in turn. With regard to the 'primary victimization' phase of the process, it may be helpful to begin by distinguishing between the 'effects' or consequences that are known to result from crimes of different kinds and their 'impact' on victims themselves. It is a relatively straightforward task (see e.g. Newburn, 1993) to identify and categorize the different types of *effects* with which various crimes may be associated, even though in practice (and particularly from the victim's own perspective) it may be much more difficult to compartmentalize them in this way. Certain crimes entail physical effects, which are likely to involve some degree of pain and suffering, and may also entail loss of dexterity, some degree of incapacity and/or possible temporary or permanent disfigurement. Many crimes also have financial effects, which may be either direct – where they are attributable to the theft of or damage to property – or indirect. Very often crime can result in additional costs that might be incurred, for example, in seeking medical treatment or legal advice, or loss of income as a result of attending to the crime and its aftermath, or possible loss of future earning potential.[39] Certain crimes can also have psychological and emotional effects upon victims including depression, anxiety and fear, all of which can adversely affect their quality of life. Finally, though it is often overlooked, crime can also adversely affect victims' social relationships with family, work colleagues and friends. In principle, at least, it should be possible to quantify most of these effects reasonably objectively, though in practice it is methodologically very difficult to do this (see Maguire, 1991: 387–402), particularly in the case of those effects that do not have direct financial consequences. The measurement of any emotional effects is particularly problematic, not least because both the emotional experience itself and the extent to which people are willing and able to discuss it are themselves highly subjective and, to some extent, culturally specific (see Wortman, 1983).

The *impact* of crime is perhaps best thought of as a product of the perceived seriousness or intensity of these effects plus their duration *from the victim's own standpoint*. Defined in this way, the term refers to an inescapably subjective assessment and evaluation by the victim of the overall consequences of the offence. This includes its meaning and significance for the victim, and whether or not it has resulted in a change of self-perception by which the victim comes to perceive himself or herself *as a victim*. Thus, the 'impact' of a crime has a crucial bearing on the way the victim interprets and responds to it during the second phase of the victimization process, as distinct from whatever tangible or intangible 'effects' may be associated with the primary phase. Unfortunately, most researchers have tended to conflate these two terms and to treat them as interchangeable, which has added to the methodological problems mentioned above, though it might help to account for the seemingly confused nature of many of the findings.

Our understanding of the process of victimization and what it entails has mainly been shaped by three very different types of research (Maguire, 1991: 387): victimization survey data, which tend to concentrate on the effects of relatively less serious 'conventional offences' and their impact on victims; in-depth qualitative studies that mostly focus on medium/serious conventional crimes and their impact on victims; and clinical studies investigating the psychological effects of catastrophic events and their impact on victims.[40] The latter include some of the most serious conventional crimes such as rape and certain 'state crimes' such as those committed in concentration camps, as well as some non-criminal catastrophic events. Not only do the various studies focus on different categories of crime victims, they also employ different methodological approaches in order to investigate different facets of the victimization process. Not surprisingly, therefore, the findings themselves are seemingly inconsistent and provide an insecure basis on which to draw general conclusions.

Victim survey studies tend to rely on telephone interview methods in order to elicit mostly quantitative data relating chiefly to the physical, financial and practical effects of certain crimes, and some more subjective data relating to their emotional impact on victims. Not only are the offences themselves mostly at the less serious end of the spectrum, however, there is also evidence (Waller, 1986) that telephone survey techniques tend to reveal lower levels of emotional distress than interviews conducted in person. The latter are favoured by most of the in-depth qualitative studies which tend to investigate the impact of offences that are either moderately serious, such as burglary (e.g. Maguire, 1980; Maguire with Bennett, 1982) or rather more serious, such as robbery, wounding and rape (e.g. Shapland et al., 1985). Moreover, studies such as these tend to be much more specific than general victim surveys, allowing plenty of time for victims to focus their thoughts and memories. Clinical studies are different again, relying as they tend to on the physiological and psychological effects and behavioural impact of very serious (and almost certainly, therefore, atypical) offences such as rape (Burgess and Holmstrom, 1974a, 1974b) or other violent crimes including torture (e.g. Eitinger, 1964; Eitinger and Strom, 1973). One additional general observation is that the effect of crime specifically on victims' social relationships with family friends and associates has largely been neglected by researchers,[41] or if acknowledged has been treated merely as an aspect of the psychological effect of crime. This is somewhat surprising as crime and its aftermath are known to be a stressful experience for victims, and social relationships are also known to be adversely affected by stress of different kinds.

What we know about the consequences of victimization

Both the effects of crime and also their impact tend to be highly offence specific. First, in terms of their initial effects, violent offences in general are, not surprisingly, frequently likely to result in physical injuries, though the degree of violence (and thus its physical effects) can vary considerably even within specific offence types. Significant physical injury is relatively unusual, however, and in 49 per cent of violent incidents reported to the British Crime Survey in 2002–3 there was no physical injury at all (rising to two-thirds of those involving robberies and common assaults (Simmons and Dodd, 2003: 77ff).[42] Eleven per cent of violent incidents reported to the BCS resulted in medical attention from a doctor (rising to 33 per cent for victims of wounding), but only 2 per cent resulted in a hospital stay (rising to 6 per cent for victims of wounding). In the BCS figures for 2000–1, the likelihood of violent offences resulting in physical injuries that require medical attention was greater for offences committed by known offenders – as in the case of domestic violence[43] (18 per cent) – than for most forms of violence committed by strangers (8 per cent) apart from muggings (18 per cent). However, the differences between these categories were much less pronounced in the 2002–3 figures (Simmons et al., 2002; Simmons and Dodd, 2003).

Even where they do not result in physical injury, however, violent offences are frequently traumatic for victims, and sometimes extremely traumatic in terms of their emotional and/or psychological impact. Thus, just under half (44 per cent) of victims of violence report that they were shocked by the incident, just under one in three (29 per cent) were fearful, one in four were emotionally upset and one in five reported that they had difficulty sleeping (Maguire and Kynch, 2000: 4ff, which is based on an analysis of data from the 1998 British Crime Survey). Threats of violence were even more likely to induce fear (in 35 per cent of victims), though in other respects their impact is somewhat less pervasive than it is for offences involving actual violence. Anger is, however, the commonest emotional reaction, as it is for all offence types, ranging from just under two-thirds (64 per cent) of victims of violence or threats of violence to just under three-quarters (73 per cent) of victims of vandalism.

The intensity of any impact that violent crime may have is both highly subjective and also, partly for that reason, much more difficult to measure. There is a tendency for survey techniques to report lower values than in-depth interviews. Nevertheless, just under one-quarter (24 per cent) of British Crime Survey victims of violence report that they were 'very much affected' by the offence, rising to just over one-third (35 per cent) in respect of those incidents that were reported to the police (Maguire and Kynch, 2000: 5). In terms of its duration, most studies report that for the majority of victims of 'ordinary' violent crime the emotional impact is particularly intense at the outset, but that after a few days the initial fear, shock and anger gives way to a longer period of nervousness, anxiety, sleeplessness, depression, fear of a repeat attack and, often, self-blaming. Some studies (e.g. Maguire, 1985; Mawby and Gill, 1987) have suggested that the duration of any serious psychological effects is unlikely to persist beyond a few months, at least in the case of 'ordinary' violent offences, and also burglary. However, one of the few longitudinal studies to have been carried out on victims of 'ordinary violence' found that over half of the sample of 216 victims who were interviewed at up to four different stages of the legal process (in some cases up to two or three years after the original offence), reported some kind of persistent emotional effects (Shapland et al., 1985).[44] One possible explanation for these inconsistent findings is that the legal process itself could resensitize victims towards, and remind them of, the effects of the offence and its impact upon them.

Other types of violent crime including rape and other serious sexual assaults have also been widely studied, using both clinical techniques and intensive interview studies and, not surprisingly, these tend to show that a large proportion of victims experience acute physical pain and suffering in addition to the increased risk of pregnancy, sexually transmitted diseases or fear of the possibility of such consequences (Newburn, 1993: 4–5; see also Katz and Mazur, 1979). The psychological effects tend to be equally profound and longer lasting, and some (e.g. Ellis et al., 1981; Burt and Katz, 1985) have suggested that they may sometimes be permanent. This is particularly true of those who have been sexually abused during childhood (Morgan and Zedner, 1992: 44–5). Relatively little research has been conducted in respect of murder and its impact on victims' surviving families and associates, and most of the studies involve clinical techniques which tend to focus on its psychological impact (see e.g. Burgess, 1975; Magee, 1983). Some studies (e.g. Malmquist, 1986) have investigated the impact on children of interspousal murders, and others (e.g. Ryncarson, 1984, 1986) have drawn attention to the psychological problems that arise in intrafamilial murders as a result of family members identifying with both the perpetrator and the victim.

Still with regard to victims of violence in general, it is easy to overlook, finally, that there are often financial consequences that result either directly or indirectly from this type of crime. One of the few studies that attempted to document these in the case of moderately serious violent offences was conducted by Shapland et al., 1985, who found that a quarter of victims reported financial loss as a result of the offence and 30 per cent incurred additional incidental financial expenditure as a result of helping the police and attending court. One category of offence that almost invariably involves potential property loss is robbery, which involves the use or threat of force in the course of a theft or attempted theft of property. A high proportion of robbery offences involve young offenders and young victims. A recent survey of police personal robbery files indicated that while cash is the most likely item of value to be taken in the course of a robbery, over one-third involved the theft of mobile phones (Simmons and Dodd, 2003: 83).

Apart from offences involving violence, the other main type of conventional offence whose effects and impact have been widely studied is burglary. This is also very likely to result in property loss, and in the 2002–3 British Crime Survey of domestic burglary victims, the three most commonly stolen items were cash (39 per cent), jewellery (23 per cent) and videos, DVDs, CDs and tapes (19 per cent) (Simmons and Dodd, 2003: Table 4.07).[45] Although it is categorized as a property offence, however, Maguire and Kynch (2000: 4) point out that the emotional reaction to burglary is very similar to that associated with violent offences. Presumably this has to do with the victim's perception that the offence involves a violation of a very precious and personal space or 'cocoon'. Thus, it is not altogether surprising that no fewer than 83 per cent of those experiencing a domestic burglary involving entry reported that they had been emotionally affected by it, and 37 per cent indicated that they had been 'very much affected' (Simmons and Dodd 2003: 60; see also Maguire with Bennett, 1982). Lesser property offences such as vandalism and theft tend, unsurprisingly, to have less of a severe emotional impact on victims, though they may be just as likely to make them angry (Maguire and Kynch, 2000: 4).

Studies investigating the impact of 'ordinary' crime have tended to show that while this varies considerably according to the type of offence, as we have seen, it appears to be less affected overall by other general factors such as the personal and social characteristics of the victim. Maguire and Kynch, for example, found that although women and poorer people were somewhat more likely to report emotional effects than men and wealthier people, the differences were not that great, and there was little significant variation according to age. When they looked beyond these broad socio-demographic categories, however, they did find certain highly specific categories of victims who were disproportionately likely to report that they had been 'very much' affected by the incidents they had experienced. Among this group of 'exceptionally vulnerable' victims who reported the highest levels of emotional impact were those who had experienced some form of 'intimidation or harassment' from the offender (or their friends or family) since the incident. Two-thirds of these victims of intimidation who reported the incident to the police said that they had been 'very much' affected by it.[46] Other 'exceptionally vulnerable' victims included the very poor, particularly those who are uninsured or have restricted mobility, single parents and those who are relatively house-bound. Serial or repeat victims were felt to be vulnerable, but not exceptionally vulnerable, while very elderly victims living alone reported levels of vulnerability that – somewhat surprisingly – were slightly lower than average.

Victims' responses to victimization

Having discussed the effects of crime and its impact on different categories of victims, we will now examine the way victims respond to their initial victimization and its impact. These responses may take a number of different forms including the possibility of changes in the attitudes and behaviour of the victim, changes in the victim's own self-perception and even self-identity, and attempts to elicit support or reactions from others including formal agencies such as the police and the courts. Once again we will consider each of these in turn.

It is reasonably well established that being the victim of a crime is frequently associated with attitudinal changes. Thus, those who have been the victim of a conventional BCS crime in the previous year are, unsurprisingly, somewhat more likely to be 'very worried' about such crimes than non-victims (Simmons and Dodd, 2003: Table 8.05). Victims of violence and victims of burglary are especially likely to be worried about those particular categories of crime, respectively, though they are also significantly more likely than non-victims to be worried about all other conventional categories of crime as well. Victims of motor vehicle crime, on the other hand, tend to be rather more specifically worried than non-victims about these particular crimes, but are only marginally more concerned than non-victims about other types of crime. Victims of crime are also more likely than non-victims to perceive that they are at risk of being victimized in the future, and once again the general pattern for different offence types is broadly comparable to that described above. Moreover, victims of violence and burglary are also far more likely than non-victims[47] to be afraid of walking alone in the area after dark and to feel insecure when alone at home during the night, whereas victims of motor vehicle crime do not feel any less safe than non-victims in either respect.

In terms of behavioural changes, such evidence as there is mostly relates to the more serious kinds of conventional offences and is mainly based on intensive interview studies involving victims of more serious forms of violence including rape. Shapland et al. (1985), for example, found that 14 per cent of victims experiencing some form of assault responded by going out much less frequently than before the offence. Rape victims appear to be particularly likely to undergo major behavioural changes including moving house or changing jobs. Williams and Holmes (1981), for example, found that one in four victims identified in a sample drawn from police records moved house following the assault, while Burgess and Holmstrom (1976) found that just under half of their small sample of rape victims (19 out of 45) had changed jobs within six weeks of the attack. Other behavioural effects include withdrawal from social contacts and drug or alcohol abuse (Peters et al., 1976; Herman, 1981; Briere, 1984, all cited in Newburn, 1993).

With some types of offences the behavioural consequences can be even more severe. This is particularly true of crimes involving serious physical or sexual abuse that is directed against child victims. In both instances[48] there is evidence that a cycle of abuse may be instigated, whereby some of those who have been victimized as children go on to perpetrate the abuse against succeeding generations of victims. Indeed, this is another illustration of the fact that, in reality, victims and offenders often belong to overlapping categories rather than the mutually exclusive camps to which they tend to be assigned by popular stereotypes. More generally, another behavioural response that is not restricted to a particular category of offence types is for the victim to engage in direct retaliatory action against the offender or suspected offender (as discussed by Miers, 2000). While such behaviour may be relatively uncommon, it too serves as a reminder that we should not rush to dichotomize too rigidly between victims and offenders when considering how each needs to be dealt with.

Quite apart from any direct behavioural consequences it might have, however, one of the most important issues when considering the impact of a specific criminal offence is whether it causes the person(s) against whom it is directed to think differently about themselves. Does it result in them seeing themselves as 'a victim' and actively seeking to assume the identity and status of a victim, with all that that entails, or not? And, if they do seek such status, will it be conferred on them by those who have the power to authoritatively bestow it?

Becoming a victim, in other words, is a social process that starts with a criminal offence but also requires a cognitive decision by the person(s) against whom it is directed to see themselves as, and assume the status of, victims as part of their strategy for coping with it. Not everyone who has been offended against will necessarily regard themselves as a victim. Some, for example, may not recognize that they have in fact been offended against.[49] This could be because the crime itself might not conventionally be recognized as such, as in the case of 'corporate manslaughter'. Or it might be that the behaviour in question forms such in intrinsic part of their everyday experience that the person against whom it is directed does not consider it to be criminal or even abnormal. Children who have been sexually abused by a relative, for example, may not appreciate at the time that they have been victimized. Similarly, women who were raped by their husbands or beaten by their partners were not, until relatively recently, encouraged to think of themselves as victims of criminal offences. Others may consciously reject the victim 'label', either because they consider it to be pejorative or because they prefer to pursue or promote other 'coping strategies'. Some of those who work with women who have experienced rape or domestic violence, for example, have deliberately renounced the 'victim' label and prefer to use the term 'survivors'. Still others may consider a potentially victimizing incident too trivial to bother about or would prefer to deal with it themselves. For example, over half (55 per cent) of those who had experienced a potentially victimizing incident over the previous 12 months reported that they did not want any help or support in dealing with it (Maguire and Kynch, 2000: 8).

Reflections such as these may help to explain the well-known phenomenon that a majority of all conventional crimes (57 per cent in 2002–3) are not reported to the police by those who experience them (Simmons and Dodd, 2003: 11). In the survey conducted by Simmons and Dodd, for most crimes (69 per cent), the main reason for not reporting the matter was because the incident was considered too trivial, there was no real loss or the police were thought to be unable to do much about it. However, decisions not to report a matter are not solely decided on the basis of how serious the 'victim' – or others – might consider it to be. Many incidents that would generally be thought of as serious in terms of their offence classification – such as robbery, wounding and burglary – for example, go unreported, and the main reason for this[50] is that the victim considers it a private matter that is best dealt with by themselves. Even when a given incident is considered by victims themselves to be 'serious', many still choose not to report it. Indeed, in the 2001 BCS, over one-third of offences (37 per cent) that fell in the top band of seriousness (as defined by victims) went unreported, and the same was true of over half (54 per cent) of those in the medium band of seriousness (Kershaw et al., 2001: 11).

Assuming that a person who has been offended against does actively seek to be recognized and treated by others as a victim, this will normally set in motion a range of other processes over which the victim has little or no control. These processes may or may not result in victim status being granted but, even where successful, they may inflict additional costs and further hardship on the victim: a consequence that is often referred to as 'secondary victimization'. We will examine the phenomenon of secondary victimization in more detail in subsequent chapters. But in the meantime this review of the victimization process may help us to identify an additional range of criteria by which we may seek to assess the performance of various victim-focused measures (including restorative justice) that are designed to alleviate the harmful consequences of victimization. The most obvious of these concern the extent to which they are capable of addressing the following kinds of harm that may result either directly or indirectly from the commission of a criminal offence:

- financial loss or additional short or longer term economic hardship
- physical harm including pain and suffering plus any longer term incapacity
- short and longer term psychological and emotional effects
- damage to social relationships, particularly those involving the victim and other family members, colleagues and acquaintances but also including the offender where known to the victim
- subjective impact of any of the above from the victim's own standpoint
- any longer term legacy including feelings of insecurity, concern about crime in general or fear of being (re-)victimized
- any negative consequences that might be associated with a person's self-perception as a victim
- the negative consequences associated with any possible 'secondary victimization'.

Victimology and its variants

Victimology as a field of study is a recently developed subdiscipline of criminology. Whereas the latter is very broadly concerned with the study of crime and criminals, victimology focuses equally broadly on crime and its victims. As within criminology itself, however, individual victimologists have tended to focus on very different sets of issues, as a result of which a number of variants within the subdiscipline may now be differentiated.

The position within victimology is further complicated by the fact that the academic study of victimology is closely intertwined with – and is consequently almost impossible to disentangle from – the equally diverse philosophies and practices that have been adopted by various sets of activists who have championed the cause of victims (Fattah, 1989). In this section, three principal variants within the field of victimology – positivist, radical and critical victimology – are briefly described and linked with the discrete tendencies within the diverse victims' movement with which they are most closely associated.[51]

Positivist victimology

Positivist victimology, like its counterpart in criminology (see Cavadino and Dignan, 2002: 49), is influenced by the view that crime, along with all other natural and social phenomena, is *caused* by factors and processes which can be discovered by scientific investigation. But whereas positivist criminologists attribute the causes of crime to various forces (including environmental and genetic factors) that act upon *offenders* and are beyond their control, early positivist victimologists were interested in the possibility that certain *victims* might in some way contribute to their own victimization. Von Hentig (1941, 1948) and Mendelsohn (1956, 1974), for example, were interested in observing and identifying regularities or non-randomized patterns of victimizing events, and in linking these to particular types of victim who could then be categorized within various typologies.[52] For instance, victims were classified according to how 'victim prone' they were, in von Hentig's case, or even (and far more controversially) according to the degree of 'culpability' exhibited by the victim, in Mendelsohn's case. The influence of positivist victimology can be discerned at the policymaking level with regard to both the development and deployment of victim survey techniques and also the launch of official campaigns to encourage victims who may be susceptible to various types of victimization to take steps to reduce the risks involved.[53]

A major weakness with positivist victimology, however, is that it assumes that the identity of victims is self-evident, since it is linked to the harm that they have sustained and the fact that their status is defined and recognized by the criminal law. Thus, there is a tendency to concentrate almost exclusively on victims of conventional interpersonal crimes, particularly those involving violence and predatory attitudes towards the property of others. There is also a tendency to view the criminal justice system in relatively unproblematic terms as the ultimate guarantor of retributive justice, thereby assuming that what victims want above all else is to see their offenders being punished for their crimes (Karmen, 1990: 11). These assumptions are reflected in those elements within the victims' movement that have assertively and, in some cases, aggressively, championed the interests of particular groups of victims. Examples include the Victims of Violence organization in England and Wales during the early

1980s (Jonker, 1986) and a more recent pressure group, the Victims of Crime Trust. In the United States the Justice for All pressure group actively campaigns in support of the death penalty.

Positivist victimology can be criticized for failing to realize the extent to which our assumptions about the identity of victims are contingent rather than self-evident. For they are shaped not only by the law itself but also by the pressures that may be brought to bear on the state and the legislature by different organizations and individuals seeking to influence that law. Moreover, it fails to appreciate the fact that both the state itself, through its agencies, and also the legal and penal processes that it sanctions may themselves create new victims and also further victimize those who have already been victimized by an offender. It also fails to acknowledge the process of social construction that is involved in the labelling of victims – both by themselves and also by others – and the aforementioned possibility that some who are victimized may nevertheless actively resist or even reject the label altogether.

Radical victimology

Radical victimology likewise resembles its criminological counterpart in rejecting the theoretical underpinnings of positivist victimology. Instead of seeing victimization as a product of the personal attributes of individual victims, early radical criminologists such as Quinney (1972) drew attention to structural factors relating to the way society is organized, and also the role of the state itself and the legal system in the social construction of both victims and offenders. Viewed from this perspective, the definition and identity of victims is far from self-evident since it extends to those who are oppressed, and thus victimized, both by 'the powerful', and also by those who act on behalf of the state, including the police and correctional agencies. For many radical criminologists (see, for example, Taylor et al., 1973; Platt, 1975; Pearce, 1976), such insights resulted in a tendency to see offenders as the principal victims of state oppression and to downplay or ignore altogether those who were in turn victimized by them. For others, including a group who became known as 'radical left realists' (see, for example, Lea and Young, 1984; Young, 1986) the findings of the first British Crime Survey alerted them to the fact that most predatory crime was directed not against the wealthy bourgeoisie but against the poorest members of society who tend to live among those responsible for such crime. Other radical victimologists have been motivated less by empirical findings than their own normative predilections. Robert Elias (1985) for example, sought to place a human rights perspective[54] on the victimological agenda. His aim was partly to devise a more objective and less parochial criterion by which victimization might be defined and measured, and partly to mobilize support in favour of measures 'to relieve human suffering' on the part of victims.

This realignment within the field of radical victimology is also reflected in certain specific tendencies within the wider victims' movement. At a political and policymaking level the concerns of new left realism were mirrored in a commitment to improving the lot of 'ordinary' victims without necessarily adopting the highly repressive responses towards offenders that are associated with more conservative law and order advocates. At a practitioner level, the quest for a human rights approach was manifested in a search for more constructive ways of dealing with both victims and offenders that sought as far as possible to meet the needs and interests of both. Thus, certain strands within radical victimology are reflected in more liberal approaches with regard to penal policy, such as the promotion of state-funded compensation schemes, support for restitution or compensation for victims by their offenders and even attempts at reconciliation (see also Karmen, 1990: 8). In this respect, some of the early progenitors of the restorative justice movement espoused aims that were certainly consistent with, even if they were not directly inspired by, some of these developments within radical victimology.

However, radical victimology has in turn been criticized for its partial and incomplete portrayal of the processes of victimization since it tends to confine its analysis to the impact of social class relationships while neglecting other factors such as gender, race and age (Jefferson et al., 1991; see also Mawby and Walklate, 1994: 16). Attempts to overcome these limitations have drawn on two main perspectives: the first derived from an approach within critical criminology that is known as 'symbolic interactionism' (see e.g. Miers, 1989, 1990a); and the second from feminist accounts (see e.g. Mawby and Walklate, 1994). Despite the differences between them, both approaches have appropriated the label 'critical victimology', which represents the third main variant within the field of victimology.

Critical victimology

For David Miers, the key questions for a critical victimology are 'who has the power to apply the label?', and 'what factors are significant in determining whether or not to bestow it?'. While acknowledging that such questions represent an advance on positivist victimology by emphasizing the contingent and culturally specific nature of our assumptions about who victims are, Mawby and Walklate do not accept that it takes us far beyond the portrayal provided by radical victimologists. This is mainly because it fails to explain how those labels are constituted and why it is that certain conceptions of who, really, are the victims, come to prevail at different times and in different sets of social and political circumstances.

Mawby and Walklate (1994) themselves have been inspired by a feminist perspective rather that one derived from symbolic interactionism as in David Miers's case. Although not initially directly concerned with criminal victimization per se, feminism did highlight the importance of neglected issues such rape, sexual harassment, domestic violence and child abuse. It also drew attention to an additional pervasive mechanism – patriarchy – which, like social class, helps to shape both the process and pattern of victimization and also our ability or willingness to recognize them for what they are. It is by no means the only one, however. Race, for example, is another factor that, like gender, is implicated in the process of victimization and, through its effect on social attitudes, one that may also obscure these processes[55] unless and until they are revealed by campaigners, social commentators and other opinion formers.

Critical victimology has highlighted the importance of historical and cultural contexts in shaping both victimizing practices and our sensitivities towards them. Even more importantly, perhaps, critical victimology should alert us to the fact that concepts such as 'victim' and 'victimization' are contested and, being historically and culturally specific, are both malleable and far from universal. It is also worth pointing out that, perhaps because of the sympathy that it evokes, the image of 'the victim' is capable of being invoked and sometimes even manipulated or exploited, whether to serve the interests of victims per se, particular groups of victims or even other objectives altogether. We will come across examples of all of these tendencies in the two chapters that follow, which examine 'victim-focused policymaking'.

Summary

In this chapter we have examined some of the factors that have contributed to the increasing 'visibility' of crime victims in recent years, both as the subject of media attention and also (as we shall see in the next three chapters) as the object of public policymaking. We have examined the concept of the victim, both in terms of the idealized imagery that is often deployed when talking about victims, and also in terms of the empirical data that are available with regard to those categories of victims who are most likely to feature in victim surveys. Questions have been raised about the adequacy of conventional conceptions of crime victims and whether these need to be extended. Attention has also been drawn to the challenges such questions may pose for the exponents of all three victim-focused approaches featured in this book and, in particular, for restorative justice theorists, advocates and practitioners, which is a topic we shall return to in Chapter 6.

We have examined the process of victimization itself, both in terms of its consequences for victims and also with regard to the different responses that it may elicit from victims themselves. This assessment has also generated an additional set of criteria by which the performance of different types of victim-focused measures might be judged. Finally, we have briefly examined the field of study that is known as victimology, including some of its more important variants. In succeeding chapters the focus switches from victims as the subject of academic scrutiny to victims as the object of endeavours by campaigners, policymakers and practitioners to promote, formulate and implement reforms are claimed to address the concerns, interests and needs of victims in a variety of different ways.

Notes

1 At least not directly; victims did, of course, benefit indirectly from many of the welfare provisions introduced during this period, including free healthcare, income maintenance and unemployment benefits.

2 Whether domestic or international. The international human rights instruments that proliferated during the early post-war period did not contain any specific measures relating to crime victims either.

3 Or as Rock (1990: 270) has more cynically put it: 'It was a form of Danegeld that was supposed to enlarge the Welfare State and ease the passage of penal reform.'

4 One notable example was the part played by the mother of Jamie Bulger in campaigning against the release of two young men who had been convicted of murdering her 2-year-old son in 1992 while they themselves were only 10 years of age. This culminated in a letter-writing campaign orchestrated by the *Sun* newspaper, which was intended to influence the Home Secretary's decision on when they should be released.

5 One example is the call for a law giving parents controlled access to information relating to convicted child offenders living in their neighbourhood. The campaign for the introduction of a 'Sarah's Law', following the murder of Sarah Payne in July 2000 followed the adoption of a similar law known as Megan's Law in the USA, and was supported by the *News of the World* as well as by parents of the murdered victim.

6 The first refuge for battered women in Britain was established in Chiswick by Erin Pizzey in 1972 (Pizzey, 1974), and served as a model for a network of some 250 projects running 400 safe houses. These are co-ordinated by the Women's Aid Federation, which was founded in 1974. In 2000 refuges took in 54,000 women and children in England alone, and offered support or advise to 145,000 others who contacted them (Zedner, 2002: 434). Similar refuges had also been set up in the USA since the early 1970s (Fleming, 1979; Walker, 1979).

7 The first rape crisis centre opened in London in 1976, offering practical legal and medical advice, together with emotional support, to women who have been sexually assaulted or raped. Just over a decade later 40 similar centres had been established (Zedner, 2002: 434).

8 See, for example, Philip Priestley's (1970) pamphlet, entitled 'What about the victim?'.

9 In England and Wales the level of recorded crime experienced an elevenfold increase, from 500,000 in 1950 (Barclay et al., 1995: 2) to 5.5 million notifiable offences in 1993 (Barclay, 1995: 38). This was matched by an increase in the rate of recorded crime from roughly one offence per 100,000 population in 1950 to ten per 100,000 in 1993, though since then there have been falls in both the number of offences and also offence rates.

10 Another concern, which has also resurfaced in Britain more recently, was that victims may become reluctant to co-operate with judicial proceedings by reporting crime and testifying in court.

11 Annual national crime surveys have been conducted in the USA since 1972, though they are now known as National Crime Victimization Surveys.

12 For example those conducted under the auspices of the International Crime Victim Survey (ICVS) programme (see van Dijk and Mayhew, 1992; Mayhew and van Dijk, 1997; see also Mayhew, 2000: 92; van Kesteren et al., 2000; van Dijk, 2000). See also the ICVS website at: http://ruljis.leidenuniv.nl/group/jfcr/www/icvs/.

13 See in particular Smart (1977), Edwards (1981) and Adler (1987).

14 See also Crawford (2000: 286), who pointed to the 'double whammy' effect whereby high crime areas are not simply afflicted by higher levels of crime but also experience a greater concentration of multiple and repeat victimizations than low crime areas.

15 See, generally, on the reporting of crime by the media Ditton and Duffy (1983), Soothill and Walby (1991: ch. 8) and Wykes (2001).

16 Moral entrepreneurs are individuals or groups who seek to persuade a society to adopt policies that reflect their moral standpoint, one example being Mothers Against Drunk Driving.

17 A notable exception is Richard Young (2000, 2002), who is one of the few to have questioned the assumptions on which restorative justice's concept of victimhood has been based.

18 This is not the only methodological defect. Another has to do with variable rates of reporting to BCS interviewers. For example, some respondents may tend – for obvious reasons – to under-report offences committed by members of the same household. Conversely other respondents – notably well-educated, middle-class victims – appear to be more able and willing to report offences.

19 The British Crime Survey began in 1982 and continued to measure both reported and unreported crime every two years before moving to an annual cycle in 2001. However, the first major victim survey in Britain was conducted in London in the mid-1970s (Sparks et al., 1977).

20 This is partly due to the relative infrequency of such offences, rendering hazardous the making of estimates based on small samples. An additional consideration relates to concerns about the willingness of victims to disclose such potentially sensitive information (see Stanko, 1988). More recently, however, offences such as these have been included in supplementary surveys conducted as part of the regular B.C.S. See, for example, Myhill and Allen, 2002; Walby and Allen, 2004.

21 Though the 2001 sweep included a booster sample of young people to enable their experiences of crime to be canvassed.

22 Including prisons which – as the work of O'Donnell and Edgar (1996, 1998) and Edgar et al. (2003) have shown – are far from crime free.

23 Thus, it almost certainly systematically excludes many of the most heavily victimized populations including those in care, the homeless, squatters and other geographically rootless people including travelling families and illegal aliens.

24 Though there has also been a commercial victimization survey (see Mirlees-Black and Ross, 1995).

25 However, the overall level of risk for both groups is relatively small, being 4 per cent for all adults, 5.3 per cent for men and 2.9 per cent for women (Simmons and Dodd, 2003: Table 5.01).

26 The gap has narrowed since the previous year, however, when women were victimized in no fewer than 82 per cent of assaults involving domestic violence (Simmons et al., 2002: 57).

27 The British Crime Survey utilizes the ACORN system for categorizing residential neighbourhoods, which is based on demographic, employment and housing characteristics that are derived from census data.

28 This was the lowest rate ever recorded by the BCS, which had previously recorded an increase in the percentage of adults who had been victimized in respect of such offences from 27.7 per cent in 1981 to 39.3 per cent in 1995. Since then, however, it has fallen in every subsequent sweep of the survey (Kershaw et al., 2001: 21).

29 They include residential burglary, criminal damage directed against a private individual and unlawful taking of a motor vehicle. Moreover, significant differences in prevalence rates were found across a range of census enumeration districts that were characterized by widely varying overall property crime rates.

30 The United Nations Declaration of Basic Principles of Justice for Victims of Crime and Abuse of Power did include within the definition of 'victim' the immediate family and dependants of the direct victim, and also those who suffer harm trying to assist victims in distress or in seeking to prevent victimization. However, the relatives of homicide victims were not included among those who were entitled to make victim personal statements in court (see below) on the grounds that the 'real' victim had been killed (Rock, 2002a: 15).

31 The award of £300,000 compensation to a former police officer who had allegedly been traumatized by his experience while attending a disaster at a football stadium in Sheffield in which 96 people died in 1989 provoked anger on the part of the Hillsborough Family Support Group. They refused to accept that the police, whom they held partly responsible for the tragedy, could also be treated as victims, and were also aggrieved at the size of the award compared with the amounts paid to survivors or the relatives of those who died, many of whom received nothing.

32 See, for example Gampell (1999: 28), who is the director of the Federation of Prisoners' Families Support Groups.

33 See, for example, the work of INQUEST, which is briefly described by Ruggiero (1999: 27).

34 A term which includes acts of pollution, health and safety infractions and corporate fraud, all of which can inflict extremely serious harm on large numbers of victims on a scale that is rarely matched by most conventional crimes and public order offences.

35 In Britain alone they include various disasters: on the railways, such as Clapham, Hatfield, Paddington, Potters Bar and Southall; at sea, such as the Zeebrugge ferry sinking and the explosion on the Piper Alpha oil platform; and even on the River Thames, in the case of the sinking of the *Marchioness* riverboat (see also note 32). In other countries, including the USA, such corporate wrongdoing is more likely to be punishable under the criminal law.

36 See also Cohen (2001), who has written more generally on the subject of 'state-sanctioned violence'.

37 Although not covered by the standard British Crime Survey, there are also comparable crime surveys covering corporate victims (e.g. Mirlees-Black and Ross, 1995). It is also important to remember that crimes directed against corporations often have an impact on the people who work within them and have to deal with them.

38 Richard Young (2000: 229) has performed a valuable service in questioning the validity of the simplistic image of crime as something that is committed against a single, individual, identifiable victim.

39 NB The financial consequences may thus be borne not just by the victim and any dependants but also by financial institutions such as insurance societies and, indeed, by society as a whole, in cases where the victim suffers a permanent loss of productivity or becomes notably dependant upon financial support from the state or other bodies.

40 It is only relatively recently that research into the consequences of primary victimization – whatever form it takes – has been undertaken.

41 But see Morgan and Zedner (1992: 28–31), who are among the few to have commented on the stress that crime may place on family relations, its capacity to rupture them, and the effect of any resulting dislocation on other members of the household, many of whom are children.

42 It must be remembered, however, that the British Crime Survey does not attempt to measure the incidence or effects of some of the most serious crimes such as murder.

43 The corresponding figure for cases involving 'acquaintance violence' was 12 per cent.

44 Long-term psychological reactions to crime have also been reported as routine occurrences among victims of various types of crime in other studies (see, for example Frieze et al. 1987; Norris et al., 1997).

45 Just over half (52 per cent) of domestic burglaries reported in the 2002–3 British Crime Survey interviews were covered by insurance.

46 Categories of victims with the highest reported levels of intimidation included people living in poorer households, those in 'striving' areas, black or Asian victims, and victims of violence. See also Tarling et al. (2000) for further findings on victim and witness intimidation that are likewise derived from the British Crime Survey.

47 NB This is not to deny that some non-victims of crime are also concerned about their personal safety; nor that they may worry about the risk of victimization and, in some cases, modify their behaviour or lifestyle accordingly. To this extent they too may be counted as 'indirect victims of crime', even though they have not been victimized and may not be related to or closely associated with anyone who has been.

48 In respect of physical abuse, see Morris and Gould (1963) and Kaufman (1985). In respect of sexual abuse, see Goodwin (1982) and Eve (1985). See also Widom (1991).

49 Victims of corporate fraud, for example, as mentioned above.

50 Cited by 47 per cent in the case of violent offences (Simmons and Dodd, 2003: 12).

51 This section draws heavily on the very helpful typology that has been developed by Mawby and Walklate (1994: 8ff). See also Miers (1989, 1990a) and Walklate (1999).

52 The use of techniques that are derived from the natural sciences, such as

'objective' observation and attempts to develop appropriate taxonomies, are also characteristic features of the positivist's approach.

53 One example has been the advice issued to mobile phone owners not to carry them too prominently or use them too ostentatiously in public, which is intended to reduce the risk of falling victim to this widely prevalent form of robbery.

54 Elias's approach also has a counterpart in the field of radical criminology: see in particular Schwendinger and Schwendinger (1975).

55 The events surrounding the murder of the black teenager, Stephen Lawrence, and its handling by the authorities, provide one obvious example.

Further reading

Christie, N. (1986) The ideal victim, in E. Fattah (ed.) *From Crime Policy to Victim Policy*. Basingstoke: Macmillan.

Mawby, R.I. and Walklate, S. (1994) *Critical Victimology*. London: Sage.

Newburn, T. (1993) *The Long-term Needs of Victims: A Review of the Literature*, Home Office Research and Planning Unit Paper no. 80. London: Home Office.

Rock, P. (2002a) On becoming a victim, in C. Hoyle and R. Young (eds) *New Visions of Crime Victims*. Oxford: Hart.

Walklate, S. (2004) Justice for all in the 21st century: the political context of the policy focus on victims, in E. Capes *Reconciling Rights in Criminal Justice: Analysing the Tension between Victims and Defendants*. London: Legal Action.

Zedner, L. (2002) Victims, in M. Maguire, R. Morgan and R. Reiner (eds) *The Oxford Handbook of Criminology*, 3rd edn. Oxford: Oxford University Press.

chapter two

Victim-focused policymaking: the 'welfare approach'

The welfare model
Criminal injuries compensation scheme
Victim support
Conclusion
Notes
Further reading

In the next three chapters the spotlight switches focus from victims themselves to the policymaking process. Until 40 years ago victims scarcely appeared at all on the policy agenda whereas offenders featured prominently in a steady and seemingly ever-increasing stream of legislative initiatives. In recent years, however, there has been a momentous sea change in the orientation of policy in this area as an early trickle of victim-focused initiatives, that was initially rather tentative and intermittent, has turned into a virtual torrent that now seems unstoppable.

This dramatic reorientation of the policy agenda is symbolized in a recent White Paper, 'Justice for All', the professed aim of which is to 'rebalance the system in favour of victims, witnesses and communities' (Home Office et al., 2002a). The change of tack is also reflected at an institutional level within the heart of government following a major restructuring of the policymaking machine itself. What was once a relatively anonymous section within the Home Office known as C4, whose responsibilities encompassed the higher courts and jury matters, aspects of the criminal law and its review and (almost as an afterthought) the criminal injuries compensation scheme, has now become the Justice and Victims Unit. This much higher profile unit retains responsibility for procedures in the criminal courts but is also responsible for policies relating to the victims of crime more generally, including compensation for victims and providing financial support for selected victim-focused organizations. At one level this institutional change can be seen as a manifestation of the government's professed commitment to the pursuit of what it was once wont to call 'joined-up government', in which departments and agencies are reconstituted around substantive areas of policy formation.[1] At another level, however, it appears to herald an important shift in policy *priorities* as victim issues are now being accorded unprecedented prominence.

The radical change in the direction of public policy with regard to victims has not happened overnight and is not the product of a seamless, pre-planned and rational policymaking process. Nor are victim-focused initiatives all 'of a piece' in terms of their philosophical underpinnings, their intended aims, the means by which they are intended to operate or their practical impact on victims themselves. Some measures such as state-funded compensation schemes and voluntary victim assistance schemes, for example, operate outwith and largely independently of the existing criminal justice system. Other measures, such as court-ordered compensation provisions or the introduction of victim impact statements have been accommodated within the existing criminal justice system in at least some common law jurisdictions. Still other initiatives, including a number of restorative justice processes such as victim–offender mediation and family conferencing have a much more uncertain relationship with the criminal justice system. For all these reasons, care is needed in tracing the shifts in the policymaking process from a time when victims were off the policymakers' radar screen to an era in which they appear to have become the principal beacon for setting the direction of public policy in this area. In order to chart these important developments, and to assist in their understanding, it might be helpful at this point to refer back to the analytical framework that was set out in the Introduction. The rest of this chapter will concentrate on a range of victim-focused initiatives that are best characterized in terms of the 'welfare model'.

The welfare model

The term 'welfare model' is used here in a broad non-technical sense to encompass the provision of various services and benefits to victims of crime by means of agencies and procedures that have been set up specifically for this purpose. These agencies operate independently of the criminal justice system and do not directly depend on the outcome of judicial processes. Victims of crime may in addition, of course, benefit incidentally from various universal 'welfare' services in the traditional sense, such as the national health service if they sustain injuries needing medical attention, for example. We noted in Chapter 1 that crime victims did not originally feature among the particular 'victims of misfortune' for whom the state was prepared to make special provision in response to the Beveridge Report 1942. Nevertheless, the first specifically victim-focused initiatives of the present era were those associated with the welfare model, the two most important of which are the criminal injuries compensation scheme and the network of victim support schemes. These are considered in more detail below. They share the common aim of providing help for victims in the aftermath of an offence, though the form of assistance is different in each case. The institutional framework within which they operate is also rather different, but both function independently of the police and courts or, at any rate, at arm's length from them.

Criminal injuries compensation scheme

Philosophical underpinnings and origins of the scheme

The criminal injuries compensation scheme (CICS) was introduced in England and Wales in 1964[2] on a non-statutory basis, and was founded on the idea that the state should in principle undertake to provide financial compensation to certain victims of violent crime. Margery Fry is generally credited with instigating the proposal, and actively campaigned in favour of such a scheme over many years. She initially favoured a revival of the concept of reparation whereby offenders are expected to provide financial compensation to their victims, and in this sense can be seen as an early progenitor of the restorative justice movement (Fry, 1951: 124–6). Realizing that most offenders would be unable to afford to make financial reparation, however, she began to argue instead for *the state* to assume responsibility for providing compensation for victims of violence. Her original proposals were founded on an explicit 'welfare model' since she invoked the doctrine of collective responsibility for providing for sickness and injury that underpinned the newly introduced welfare state. Moreover, she linked this to the principle of national insurance, which provided the mechanism for 'risk sharing' by spreading the burden of risk among the population at large, instead of allowing it to be borne by the unfortunate individuals who became victims of violent crime. Indeed, the model she advocated was based on the then recently introduced Industrial Injuries Scheme that had been set up under the post-war National Insurance Acts (Fry, 1957, 1959).

As Duff (1998: 108–11) has pointed out, this model has important implications for the scope of the scheme, the basis on which eligibility is calculated and also, therefore, the level of any payments that might be made under it. Here, the crime victim is characterized as a needy supplicant who, in the event of a 'loss of faculty', might be entitled to a periodic pension, and, possibly, to short-term benefit payments based on 'incapacity for work'. This was not the basis on which the scheme was eventually implemented, however, which rejected the industrial injuries analogy. It adopted, instead, a common law model in which damages are calculated on the basis of the civil damages that would be payable if a person were injured as the result of another person's negligence. This too had important implications for the basis on which eligibility was originally calculated and, hence also, on the level of payments paid by the scheme. For civil law damages are payable in a lump sum rather than in the form of a periodic pension and, unlike the industrial injuries scheme, are much more generous since they include payment for pain and suffering, and also loss of earnings, in addition to compensation for loss of faculty.

The scheme was initially administered by a body known as the Criminal Injuries Compensation Board, a quango[3] whose members were appointed by the Home Office. Somewhat anomalously, however, the government, which introduced the scheme in 1964, emphatically rejected the idea that the state owed any legal liability to victims, even though it is possible to construct a plausible argument in support of such a principle.[4] Since it had also rejected the national insurance rationale that could be linked with an extension of the distributive justice principle underlying other aspects of the welfare state, this left the new scheme without a clear and defensible justification. Not surprisingly, perhaps, the charge of 'theoretical incoherence' has continued to dog it ever since (see Atiyah, 1970; Duff, 1998).

When it was first introduced, the scheme was premised on the assumption that the payment of compensation to victims of violent crime was a privilege rather than a right. Consequently, the Criminal Injuries Compensation Board, as it was then known, technically awarded payments initially on a discretionary ex gratia[5] basis only. In the absence of a logically defensible rationale on which to base the scheme, commentators have suggested that its introduction owed more to pragmatic considerations. Indeed, Miers (1978: 55, 1980) has linked it to an incipient process involving the 'politicisation of crime victims' in response to which the government came to accept the need to do 'something' for victims that went beyond the universal benefits to which they were already entitled under the welfare state. State-funded compensation, in other words, is seen as a mainly symbolic gesture – though it does also confer significant material benefits on the recipient – that represents and manifests society's empathy for and solidarity with the unfortunate victim of violent crime (see also Duff, 1998: 107). Hence also the rather intuitive adoption of the common law principle of civil damages as the initial yardstick by which to assess the value of any compensation payments, though this was to sow its own tensions as the number of claimants and consequent level of expenditure increased over the years.

When viewed in this way, state-funded compensation can be seen as an embodiment of society's resolve to repair the harm that has been caused by an offence, at least insofar as this can be achieved by purely financial means. At the same time it also serves symbolically to reforge the social bonds that bind people together. This characterization also helps to explain why the principle of state-funded compensation is sometimes confused with the concept of restorative justice since there is a high degree of congruence between the two, at least in terms of their ultimate aims. No attempt is made to engender personal accountability on the part of the offender, however, or to involve either party in a decision-making process that seeks to address the harm caused by an offence, and this makes it appropriate for them to be placed in separate conceptual categories.

Strengths and weaknesses of the CICS

Despite its theoretical incoherence, the state-funded criminal injuries compensation scheme enjoys one crucial advantage as a means of serving the interests of victims that is not shared by any other initiative, whether belonging to the criminal justice model or the restorative justice model. For a victim's entitlement to any award under the former scheme is – unusually – not dependent on the statistically highly remote possibility of an offender being apprehended,[6] prosecuted, convicted, ordered to pay compensation and having the ability to pay. Nor does it depend on an offender's willingness to participate in any form of restorative justice process, or on a decision taken by others that such a process might or might not be suitable. A state-funded compensation scheme, in other words, is – in certain respects at least – able to serve the interests of victims in a way that no restorative justice or conventional criminal justice initiative could hope to emulate. As such it is, in principle, capable of complementing various other victim-focused initiatives in a quite distinct way, and there would certainly be a strong case for retaining such a scheme even if the criminal justice system were to be radically reformed in the light of restorative justice precepts (see also Chapter 6).

Having said that, however, the criminal injuries compensation scheme is by no means perfect and, throughout its history, has never been entirely immune from tension and contradictions. One of the scheme's most serious limitations relates to its eligibility criteria. These were, from the outset, drafted in such a way as to strongly favour the interests of those conforming to Christie's stereotypical 'ideal victim' (see Chapter 1), at the expense of those who might in some way be deemed to be 'undeserving'. Indeed, the principle of 'desert' has, over the years, featured rather more prominently among the scheme's eligibility criteria in many respects than that of 'welfare need'. This was particularly true of the original eligibility rules, which explicitly allowed the then Criminal Injuries Compensation Board to withhold payment from victims whom they considered to be undeserving with respect either to their character or their lifestyle (Miers, 1978: 177, 1990b: 75–99). Thus, for example, the claims of prostitutes who were victims of sexual assault were liable to be rejected or reduced on the ground that their lifestyle took them out of the category of blameless victims.[7] Still more controversially, even the claims of non-prostitute victims of sexual assault were liable to be scrutinized with particular care to determine, for example, whether the victim might have borne any responsibility as a result of provocation (Williams, 1972: 20, 34).

Another category of victims whose claims were likely to be rejected out of hand in the early days of the scheme was that of assault victims where the assailant was living with the victim as a member of the same family. This 'familial exclusion clause' also betrays a preference for 'ideal victims' who, it will be recalled, are those victimized by 'unknown' offenders, though this particular rule was abolished in 1979 (Rock, 1990: 271). Provisions allowing the authorities to exclude claims based on the victim's 'undeserving' character or lifestyle were also abolished when the criminal injuries compensation scheme was reformed and reconstituted on a statutory footing in the mid-1990s. But even then the principle of withholding payment from 'undeserving' victims who fall outside the stereotypical image of the 'worthy' victim was retained in provisions authorizing the Criminal Injuries Compensation Authority[8] to withhold payment from those with unspent criminal convictions. Moreover, payment may still be denied even if the convictions relate to minor non-violent offences that have no bearing on the injury that is the subject of a claim.[9] Although some (see e.g. Zedner, 2002: 442) have justifiably questioned the logicality of such a principle, it again reflects a preference for denying claims by those who do not conform to the 'innocent victim' stereotype. This includes both the category of 'delinquent' victims who, as Miers (2000: 90) reminds us, resemble offenders too closely (and might even themselves have been formally so categorized in the past) and, a fortiori, the category of offender claimants. Moreover, victims who take the law into their own hands and suffer personal injury as a result would also be refused compensation since the 'politicization of the victim of crime' requires that the taxpayer be asked to compensate only those victims who present 'deserving' characteristics (Miers, 2000: 90). Just under 10 per cent of applications each year are rejected on the ground that the victim was not 'blameless'.

If the concept of the 'ideal victim' has loomed large in the philosophy and practice of the criminal injuries compensation scheme, the same might also be said of the concept of the 'ideal offence'. Ever since its inception, compensation has been restricted to victims of crimes of violence, which clearly fall into the category of a stereotypically 'predatory offence', though some have questioned the rationale for denying assistance to other categories of victims (Ashworth, 1986; Duff, 1987). This restriction also gave rise to definitional problems in the early days of the scheme, which adopted a very legalistic interpretation of the 'offence' requirement. This led it to exclude claims by victims of offenders who lacked the requisite *mens rea* to commit an offence in law, either because they were too young or because of a lack of mental capacity. However, the scheme was subsequently amended to include such victimizing events (Miers, 1990b: 127; see also Criminal Injuries Compensation Authority, 2001: para. 7.10, para. 10 of the scheme). Victims who are injured as a direct result of a crime of arson may also qualify for compensation even though this is not technically an offence involving violence. However, a less generous line has been taken with other injuries even where these are caused by criminal breaches of certain regulatory requirements (the Factories Acts, for example), since these are not defined as violent offences. Distinctions such as these, although seemingly illogical, may also be explained on the basis of the 'ideal offence' principle. Although victims are only compensated in respect of injuries that are directly attributable to a crime of violence, this may include certain categories of indirect or secondary victims: for example those injured while attempting to catch an offender. In exceptional circumstances, this could also extend to police officers or firefighters who are injured in the course of their duties. Nevertheless, over 90 per cent of applicants are victims of a restricted range of violent offences (mostly involving assaults) that are set out in ss. 18, 20 or 47 of the Offences against the Person Act 1861 (Miers, 2000: 89).

Another set of limitations associated with the criminal injuries compensation scheme relates to the type of assistance that is available, which is restricted to financial compensation, and also the basis on which any such awards are calculated. Although financial compensation confers a material benefit – that in some cases can be substantial – on the recipient, money alone is incapable of meeting many of the other physical, emotional or practical consequences of an offence. Moreover, the process of applying for compensation can be very time consuming and delays were a particular problem under the old pre-1996 scheme, which was criticized for its inefficiency (Home Office Management Advisory Services, 1991).[10] Another criticism that has been levelled against the scheme relates to the paternalistic way in which it was set up without any reference to victims themselves (Shapland, 1981). Moreover, the scheme was launched without any attempt to ascertain whether financial compensation from the state (as opposed to the offender) is capable of alleviating the victim's suffering, restoring their sense of moral worth or overcoming any reluctance to co-operate with the criminal justice system.

With regard to the calculation of any award that might be payable, the scheme has always been subject to a minimum award threshold, which currently stands at £1000. As a result, compensation is effectively denied to the great majority of victims of minor assaults and robberies who might otherwise have been eligible. Despite such overt 'rationing' devices, demand for the scheme grew rapidly during the latter part of the twentieth century and, because of this, a new tariff system was introduced in 1995, which replaced the old common law approach based on the civil damages principle. The twin aims of the reform were to curtail the rapidly escalating costs of the scheme and to improve its administrative efficiency by simplifying the process of calculating awards.

The switch to a tariff-based approach and its consequences

Under the tariff system, over 300 different types of injury are listed, all of which are grouped into 25 bands comprising injuries of comparable seriousness (see Criminal Injuries Compensation Authority, 2001). Each band equates with a tariff level ranging from £1000 to £250,000 but, unlike the old system, separate payments are not normally made in respect of loss of earnings or expenses, so the new system is significantly less generous than its predecessor in this respect. However, the most severely injured victims – those who are incapacitated as a result of their injuries for longer than 28 weeks – do qualify for loss of earnings and other earnings, such as the cost of care provision. This is in addition to the basic lump sum, but is subject to a maximum payment of £500,000, which is twice the highest tariff level. This exception was introduced as a concession by the Conservative government – which introduced the new tariff system in 1995 – following an outcry over the original proposals, which were denounced as a crude attempt to decrease public expenditure at the expense of victims.

However, as Duff (1998: 125ff) has pointed out, the switch from a common law based approach to a twin-track or hybrid tariff system has rendered the philosophical basis of the scheme even less theoretically coherent than it was before. Moreover, because the level of compensation is no longer tailored in the great majority of cases to the individual circumstances of the claimant, the scheme as a whole has become significantly less victim centred than it was when first introduced. Thus, the new scheme introduces an additional degree of ambiguity by making it appear as if the level of compensation is determined less by the victim's particular plight than by the gravity of the offence. Furthermore, there is also a danger that, if tariff levels fail to keep pace with inflation,[11] the gap between them and common law damages awards will steadily increase over time, thereby reducing the material benefit available to victims and rendering the symbolic function increasingly tokenistic.[12]

A further limitation of the criminal injuries compensation scheme relates to the issue of access to the scheme and the way this is regulated. When first introduced, the onus was firmly on victims to apply for compensation, but few were aware of the scheme unless officials took the trouble to inform them of its existence. Consequently, the take-up rate was, not surprisingly, found to be very low (Shapland et al., 1985). By 1999, however, there were over 43,000 successful claimants and £206 million was paid in compensation (Home Office, 2000a).[13] Even though the existence of the scheme and its operation are now much more widely publicized than at any time in the past,[14] the police still effectively act as gatekeepers to it, and concerns have been expressed about the way they perform this role (Newburn and Merry, 1990; Zedner, 2002: 442). For example, they may fail to inform, or seek to deter, those they consider to be inappropriate claimants. Rather more proactively, they may also pass on information (for example, relating to an applicant's previous criminal history) that could have a bearing on the success of any application to the Criminal Injuries Compensation Authority.

Finally, Rock (1990: 275) has suggested that, in its early years, even the very existence of the scheme acted as a block on any further victim-focused initiatives. For it enabled government officials to persuade themselves, and also to try to convince others, that it was doing all that could reasonably be expected to meet the needs of victims. Helen Reeves, who was the first national development officer for the National Association of Victim Support Schemes, certainly took the view in 1986 that the existence of the scheme made it harder to elicit government support for her organization, which was soon to become much better known as Victim Support.[15]

Victim Support

Origins and expansion: from local initiative to nationwide key player

Victim Support represents a very different form of welfare-oriented approach towards the victims of crime; its main characteristics include the provision of *services* (as opposed to financial compensation) by a network of local *community-based voluntary organizations* (as opposed to the state) that are *independent* of the criminal justice system. The organization has been in existence for just 30 years since the first local scheme was established in Bristol in 1974 (Gay et al., 1975; Holtom and Raynor, 1988). During the intervening period it has achieved a phenomenal rate of growth with regard to both the size and scale of its operations, and this expansion has been matched by equally profound changes in its source of funding, modus operandi and also (albeit to a somewhat lesser extent) in its operating philosophy.

The number of local victim support schemes and branches increased from 34 in 1979 to 305 in 1987 (Rock, 1990: 212) and by early 2003, 389 schemes were listed on Victim Support websites for England and Wales (including Northern Ireland and the Channel Islands) and Scotland.[16] During the financial year 2002–3, the organization employed 1155 people and co-ordinated a total of just under 12,000 volunteer supporters (making a total of just over 13,000 people in total) who between them offered a range of support services to nearly one and a half million (1,404,130) victim referrals (Victim Support, 2003a). The referral rate was 12 per cent higher than in the previous year, and represents an increase in the number of victims who were 'offered assistance' of more than 75 per cent since the previous decade (1992–3). In 1980 a mere 12,000 victims (in round figures) had been referred to Victim Support.

Much of this expansion has been made possible by Victim Support's continuing success over the years in securing increasing levels of public funding from successive governments. One of the most notable upward hikes in recent years was a more than twofold increase in funding from £11.7 million in 1997 to £28 million by April 2002 (Home Office et al., 2002a: para. 2.13), though it had more or less levelled off the following year.[17] During this same period victims were accorded a much higher profile on the criminal justice policy agenda and there were also signs of a potentially equally significant shift in the direction of Victim Support's own policy stance.

In its early days, Victim Support was an avowedly apolitical voluntary sector organization offering a fairly limited range of services to an equally restricted victim clientèle. Over the intervening years, however, all these original attributes have undergone a significant transformation. In terms of its operating philosophy, Victim Support originally adopted a predominantly personalized 'befriending' role that was founded on principles of 'good neighbourliness' and placed a heavy emphasis on contacting victims individually to offer them practical advice[18] and emotional support in a face-to-face meeting (Maguire and Kynch, 2000: 14). Local victim support schemes were initially heavily dependent upon the police for their referrals, and this resulted in a tendency to concentrate on victims who conformed to an 'ideal-typical' stereotype, the vast majority of whom consisted of domestic burglary victims. Schemes also had to contend with a variety of other problems including irregular referral rates, reluctance on the part of the police to pass on 'confidential' victim contact information and an insistence on eliciting prior consent from victims before passing on their details to Victim Support. Although these problems were eventually overcome, similar difficulties have been encountered by a number of restorative justice initiatives, as we shall see in Chapter 4.

A major breakthrough for Victim Support took the form of a gradual willingness on the part of the police during the 1980s to adopt an 'automatic' referral system encompassing several major categories of crime; a policy that was ultimately endorsed by national police representatives. This policy was incorporated in a Code of Practice (Victim Support, 1995b) and includes the following offences: arson, assaults (other than domestic violence),[19] burglary, criminal damage against private premises, robbery and theft from the person. The most obvious effect was to 'open the floodgates' in terms of the number of referrals received by individual victim support schemes, since they were all expected to commit themselves to the Code of Practice. But an indirect consequence was to pass the responsibility for 'gatekeeping' from the police to each local co-ordinator, who henceforth had to decide not only which victims should be offered assistance but also, because of the numbers involved, the kind and intensity of service that was on offer.

By the late 1980s, Victim Support was receiving government support on a scale that was large enough to deliver some degree of assistance for victims on a national basis. However, this simply increased the responsibility to demonstrate that public money was being spent in a principled, responsible, equitable and effective manner. Moreover, the publication of the Victim's Charter in 1990, which was updated in 1996, set out the standards of service that victims who were covered by its Code of Practice (see above) were entitled to expect (Home Office, 1996: Standard 25). For its part, Victim Support accepted a commitment to provide services to '*all* victims of crime', and to ensure that '*all* victims are provided with appropriate information, recognition and support' (Victim Support, 1995a; emphasis added).

Assessing the performance of Victim Support[20]

The inclusion of relevant questions in the British Crime Survey makes it possible in principle to monitor the performance of Victim Support in discharging these responsibilities, and this was assessed in a report based on data provided by the 1998 survey (Maguire and Kynch 2000).[21] With regard to the pattern of contact with victims, the vast majority of those who recalled some contact from Victim Support had reported the incident to the police.[22] Allowing for the fact that not all incidents that are reported to the police are recorded by them as crimes, Maguire and Kynch estimated that the contact rate in respect of 'recorded' offences was around 29 per cent.[23] Although somewhat lower than the estimate of 45 per cent that is derived from Victim Support's own referral statistics, they point out that much of the difference is likely to be accounted for by a failure to recall having received a Victim Support leaflet.

With regard to those offences that are recorded by the police, the study concluded that Victim Support were reasonably successful in striking an appropriate balance between the aim of offering assistance to every type of victim and that of targeting resources on those most in need. Thus, those most likely to be contacted included victims of burglary (53 per cent estimated contact rate), wounding or robbery (43 per cent) – which, as we saw in Chapter 1, are the offence types that are likely to provoke the greatest emotional reaction – and also theft from the person (45 per cent). Moreover, victims reporting the highest levels of emotional impact and expressing the greatest level of need – for example, victims of more serious offences, poorer victims and those belonging to exceptionally vulnerable groups – were on the whole most likely to be contacted. However, the organization was less effective in targeting other groups reporting high levels of impact and need, such as male victims of violence and victims of serial offences, threats and intimidation. To this extent Victim Support could still be said to be mainly targeting 'stereotypically ideal' victims as opposed to those (including young unemployed males and those subject to chronic processes of victimization) who fit less comfortably into this category.

Victim Support referral statistics for 2002–3 suggest that just over 30 per cent of referrals related to violent (including sexual) offences, and 28 per cent related to burglary (Victim Support, 2003a). Theft and criminal damage offences accounted for most of the remainder. Domestic violence (which falls outside the 'automatic referral' category) accounted for just over 5 per cent of the total, and racially motivated crimes for just under 2 per cent, though numerically the latter category had increased tenfold since 1992–3. The latter figures appear to reflect a willingness to extend the scope of the service beyond the traditional category of 'stereotypical' offence types, though they still account for only a small proportion of all referrals.

As for the mode of contact, the Maguire and Kynch survey found that the commonest method involves a letter and/or leaflet (69 per cent). Only

13 per cent of initial contacts took the form of an 'unannounced visit' from a volunteer, the remainder of contacts being made by telephone. But when follow-up visits are included, the proportion of victims who received a visit from a volunteer was 26 per cent, which is broadly in line with earlier findings. Once again, the survey concluded that the organization was reasonably successful in contacting and visiting those reporting the greatest impact or who expressed a wish for assistance. Among those who recalled some contact with Victim Support, 58 per cent rated the service as 'fairly' or 'very helpful'. For those who were contacted by telephone, the figure was higher (69 per cent), and higher still in respect of those who received a visit (80 per cent). Even among those who just received a letter or leaflet, the 'satisfaction rating' was 46 per cent. The survey also reported an increasing public awareness of the service; 79 per cent of victims had heard of Victim Support compared with only 32 per cent in 1984.

An expanding agenda

In recent years Victim Support has sought in various ways to improve the accessibility of its service, increase the range of victims it is able to assist and also expand the type of service that it provides. In 1998 a new national telephone helpline, Victim Supportline, was launched with the aim of encouraging self-referrals and extending the service that is offered to the very many victims (nearly 55 per cent) who choose not to report an incident to the police. Although the number of calls has doubled since its introduction, it has been relatively slow to take off and the proportion of self-referrals or referrals from other agencies remains very small at just under 2 per cent of the total in 2002–3 (slightly down on the 2001 figure of 3.4 per cent; Victim Support, 2003a). However, almost half of all calls related to violent crime, and increases were recorded in respect of domestic violence, child abuse and rape. Over half of those using the service were referred on or directed to their local Victim Support scheme for further assistance.

In addition to the service it provides directly for victims, Victim Support also hosts and supports a small self-help group: Support after Manslaughter and Murder (SAMM), which was registered as a charity in 1990. This organization offers those who are bereaved as a result of murder or manslaughter emotional support from volunteers who are uniquely qualified to do so, having themselves lost relatives in this way. SAMM is funded by charitable donations and (since 1999) by a small grant from the Home Office, which is also administered on its behalf by Victim Support. In addition to its highly regarded victim assistance and support role, SAMM also adopts a rather more controversial victim advocacy stance, and has been criticized in this regard for advocating harsher punishment for offenders (see for example, Williams, 1996).

One of Victim Support's principal strengths over the years has been its ability to identify genuine needs that are not being met, show how they might be addressed, raise funding from central government to enable this to happen and then set up and manage the new service (Williams, 1999a: 90ff). A classic example is the Witness Support initiative, which grew out of a recognition on the part of local schemes that victims were often ill-informed about the way their case might be dealt with in court and frequently had distressing encounters with offenders or their supporters while attending court.[24] After establishing a demonstration project that showed how these needs might effectively be met, Victim Support success-fully obtained funding for a network of Witness Support schemes and achieved nationwide coverage in respect of Crown Courts by 1996. Wit-nesses and victims, most of whom are referred by the Crown Prosecution Service, are offered support both before (for example, in the form of information and pre-trial visits to court), during and after trial. By the end of March 2002, Victim Support had achieved its target of setting up a Witness Service in every magistrates' court in England and Wales in add-ition to those already established in Crown Courts (Victim Support, 2002a: 16). The new service is separately funded and administered, with its own local committee structure and volunteers, which reduces the risk of role conflict that might otherwise arise.

This relatively uncontroversial, service-oriented approach combined with a reputation for efficiency has enabled Victim Support to establish itself as one of the 'key players' within the criminal justice system even though not strictly part of the system, and despite its formal status as a voluntary organization. Its membership of the government's interdepart-mental Victims Steering Group affords further evidence of the degree of influence it has managed to secure within policymaking circles. For the most part this has been achieved without any overt political lobbying or campaigning 'victim advocacy' work. In recent years, however, there have been growing signs that the organization is prepared to adopt a more part-isan, proactive approach, and this is reflected in its willingness to add an increasingly overt rights-based discourse to the vocabulary it uses. The first indication that it might be prepared to adopt a more oppositional stance came in 1995 when it spoke out against government proposals to reduce the level of compensation awarded to victims under the criminal injuries compensation scheme (see above). It also broke new ground in the same year by launching a campaign promoting the introduction of new enforce-able rights for victims of crime (Victim Support, 1995a). They included a 'right' to be treated with 'respect, recognition and support', to be heard, to receive protection from criminal justice agencies, to be kept informed about the progress of their case and also to receive compensation.[25]

Since then, Victim Support has increasingly turned its attention towards the needs of those victims who have no involvement of any kind with the criminal justice system, and who actually constitute the great majority of all victims. Thus, in respect of crimes against individuals and their prop-erty, it is estimated that out of every 100 such offences, 54.8 per cent are never reported to the police, which is the normal prerequisite for any kind of formal victim-focused intervention to take place.[26] This leaves just over

45 per cent that are reported to the police. Only just over one-half of these are recorded as crimes by the police, however, which accounts for under one-quarter of the original total (24.3 per cent). Just over one in 20 (5.5 per cent) are 'cleared up' or detected. Only 3 per cent result in an offender receiving a caution of conviction in respect of the offence they have committed.

This phenomenon, which is usually referred to as the 'attrition rate' (Home Office, 1999a)[27] is extremely important because it underlines the serious limitations to which virtually all victim-focused initiatives are subject, regardless of the approach or model with which they are associated. Initiatives linked to the criminal justice model are particularly deficient in this respect since at best they normally only apply in respect of offences that are brought to the attention of the police and, in reality, are only likely to benefit a small subset of these. Initiatives linked to the welfare model are likewise normally restricted in scope to offences that have at least been reported to the police (apart from limited initiatives such as the Victim Supportline, described above). (The extent to which restorative justice initiatives are subject to the same limitations will be assessed in Chapter 6.) In view of these limitations, Victim Support is correct in drawing attention to the needs of the great majority of victims whose offences receive no (or virtually no) intervention from the criminal justice system whatever.

In order to meet *their* needs, Victim Support published a manifesto in 2001, which reiterated the 1995 proposals calling for legislation to protect victims' rights, and also argued for a Commissioner for Victims of Crime (Victim Support, 2001). The government had already indicated that it favoured the introduction of a Victims' Ombudsman, whose primary task would presumably be to investigate complaints (Home Office, 2001a: para. 3.129). However, Victim Support argued for a commissioner who would, in effect, champion the best interests of crime victims in a wide variety of ways extending far beyond the traditional task of dealing with unresolved individual complaints. They include the scrutiny of proposed legislation to assess its probable effects on victims of crime;[28] responsibility for ensuring that agencies changed any policies or procedures that had not been proved to take account of the needs and interests of victims; action to tackle secondary victimization; the conduct of enquiries into matters of public concern that could not be resolved by means of individual cases; and the bringing of test cases. At the time it seemed unlikely that such a wide-ranging and radical 'shopping list' would be accepted in its entirety, even by a government that professed itself to be committed to 'rebalancing' the criminal justice system in the interests of victims, witnesses and communities. Nevertheless, the government's initial response, which appeared in the White Paper 'Justice for All', suggested a willingness to make some major concessions to these demands (Home Office et al., 2002a: paras. 2.45, 2.46). These and subsequent developments are dealt with more fully in Chapter 3.

Finally, in a policy report published in February 2002, Victim Support returned to a more traditional 'welfarist agenda' by setting out a wide range of social entitlements which should be available for all victims of crime irrespective of any involvement on the part of the criminal justice system (Victim Support, 2002b). For example, it argued that crime victims should have access to free healthcare services geared to meeting their needs (including access to counselling and psychiatric services) and that the government should adopt an integrated approach to ensure that those needs are actually met. Within the housing sphere, it argued that greater priority should be given to meeting the housing needs of crime victims (including the right to move to new and safer accommodation and new obligations on social landlords to meet minimum standards of security and repair). Finally, within the financial sphere, it argued that the benefits system needs to be overhauled to ensure that victims' needs are recognized and addressed, and that social landlords should be required to introduce contents insurance for tenants renting their properties.

Recent initiatives such as these show an increased willingness on the part of Victim Support to pursue a hybrid approach that combines its traditional victim assistance function with a much higher profile policy advocacy role. At one time this might have been viewed as an uncharacteristically reckless, 'high-risk' strategy since too much boat rocking could have jeopardized hard-won policy gains and influence. In the rapidly changing policy climate of recent years, however, such a shift appears to reflect a shrewd acknowledgement that there is no longer any need for the covert and defensive strategies that may have served the organization so well in the past. It also suggests that there may be more to be gained by not simply contributing to the fast-moving debate over victims' needs and entitlements but by seeking, wherever possible, to influence and set the terms of the policy agenda.

Other service-oriented victim assistance organizations

For many years Victim Support was the only victim assistance organization in receipt of regular government funding. While this state of affairs continued, it was considered to be the sole standard bearer for the 'official' wing of the victims' movement since it was the only organization formally recognized by policymakers as representing the interests of victims. There were other sister organizations such as Rape Crisis and Women's Aid, but as long as these were denied both funding and any degree of political recognition, they were apt to be characterized as belonging, in Robert Elias's (1993) terminology, to the 'hidden' or 'unofficial' victims' movement (Williams, 1999a: 70ff).

There are growing signs, however, that this formerly rigid dichotomy between an 'official', 'authorized' victims' movement and a 'samizdat' hidden wing of the same movement may be dissolving in the changed political climate with regard to victim issues. One harbinger of change is the fact that the Home Office was eventually persuaded – for a short time at least – to directly fund the Rape Crisis Federation, after years of refusal. Another is the increased willingness of victims' organizations to work together across the erstwhile 'binary divide', one example of which is the very close collaboration referred to earlier between Victim Support and Support after Murder and Manslaughter.

Of the other main 'service-oriented' organizations, the two best known and longest established are the Women's Aid movement and the Rape Crisis movement, both of which have combined the support they offer to individual victims of particular kinds of offences with a much more overtly political stance. The Women's Aid movement originated during the 1960s and 1970s at a time when feminist activists and campaigners began drawing attention to the plight of victims of domestic violence and abuse. They not only drew attention to a category of victims who were neither recognized nor catered for – because they fell outside the conventional 'ideal victim' stereotype – but also provided practical support in the form of 'refuges', information and advice and a collectivist philosophy based on self-help and mutual support. From the first refuge for battered women founded by Erin Pizzey in 1972 (Pizzey, 1974; see also Chapter 1), a network of 250 refuges has developed covering the whole of the United Kingdom. A national Women's Aid Federation was established in 1974, and the movement's activities also include educational and campaigning work, although continuing difficulties in obtaining regular core funding inhibit both the scale of its activities and the level of provision it is able to furnish in its refuges.

Rape Crisis Centres first developed in London during the 1970s, and now number around 37 local groups in England and Wales, with a further 5 groups in Scotland. The centres offer counselling, information about legal and medical matters plus emotional and practical support, for example, by accompanying women to police stations, courts, hospitals or special clinics. A key aim is to re-empower women who have experienced a debilitating loss of control at the hands of an attacker. The centres were for a time supported by a national Rape Crisis Federation that was established in 1996 but which closed, following a withdrawal of Home Office funding, in autum 2003 (Jones and Westmarland, 2004). In addition to the practical and emotional support provided for victims,[29] the movement also adopts a campaigning and educational role that seeks to challenge common misconceptions about rape by attributing responsibility to acts of male aggression and power that are rooted in deeply entrenched social attitudes towards women.

Victim lobby groups

All the organizations that have been described so far in this chapter aim to provide practical assistance and support to victims of crime and, although their approaches and methods differ considerably, as we have seen, this overarching 'service orientation' places them firmly within the 'welfare model'. The same cannot be said of all victim-oriented organizations, however, some of which have a radically different set of priorities and thus belong to a very different tradition. Victim lobby groups, for example, exist primarily to promote the interests of victims, or particular groups of victims, by means of political or media lobbying which in some cases is conducted in a highly polarized and partisan manner.

One victim lobby group, the Zito Trust, was founded in 1994, two years after Jonathon Zito was killed by a man who suffered from schizophrenia. It seeks to highlight issues relating to mental illness and the care of those affected by it, and campaigns in a vigorous but generally responsible way behind the scenes for the reform of mental health law and policy. It also campaigns to improve the treatment afforded to patients with mental illness, the support given to their carers and the level of provision for people who are victimized as the result of a breakdown in community care arrangements.

Other victim lobby groups adopt a much higher public profile and employ far more confrontational and unashamedly partisan tactics. This has been particularly true in the United States, where the victim movement has tended to assume a much more assertive and political stance in its support for victims. One highly influential organization is the National Association for Victim Assistance (NOVA), which was established in 1976 and has campaigned vigorously for new legislation to promote victims' rights and improve victim support measures. Many campaigning groups or 'victim advocacy' projects do not simply draw attention to deficiencies in the way the criminal justice system deals with victims but demand a fundamental overhaul so that it not only addresses the perceived needs and rights of victims but is far more punitive in the way it deals with offenders.[30] In some states this extends to campaigning for the retention or reintroduction of the death penalty.

In Britain this radical oppositional standpoint is confined to a few small pressure groups, of which the Victims of Crime Trust, founded in 1994 by a former British Transport Police officer, is one of the best known examples. Although it claims to represent and provide support to over 200 victims, many of whom are the relatives of murder victims, it is best known for its outspoken campaigning in pursuit of a highly partisan 'law and order' platform. While this is ostensibly conducted on behalf of and in the interests of victims, many of the issues on which the trust campaigns[31] appear to have little direct relevance to individual victims and seem to be part of a more general campaign to popularize punitive attitudes towards offenders. Victim lobby groups of this kind have very little in common with the welfare model that provided the focus for the present chapter. However, they do anticipate a switch of focus towards the contrasting criminal justice model, which is the subject of Chapter 3.

Conclusion

In this chapter we have turned the spotlight on two important sets of victim-focused initiatives that seek to put right the harm caused by an offence, and which are thus clearly *compatible with* restorative justice initiatives since they share the latter's 'harm redressing goal'. However, in most other respects the provision of state-funded financial compensation for the victims of violent offences and the rendering of advice, emotional support and practical assistance by voluntary networks such as victim support represent a conceptually quite distinct approach.

Readers may find it helpful at this point to refer once more to Table I.1 (pp. 6–7) in the Introduction, which seeks to encapsulate some of the distinctive features associated with this welfare model. Thus, both sets of initiatives derive from a very different *welfare-based* philosophical tradition that focuses exclusively on meeting the needs of victims without making any attempt to promote the accountability of the offender, which is another hallmark of the restorative justice approach. In terms of process, as we have seen, each of the welfare-based, victim-focused measures has its own modus operandi. Although the role assigned to the victim is different in each case, neither initiative seeks to involve victims in a restorative justice style inclusive decision-making process. Although both sets of welfare-based initiatives operate in rather different institutional contexts, they subsist almost entirely outwith the criminal justice process[32] (which is true of some but not all restorative justice approaches). Consequently, in view of these important differences between the different approaches, it seems sensible to assign the two main welfare-based initiatives we have examined in this chapter to a conceptually distinct model, which is how they are depicted in Table I.1 (pp. 6–7).[33]

Notes

1 Another manifestation of the same commitment is the interdepartmental Victims Steering Group, which consists of representatives of most of the major departments and agencies with responsibilities for victims, and which meets twice a year.

2 It was not quite the first such scheme in the world since New Zealand had set up its own scheme a few months earlier as a result of the Criminal Injuries Compensation Act of 1963. However, the latter was itself directly influenced by the policy debate that had been initiated in England by Margery Fry's proposals during the 1950s. See Rock (1990) for a detailed account of the origins of the scheme; see also Miers (1990b, 1997) and Duff (1998). The position with regard to other European criminal justice systems is set out briefly in Brienen and Hoegen (2000: 1097–8).

3 The acronym stands for Quasi-Autonomous Non-Governmental Organization,

which is a non-departmental public body that is appointed by the government to undertake some activity but is expected to exercise its functions independently.

4 'Social contract' theory furnishes one such rationale, premised on the reciprocal obligation that is owed by the state to protect its citizens from violent crime at the hands of their fellow citizens in return for their obedience to it. Since its citizens are obliged to renounce the use of violence and look to the state for protection, they could argue that they are entitled to compensation from the state when it fails to comply with this duty to protect them.

5 As an 'act of grace' rather than arising from any obligation, and with no acceptance of legal liability on the part of the state. Though as a public body with a duty to act judicially, the English courts quickly established that the board was subject to judicial review, which means that its decisions could be challenged if it could be shown to have exercised its discretion unlawfully. See *R. v. Criminal Injuries Compensation Board, ex parte Lain* [1967] 2 QB 864.

6 However, there are stringent reporting requirements, non-compliance with which on the part of the injured victim will preclude an award that might otherwise have been made.

7 In one case an applicant's award for loss of society was halved because the deceased victim was a prostitute and dealt in drugs (Miers, 1997: 160).

8 Created under the Criminal Injuries Compensation Act 1995, the Criminal Injuries Compensation Authority is successor to the original Criminal Injuries Compensation Board, which administered the non-statutory scheme that was originally introduced in 1964.

9 Paragraph 13(e) of the scheme. See Criminal Injuries Compensation Authority, (2001: para. 8.15–8.16), which explains the scale of any reductions that may be imposed on the basis of previous criminal convictions.

10 Even under the new tariff scheme, the target that was set in 1998–9 for issuing first decisions within 12 months of receipt of a claim was only 90 per cent. And the actual performance was worse, with only 81.7 per cent of claims being met within the target. The shortfall was partly due to staff recruitment problems and partly because of the need to divert resources to deal with the backlog of cases still to be determined by the outgoing Criminal Injuries Compensation Board. (Home Office annual reports available online at: www.archive.official-documents.co.uk/document/cm46/4657/ghome.pdf)

11 Such a risk appeared to be particularly acute when the new system was introduced since the Conservative government of the day was committed to reducing public expenditure as a matter of principle. Following a consultation exercise in 1999, however, the then relatively newly elected Labour government announced plans to extend the scope of the criminal injuries compensation scheme by increasing most tariff levels by 10 per cent, with additional significant increases for particular categories of victims. They include victims of rape, sexual assault and child abuse and those sustaining serious multiple injuries (Home Office, 2001a: para. 3.120).

12 N.B. In 2004, the government published a consultation paper that contained a range of options for further reform of the Criminal Injuries Compensation Scheme (Home Office, 2004). Among the proposals were measures to make the scheme more focused by transferring to employers the responsibility for compensating workers who are injured in the course of their employment, and also to improve the efficiency of the scheme. The funds released from this and other sources (including a surcharge on convicted offenders) could then be used to

finance a Victims' Fund for England and Wales, the purpose of which would be to fund a range of services to support victims of crime and also to prevent repeat victimization.

13 The government claimed that this was more than was paid out by all the other European schemes added together (Home Office, 2001a). Others, including Victim Support, were less impressed, pointing out that, as a percentage of all crime victims, only a fraction of 1 per cent received state compensation. Even if the analysis is restricted to victims of violent crime, which is arguably a fairer basis of comparison, the proportion of victims who receive compensation from the state is still less than 1.5 per cent (calculations based on British Crime Survey data contained in Kershaw et al., 2001).

14 See, for example, cjs online, the criminal justice system website at: www.cjsonline.org/citizen/victims/compensation.html

15 Victim Support continues to be critical of certain aspects of the scheme, particularly with regard to victims in receipt of means-tested benefits, which may be reduced where compensation of more than £3000 is awarded (Victim Support 2003b).

16 See www.victimsupport.org/site_home.html for Victim Support England and www.victimsupportsco.demon.co.uk/main/intro.html for Victim Support in Scotland. However, the growth in the number of schemes may now be at an end and could fall somewhat in the future as individual schemes reorganize under area management.

17 Although Victim Support does also rely on other sources of funding, including donations elicited from national and local fundraising campaigns and also trading activities, these are dwarfed in scale by the organization's heavy reliance on central government grants. In 2002–3, these accounted for over 96 per cent of its incoming resources of around £30 million (Victim Support, 2003a: 3).

18 For example, in assisting people with Criminal Injuries Compensation claims. Just under 14,000 people were helped in this way in 2001–2 (Victim Support, 2002a: 15).

19 Such offences may still be referred to Victim Support, as we shall see, but only with the consent of the victim. The same is also true of sexual offences (including rape), manslaughter, murder and road deaths (which may or may not involve a criminal offence).

20 One of the earliest studies of victim support schemes was undertaken by Maguire and Corbett (1987), and is still one of the most comprehensive surveys of its kind.

21 However, Maguire and Kynch (2000: 2) themselves warn against reading too much into the findings since victims with experience of Victim Support constitute a relatively small proportion of the total sample. Thus, only 400 victims from the 15,000 households canvassed recalled any contact with Victim Support, and only 101 of these were able to recall face-to-face contact with a volunteer.

22 Around the time of the 1998 survey, Victim Support had recently introduced a new method of initiating contact – Victim Supportline (see below) – one aim of which was to encourage self-referrals and thus extend the scope of the service to those who may not even have reported an incident to the police. But this had not been in place long enough for its effects to be assessed.

23 If the contact rate is calculated on the basis of all BCS crimes that are known to the police, however, then the reported 'strike rate' becomes a much more

modest 10 per cent. NB If *all* BCS incidents whether reported to the police or not are included the reported contact rate would be only 4 per cent.

24 NB These are examples of 'secondary victimization' (see Chapter 1) on the part of the criminal justice system.

25 Support for such 'rights' forms an important part of the conceptually distinct 'criminal justice model', and the issues this raises will be examined in Chapter 3.

26 But see the recent introduction of the Victims Supportline above.

27 More recently the government has taken to talking of 'The Justice Gap', which is the difference between the number of offences recorded by the police and those for which an offender is dealt with by means of a caution, conviction or has offences taken into consideration by the court (Home Office et al., 2002c). By excluding offences that are neither reported to the police nor recorded by them, the 'gap' revealed is smaller than that disclosed by the attrition rate since it suggests that just under one in five (19.8 per cent) of offenders are brought to justice. But this more selective presentation of the data excludes the interests of those victims whose crimes are not recorded by the police and may not even be reported to them, and is therefore incomplete and misleading from a victim-focused perspective.

28 This would almost be akin to a requirement to conduct a 'victim impact assessment' in respect of each new piece of legislation.

29 Or 'survivors' as the federation prefers to call them, because it is seen as a less disempowering term.

30 For example, Families and Friends of Murder Victims and Mothers against Drunken Drivers (MADD), which calls for tougher sentences for those convicted of drink driving offences. However, as Zedner (2002: 432) points out, there are exceptions and some groups, such as Parents of Murdered Children, refrain from active political involvement.

31 Recent examples include an attempt by prison inmates to invoke human rights legislation as a means of challenging the policy of prison authorities to restrict access to pornographic material; a prison charity which distributed to prison inmates a crossword puzzle featuring clues about criminal offences; and Jeffrey Archer's plans to publish a book based on his experiences in Belmarsh prison.

32 In the case of Victim Support, however, recent innovations such as the introduction of witness support schemes necessarily entail some limited involvement with criminal justice processes, albeit not in any formal capacity.

33 As opposed to lumping together all actions that aim to do justice by repairing the harm that has been caused by a crime, as some have argued (Bazemore and Walgrave, 1999: 48).

Further reading

Duff, P. (1998) Criminal injuries compensation, *Oxford Journal of Legal Studies*, 18: 105–42.

Miers, D. (1997) *State Compensation for Criminal Injuries*. London: Blackstone.

Rock, P. (1990) *Helping Victims of Crime: The Home Office and the Rise of Victim Support in England and Wales*. Clarendon Press, Oxford.

Williams, B. (1999a) *Working with Victims of Crime: Policies, Politics and Practice*. London: Jessica Kingsley.

Victims and the criminal justice system

Only a small minority of victims have any formal dealings with the criminal justice system since, as we have seen, over half of all conventional crimes are not reported to the police. Of those that are, only 60 per cent are recorded as such by the police (Simmons et al., 2002). Furthermore, only 5 per cent of all conventional offences result in an offender being detected, and only 2 per cent result in a conviction and possible sentence. It follows that only a small proportion of all victims is likely to come into contact with criminal justice agencies other than the police. For those victims who do have dealings with the criminal justice system, however, the way they are treated is likely to have an important bearing on their ability to cope with their offence and put it behind them. It could also influence their willingness to report future crimes and collaborate with criminal justice agencies in seeking to secure the conviction and punishment of those who are responsible. Since almost 90 per cent of recorded crime is brought to the attention of the police by victims or those acting on behalf of victims (JUSTICE, 1998), victims clearly have an important part to play in the criminal justice process, particularly in those cases in which the defendant pleads not guilty. Perhaps surprisingly, in view of its dependence on the willingness of victims to co-operate, the criminal justice system's approach towards victims has in the past been characterized – at least within common law jurisdictions – at best by neglect and at times by insensitive and harsh treatment. One symptom of the low priority that has historically been accorded to victims is the tiny proportion of the total criminal justice budget that is devoted to meeting the needs of victims.[1] In recent years, however, a series of victim-focused initiatives has been introduced, as a result of which victims now enjoy a considerably higher profile within the criminal justice process than at any time in the past.

In order to make sense of these recent developments, this chapter will begin by setting out the extent to which victims' interests were neglected during the long 'era of victim disenfranchisement' that may only now be drawing to a close. The various policy initiatives – both international and domestic – that have sought to integrate victims within the criminal justice process are then briefly outlined. This is followed by an assessment of a range of victim-focused reforms that have attempted to accommodate a victim perspective within the framework of the conventional criminal justice system. The key feature of this system is its confrontational and exclusionary approach towards the treatment of offenders but, as we shall see, this also entails constraints for the full enfranchisement of victims. Those victim-focused initiatives that are associated with restorative justice processes, on the other hand, derive from very different philosophical foundations. They appear to offer the prospect of a very different set of relations between offenders, victims and other key stakeholders: one that is predicated on the basis of a much more socially inclusive approach. Even though some attempts have been made to incorporate restorative justice initiatives within the conventional criminal justice system in recent years, analytically speaking such developments belong to a quite distinct tradition and, consequently, will be dealt with separately in subsequent chapters.

Victim neglect during the 'era of disenfranchisement'

The 'era of victim disenfranchisement' began during the early part of the nineteenth century, at around the time that the state began to assume primary responsibility for the prosecution of offenders instead of leaving it up to victims themselves, or to prosecution societies acting on their behalf, as in the past. This transfer of responsibilities coincided with the introduction of professional police forces, whose task it was to investigate offences and prosecute suspected offenders. But such developments should be seen in the context of a much wider shift in the nature of penality – often referred to as the 'great transformation' – in which new institutions and techniques of social control were fashioned during the late eighteenth and early nineteenth centuries to meet the requirements of the new industrial social order. Conceptually, the reallocation of responsibility for bringing offenders to justice was signified by the fact that crime henceforth came to be viewed principally as an offence against the state, representing 'society' as a whole. Symbolically it was signified by the fact that prosecutions were brought in the name of the Crown rather than the victim. Although these developments had some advantages for victims, who were no longer responsible for conducting their own investigations and prosecutions,[2] there was also a price to be paid in terms of a distancing and disempowerment of victims from 'their' case. The subsequent neglect of victims during the era of disenfranchisement came to be reflected in terms of their status, role and entitlement to redress.

Within common law based adversarial systems of criminal justice there are only two parties to a case: prosecution and defence. Consequently, victims have no formal status within the proceedings, as is possible (at least in principle) within inquisitorial systems. Nor have victims been entitled to any special consideration or respect by virtue of the harm they might have experienced. The lack of any formal status means that in practice victims have not even been kept informed about 'their' case – for example whether a suspect had been arrested, a prosecution initiated or an offender sentenced and punished. There has certainly been no expectation that they should be consulted or provided with reasons for any of the decisions that may have been taken during the course of the case. As critics have pointed out during the more recent period of victim sensitization, the denial of such 'common courtesies' has only served to increase the feelings of victimization and helplessness experienced by many victims (JUSTICE, 1998: 34).

In the absence of any formal 'standing', the only role accorded to the victim was to provide any information that might be required by the prosecution and, if necessary, to testify as a witness in court in the event of a not guilty plea. Or, as John Braithwaite (1992: 4) more graphically put it, their presence was only required to provide 'evidentiary cannon fodder', as opposed to any expectation they themselves might have as a 'citizen with participatory rights and obligations'. The absence of any formal status has also meant that, if they were required to attend court, victims were not furnished with any special provision (such as separate waiting rooms) or facilities beyond those that were generally available, even though this might bring them into contact with defendants and their supporters. Lack of separate provision was symptomatic of a failure on the part of criminal justice officials to acknowledge the potential vulnerability of many witnesses, and their need for protection from possible intimidation by prosecution witnesses. Even inside the courtroom, the gladiatorial nature of adversarial proceedings has the effect of exposing victims to rigorous and, at times, oppressive cross-examination by defence counsel (or even, on occasion, by the defendant in person). This can often amount to secondary victimization on the part of the criminal justice system itself (Ellison, 2001: 87ff; Doak, 2003: 31), particularly in the case of rape offences (Temkin, 1987: 6–8; Soothill and Soothill, 1993).

Finally, the lack of any formal standing meant that the victim's 'entitlement to redress' was likewise exceedingly limited during the era of disenfranchisement. In theory a victim could (and still can) bring a private prosecution though, lacking the necessary resources and expertise, most victims leave it up to the police and Crown Prosecution Service to decide whether or not to initiate criminal proceedings. Prior to the victim-focused reforms of the last two decades, such decisions were taken on the basis of official assessments of what 'the public interest' demands, and not according to the desires of the victim who, in any event as we have seen, was not normally consulted.[3] In the event of a conviction, the primary issue facing the court is how to punish the offender. This decision was likewise determined chiefly on the basis of public interest considerations such as the seriousness of the offence viewed in the light of the offender's culpability, the need for proportionality and the desirability of consistency of treatment for like offenders.[4] Until recently, the interests and wishes of victims on matters of sentencing, like those relating to prosecution decisions, have at best been relegated to subordinate considerations when determining the public interest. Whatever a victim may have felt about the punishment imposed on 'their' offender, it would not normally provide any direct redress for the personal harm they may have experienced. No such provision was forthcoming from the criminal justice system during the era of victim disenfranchisement. Moreover the scope for direct redress remains extremely limited, as we shall see, despite the strengthening of victims' entitlement to financial compensation from their offenders in recent years.

In short, the conventional criminal justice system has for very many years failed victims in three principal respects. First, it has failed to acknowledge the special status of victims arising from the fact that they have personally suffered harm of some kind as a result of the offence. This failure has been compounded by a withholding of relevant information and a reluctance to provide victims with appropriate support. Second, it has denied victims any formal role in the proceedings except on the limited occasions when they were needed in order to pursue criminal justice goals, in which case their involvement was purely instrumental. Third, it has failed to provide any material redress for the personal harm that victims might have sustained. As a result, all victims were for many years disenfranchised by the system, and many felt disempowered, exploited or even traumatized as a result of their experience.

Victim-focused policy initiatives

Deeply entrenched as it was, the continuing disenfranchisement of victims came under increasing pressure during the final decades of the twentieth century in the face of rapidly changing public and official perceptions of crime victims and their entitlements (see Chapter 1). At an international level, one of the first standard-setting initiatives was the UN Declaration of Basic Principles for Justice for Victims of Crime and Abuse of Power, which was adopted by the UN General Assembly in 1985 (United Nations, 1985). The Declaration set out a number of victim entitlements including the following: access to justice; to be treated with respect; to be provided with information; to have their views considered on matters relating to their personal interests; and to restitution, compensation and assistance. The Council of Europe has also published various declarations relating to the rights of victims of crime,[5] culminating in the adoption by the Council of Ministers in 2001 of a Framework Decision on the Standing of Victims in Criminal Proceedings (EU Council of Justice and Home Affairs Ministers, 2001). This echoes the UN Declaration in certain respects since it too stipulates that legal systems should treat victims with respect (Article 2), provide them with information relating to their case (Article 4), allow them to be heard during proceedings and to provide evidence (Article 3), and should also make provision for vulnerable victims (Article 8(4)). In contrast to other international provisions, the Decision itself is binding on member states, and most of its provisions came into force in March 2002. However, the rights referred to are highly generalized (and do not, for example, require that victims should be treated as parties to a case), leaving considerable discretion for states to determine how they should be implemented.

The promulgation of victim-sensitive standards in international instruments such as these has been echoed in the adoption of various kinds of victim-focused reforms across a wide range of jurisdictions.[6] In England and Wales, the process of enfranchising victims within the framework of the conventional criminal justice system proceeded initially on a piecemeal basis, beginning with the introduction of compensation orders in 1972 (described below).[7] A series of disparate initiatives by the Home Office during the 1980s provided evidence of a growing sensitization regarding victim issues. They included the issuing of two Home Office circulars: one addressed to chief constables containing guidance on the treatment of victims of rape and domestic violence (Home Office, 1986) and one issued to all criminal justice agencies urging improvements in the way victims were dealt with (Home Office, 1988). In addition, two sets of information leaflets were prepared for victims themselves: one, entitled 'Victims of Crime', providing information about compensation; the other, entitled 'Witness in Court', explaining what was involved for those called upon to give evidence in court.

However, the first signs of a more co-ordinated approach came with the publication of the Victim's Charter in 1990 (Home Office, 1990).[8] This purported to provide a 'Statement of Rights of Victims of Crime', though critics were quick to point out that it contained no new rights, while those to which it referred were insubstantial in terms of content and in any case mostly legally unenforceable (Victim Support, 1990; Cavadino and Dignan, 1992; Fenwick, 1995).[9] Williams (1999a: 76) has correctly pointed out that in reality the initial version of the Charter did little more than set out some 'guiding principles' on the treatment of victims, record progress to date on improving the lot of victims and subtly identify areas where further progress was needed. This was accomplished by identifying a checklist of questions for criminal justice agencies to consider, several of which referred to aspects of government policy that were not yet being implemented. A second edition of the Charter, published in 1996, described itself – somewhat more modestly and realistically – as 'A Statement of Service Standards for Victims of Crime'.[10]

Further reference will be made to the content of the Victim's Charter in the following section, but an important preliminary observation at this point relates to the extremely limited and selective way in which both victims and offenders are conceptualized in both editions of the Charter. Critics have pointed out that throughout the Charter both parties are exclusively assumed to be individuals: 'natural persons' as opposed to corporate entities (Mawby and Walklate, 1994; Williams, 1999b; Edwards, 2001: 46). Thus, the only offences that are specifically mentioned in the Charter are the conventional 'predatory offences' of murder, rape, sexual and other assaults, theft and burglary, thereby omitting regulatory offences that are more likely to be committed by corporate offenders. Likewise, no reference is made to the victims of corporate crime such as company frauds, pollution and environmental offences and health and safety infractions all of which appear to fall outside the ambit of the Charter. This is in spite of the large numbers of victims involved and the fact that the harm they suffer is frequently greater than that suffered by conventional victims (Sanders, 2002: 199). In terms of its content therefore, the Charter largely embodies the stereotype of Christie's archetypal victim to which reference was made in Chapter 1. Rock (2002b) has also complained about the selectivity of the Home Office's concept of victimhood, noting the further omission of victims of road accidents and school bullying. In its review of the Victim's Charter, the Home Office indicated that it was willing to consider the inclusion of those victimized as a result of road traffic incidents, whether or not criminal charges are brought, but did not even acknowledge the case for extending the definition of victims to those affected by regulatory offences committed by corporate offenders (Home Office, 2001b).[11]

In July 2002, the government published a White Paper entitled 'Justice for All', in which it identified three key areas for reform: one was the need to 'rebalance the criminal justice system in favour of victims';[12] a second was to provide the police and prosecution with the tools to bring more offenders to justice; a third was to take tough action on anti-social behaviour, hard drugs and violent crime (Home Office et al., 2002a). All three policy initiatives were announced amid considerable publicity, but the time taken to bring the victim reforms to fruition contrasts strikingly with the rapid progress in bringing forward the other two key sets of proposals contained in the 'Justice for All' White Paper. Thus, proposals to improve the effectiveness of the criminal justice system in bringing offenders to justice[13] were set out in the Criminal Justice Bill, which was published in the autumn of 2002 and enacted in December 2003. Proposals for dealing more effectively with anti-social behaviour were announced in the spring of 2003, and the ensuing Anti-Social Behaviour Act received the Royal Assent on 20 November 2003. Meanwhile, a 'Victims of Crime Bill', which was expected to have been announced in spring 2003, was shelved in favour of the latter measure (Travis, 2003), despite promises in both the 1997 and 2001 Labour election manifestos to introduce such a Bill. It was not until December 2003 that the Domestic Violence, Crime and Victims Bill was finally published.

The Bill incorporated a number of provisions that were first announced in a leaflet called 'A Better Deal for Victims and Witnesses', published in November 2002, in which three government departments set out their plans for '[bringing] victims closer to the centre of the criminal justice system' (Home Office et al., 2002b).

The plans included four key elements, the first of which was the publication in July 2003 of a national strategy for victims and witnesses setting out key principles and a programme of initiatives for the benefit of victims both within and beyond the criminal justice system (Home Office et al., 2003). The second element was a proposal to replace the voluntary Victim's Charter with a statutory Code of Practice,[14] the details of which were outlined in the Domestic Violence, Crime and Victims Bill referred to above. However, the Home Office review of the Victim's Charter had previously expressed a preference for establishing broad guiding principles rather than creating specific legislative rights (Home Office, 2001b). The Bill itself specifically states (in Clause 23) that failure to comply with the code 'does not, in itself, give rise to any liability to legal proceedings'. Consequently, the principal 'remedies' for victims who do not receive the standards of service to which they are supposed to be entitled will continue to take the form of internal 'grievance procedures' rather than enforceable legal remedies. The only additional entitlement to supplement the complaints mechanisms that have previously been established by individual agencies themselves is a right to refer any complaint to the Parliamentary Ombudsman, which constitutes the third element in the government's four-part reform programme.[15]

The fourth and final element in the government's Victim Reform Strategy concerns the appointment of an independent Commissioner for Victims and Witnesses.[16] The 2002 White Paper described the Commissioner's task as follows: to 'champion the interests of victims and witnesses' in advising on the implementation of the new National Strategy for Victims and Witnesses, reviewing existing practices and procedures and making recommendations on victim-related policies or legislative proposals (para. 2.46). In addition, the Commissioner will be able to draw on the views of a consultative forum known as the National Victims' Advisory Panel, which was established in March 2003.[17] The Panel itself is to be put on a statutory footing by virtue of Clause 32 of the Domestic Violence, Crime and Victims Bill. Once enacted and implemented, the Bill will bring to fruition the government's gradually unfolding victim reform programme, which it hopes will ensure that victims and witnesses get a better deal from the criminal justice system than they did in the past.

Enfranchising victims: the conventional criminal justice approach

Having looked at the broad range of victim-focused policy initiatives that have been adopted in recent years, the focus shifts in this next section to the specific measures that have been introduced in order to accommodate a victim perspective within the conventional criminal justice system. The aim will be to examine their impact on victims, and to assess the extent to which they have succeeded in enfranchising victims – with regard to their status, role and entitlement to redress – at the pre-trial stage, during the court-based phase and at the post-sentence stage.

Pre-trial victim-focused measures

Measures relating to the status of victims

The publication of the Victim's Charter in 1990 provided the first formal acknowledgement that certain victims[18] might have expectations or entitlements by virtue of their status as victims, though some of its standards were so platitudinous as to be virtually worthless. The statement that '[t]he police will respond to your report as quickly as they can' (Home Office, 1996: 2), for example, has been criticized for patronizing and infantilizing victims rather than empowering or reassuring them (Williams, 1999b: 587). Another equally vacuous statement is that '[t]he police will do their best to catch the person responsible for your crime'.

The Charter did break new ground in acknowledging for the first time that victims are entitled to information: both in the form of a general leaflet called 'Victims of Crime',[19] and also in the form of feedback to keep them informed of significant developments in their case (Home Office, 1996: 2). But, as JUSTICE (1998: 34) pointed out, this amounted to little more than 'a statement of principles and intent' and, as was true of the Charter as a whole, was not linked to a timetable or additional resources with which to encourage its early implementation. In addition to these rather anodyne measures, the Home Office also introduced under the auspices of the Victim's Charter a pilot initiative known as One Stop Shop (OSS) that was aimed at further improving the provision of information to victims.[20]

One of the biggest problems in seeking to meet the informational needs of victims relates to the multiplicity of semi-autonomous criminal justice agencies, each of which has specific responsibilities at different stages of the criminal justice process but none of which has an overview of the entire process. The problem is further compounded by a failure to clearly assign responsibility for meeting the needs of victims among the various agencies with whom they have dealings (Shapland, 2000: 154). The One Stop Shop initiative's response to the problem was to vest responsibility for providing victims with information throughout a case in a single agency: the police. Under the initiative, which was piloted in five police areas, victims of certain conventional predatory offences[21] whose offender was caught and charged were asked if they wished to take part in the One Stop Shop scheme and its companion Victim Statement Scheme (dealt with later). Those opting into the OSS scheme were informed in writing by the police of the charges laid against a suspect, date of first and subsequent hearings including trial (if applicable), and outcome of the proceedings including verdict and, if applicable, the sentence imposed.

The pilot OSS initiative was evaluated and nearly half (46 per cent) of those who were eligible opted into the scheme, though a quarter of those interviewed could not remember being invited to take part, suggesting that the scheme failed to communicate effectively with a significant minority of victims (Hoyle et al., 1998).[22] A substantial majority (about three-fifths) of victims who opted into the OSS scheme found the information they were given 'very' or 'fairly' useful, and those who opted in were more likely to feel better at the end of their case than those who had opted out.[23] However, a significant minority (around 20 per cent) thought that the information they were given was 'not at all' useful. Most were aggrieved either because they had not been given enough information[24] or, in the case of one-third of those who were interviewed, because of a delay in sending it. Moreover, there was some evidence that a failure to satisfy victim expectations that had been raised by the promise of information about their case may have contributed to significantly increased feelings of dissatisfaction with regard to the responsible agency, in this case the police.

In the wake of the OSS pilot scheme, responsibility for providing victims with information about their case was shifted from the police to the Crown Prosecution Service. This was in line with a recommendation made by the Glidewell Review (1998) of the latter service, and was supported by an additional allocation of £11m (Home Office et al., 2002a: para. 2.35) to facilitate and support the 'Direct Communication with Victims' initiative. Initially this was intended to take the form of a 'one-way' channel of communication, by means of a formulaic letter from the Crown Prosecution Service to the victim, but the scheme was subsequently adapted to allow for more detailed case-specific letters backed up, where appropriate, by telephone conversations and meetings (Sanders, 2002: 214ff). This goes beyond the provisions of the Victim's Charter, under which the Crown Prosecution Service's responsibility to explain their decision with regard to prosecuting a suspect was restricted to the families of homicide victims, and even then only on request (Home Office, 1996: 3).

Measures relating to the role of victims in the decision-making process

As for the victim's role, we have already seen how, for many years, victims were not entitled as of right to play any part at all during the pre-trial phase in criminal proceedings, though they might be required to act as witnesses for the prosecution if their case proceeded to trial and this was felt necessary in order to secure a conviction. Once it is accepted that victims *might* have a role at the pre-prosecution stage, this could in principle take a number of different forms. One possibility is that victims might be invited to contribute to the decision-making process by providing purely factual information – for example, in relation to the impact of the offence – that could be relevant to the police or prosecuting authorities when determining what the public interest demands. A second possibility is that in some or possibly all cases they might be consulted and invited to express a view regarding the outcome of the decision that has to be taken but without their views being determinative in any way on the outcome. A third possibility is that victims might be invited to actively participate in the decision-making process by *requiring* criminal justice agencies to consult victims and to take their views into consideration when reaching their decisions.

The first of these options is relatively uncontroversial and, subject to appropriate safeguards, might be acceptable even to those who are generally opposed in principle to the idea of conceding participatory or 'procedural rights' to victims.[25] The second option is more contentious and opposed by many on the grounds that victims themselves are said not to wish to be given this responsibility, that it raises false and unrealistic expectations on the part of victims or that it is wrong in principle for them to be given such a responsibility.[26] The third option is the most controversial of all and is opposed by many in part because it may threaten the due process rights of offenders not to be punished more than they are objectively thought to deserve according to public interest criteria.[27] But another objection is that it injects an even greater degree of disparity into the decision-making process, thereby offending against the more general due process principle of consistency which requires that similarly situated offenders are treated alike. This would not be the case if victims were allowed to influence the decision.

As we shall see, moves to incorporate a victim perspective into the English criminal justice process have so far been confined to the more restrictive first and second options of the three possibilities that were outlined above. The Victim's Charter itself states that victims will have the chance to explain how the crime has affected them, and that their interests will be taken into account by the police, Crown Prosecutor, magistrates and judges. We will examine the way in which this is done in the next section, since the information that is provided by victims also has a bearing on the way sentencing decisions are taken. Here we focus more specifically on the extent to which victims have a right to be consulted by the police and Crown Prosecution Service during the pre-court phase of the process.

One of the most important preliminary decisions that needs to be taken in relation to a suspected offender is whether to take no formal action, administer a caution[28] or prosecute. The two most important sets of factors influencing the decision relate to strength of evidence and public interest criteria. During the era of victim disenfranchisement, as we have seen, the latter was determined without any formal reference to what the victim might desire. Nowadays, the interests and views of the victim constitute one of the considerations – together with the seriousness of the offence and the previous offending history of the suspect – that the police are expected to take into account in determining what the public interest requires (Home Office, 1994). It is important to note, however, that the *views* of the victim are not determinative, and have to be weighed against other public interest factors, and also what is thought to be best for the victim. Official attitudes concerning both sets of factors have changed over the years, particularly with regard to cases involving allegations of domestic violence or sexual violence within a domestic context. In the past there was a tendency not to prosecute in such cases, irrespective of the victim's wishes, partly because of concerns over evidential adequacy, but partly because the offences themselves were viewed less seriously. Now there is (in principle at least)[29] a presumption favouring prosecution on grounds of offence seriousness, even in cases where it may not be felt to be in the interests of the victim, and even when the latter is opposed to prosecution (Home Office, 2000b).

Until recently there was, somewhat anomalously, no corresponding requirement for the police or prosecuting authorities to consult with victims before prosecuting, as opposed to cautioning, a suspect. But this is no longer the case. Since 1992 the Crown Prosecution Service, which is responsible for prosecuting all conventional offences, has been required to take into account the interests of the victim, and to have regard to the wishes of victims who may not wish the suspect to be prosecuted. A later version of the Code (published in 2000) reiterates the formal position that the Crown Prosecution Service prosecutes on behalf of the public at large and not just in the interests of a particular individual. However, it goes on to say (in para. 6.7) that when considering what the public interest requires, the Crown Prosecutor should have regard not only to 'the consequences for the victim of any decision whether or not to prosecute', but also to 'any views expressed by the victim or the victim's family'. Another important pre-trial decision about which victims may have strong feelings relates to the charges that may be brought against the defendant and, in particular, to any changes that may be made, for example, as a result of charge or plea bargaining. At one time the victim had no say in relation to such matters, but once again this is no longer the case following the publication in 2000 of the *Attorney-General's Guidelines on the Acceptance of Pleas*.[30] The guidelines state that before a decision is taken to accept a plea in relation to a particular charge, or offer no evidence, the prosecution should 'whenever practicable, speak with the victim or the victim's family, so that the position can be explained *and their views and interests can be taken into account as part of the decision-making process*' (para. 5, emphasis added). This stops far short of giving victims a determinative say in such matters, though it is now possible for them to have some limited input into the decision-making process, at least in relation to Crown Court cases (since the Guidelines do not apply to those tried in the magistrates' courts).

As a result of the above changes, most victims[31] of offences that are normally dealt with by the police have benefited from a degree of enfranchisement at least with regard to certain important pre-trial decisions.[32] However, these changes do not apply to those victims whose offences are normally dealt with by agencies other than the police, who remain just as disenfranchised as they have ever been (Sanders, 2002: 212–13).

Measures relating to a victim's entitlement to redress from the offender[33]

Finally, the pre-trial decision-making process also has very important implications for the victim's entitlement to redress from the offender since, at present, this is only possible where the offender is ordered to pay compensation following a prosecution and successful conviction.[34] Consequently, a decision to caution rather than prosecute may deprive the victim of compensation that might otherwise have been forthcoming (Dignan, 1992: 468). This anomaly is soon to be addressed, however, as the Criminal Justice Act 2003 (Part 3, ss. 22–27) provides for the introduction of a system of conditional cautioning, which will be administered by the police on the recommendation of the Crown Prosecution Service. Under the accompanying Code of Practice that came into force on 3 July 2004 interviewers are instructed to ascertain what the victim's attitude would be regarding an offer of reparation but without giving the impression that the victim's views would be conclusive as to the outcome.

Court-based victim-focused measures

Measures relating to the status of victims

Proportionately very few criminal offences result in a suspect appearing in court, as we have seen, and even fewer of these result in a not guilty plea that would require a trial of the issues and, possibly, the summoning of witnesses including any victim(s) of the offence. However, those that do include many of the most serious high-profile offences that are most likely to be reported in the media. Consequently, cases such as these take on a totemic significance regarding the way victims are treated by the criminal justice system that far outweighs their numerical importance (JUSTICE, 1998: 58). As with the pre-trial phase, responsibility for dealing with victims during the trial phase is fragmentary and unclear, involving as it does the police, Crown Prosecution Service, court officials, voluntary organization such as Witness Support and the judiciary. This diffusion of responsibility is exacerbated by the fact that victims are by no means the only witnesses likely to be called to give evidence in a contested trial, which has tended in the past to lower their status even further in the eyes of the authorities.

It is the responsibility of the police to inform witnesses, including victims, of any court hearing, which is normally done by means of a letter and an accompanying explanatory leaflet produced by the Home Office, entitled 'Witness in Court'. Increasingly, the courts themselves may supplement this general information with their own more detailed leaflets.[35] However, this is a one-way conduit and concerns have been expressed (see, for example, JUSTICE, 1998: 63) that there is no routine mechanism whereby witnesses might inform courts directly of any health problems which might affect their ability to give evidence, and the same applies to any concerns or fears they may have about possible intimidation. The introduction of Witness Support services and their more recent extension to magistrates' courts (see Chapter 2) affords a potentially valuable means of alleviating some of the anxiety that victims are likely to experience prior to a hearing, particularly in the case of vulnerable witnesses. This potential will only be realized, however, where witnesses are informed of the service,[36] and concerns have been expressed that this does not always happen, even in the case of vulnerable witnesses (JUSTICE, 1998: 64).

A major problem in the past has been that criminal trials have tended to be organized around the convenience of criminal justice agencies, particularly the judiciary, and this has often resulted in a lack of consideration being given to other court users, including witnesses and victims. Thus, cases tend to be listed on noticeboards under the name of the defendant even though this may not have been communicated to the victim (perhaps because of concerns regarding intimidation), making it difficult for witnesses to know which courtroom they need to attend. It is even more difficult in courts that lack information points or reception areas for witnesses.[37] Moreover, because it is difficult to predict the length of a hearing, more cases may be listed than can be dealt with on a given day unless some of the cases collapse, as where a defendant decides to plead guilty. This can result in witnesses attending unnecessarily and experiencing frequent adjournments and delays before being called.[38] But if cases do collapse victims are not always informed of this straightaway, let alone given an explanation for what has happened and why their testimony will no longer be required.

Another symptom of the marginal status accorded to victims in the past was the inadequate provision of facilities such as refreshment and waiting rooms and the virtual absence of separate facilities for prosecution witnesses, even where some provision was made. This is in spite of the obvious risks of intimidation when victims are expected to mix with the general public since this will often include the defendant's family and supporters.

The situation has somewhat improved in recent years, however. In a survey conducted in 1986, Shapland and Cohen (1987) found that only 48 per cent of magistrates' courts had refreshment facilities, but in a mere 7 per cent of courts was there separate provision for witnesses including victims. By 1996, however, 88 per cent of magistrates' courts (and 92 per cent of Crown Courts) had refreshment facilities, though only 7 per cent of magistrates' courts and 10 per cent of Crown Courts[39] provide separate provision for victims and witnesses (Shapland and Bell, 1998). Greater improvements were recorded in respect of waiting facilities. In 1986, only 3 per cent of magistrates' courts had a separate waiting room, and only a further 3 per cent were able to make such space available if required. By 1996, 71 per cent of magistrates' courts had a separate waiting room, and a further 13 per cent were able to make special provision for vulnerable witnesses. Somewhat surprisingly, only 73 per cent of Crown Courts routinely provided separate waiting facilities in 1996, though almost all others could make special provision if required. The first national witness satisfaction survey confirmed these figures since three-quarters of witnesses reported that they had been allocated to separate waiting rooms (Whitehead, 2000: 3).

The lack of consideration afforded to victims at the pre-trial stage also extended in the past to the hearing itself. It was reflected in a tendency not to inform victims that they could attend and listen to the proceedings if they wished to and, even if they were told they could, in a failure to routinely make separate provision for them. Thus in 1986, 20 per cent of magistrates' courts had no one to direct a victim where to go and what to do (Shapland and Cohen, 1987: 36). Most courts (84 per cent) required victims who were not also witnesses to sit in the public gallery, where they might find themselves in close proximity to the defendant's supporters, as opposed to making space available in the body of the court itself. By 1996, however, the proportion of magistrates' courts requiring victims to sit in the public gallery was down to just over half (53 per cent), though in the Crown Court most victims (76 per cent) were still generally expected to sit in the public gallery (Shapland and Bell, 1998: 540).

One final issue relating to the status of victims during the trial phase concerns their safety and feelings of equanimity while in court. This is a matter of particular concern in the case of witnesses who are especially vulnerable, whether on account of their age, disability, the type of offence that has been committed against them or their relationship with the suspected offender. Many of the above issues relating to the facilities that are available in court and whether special provision is made for witnesses also have an important bearing on the extent to which witnesses consider themselves safe from intimidation that is perpetrated by or on behalf of the defendant. However, it is important to remember that many witnesses find the whole process and court environment intimidating, whether or not they also experience intimidation at the hands of an individual. In the first national witness satisfaction survey 25 per cent reported feeling intimidated by an individual[40] compared with 18 per cent who felt intimidated by the process and 5 per cent who were intimidated by both an individual and the process (Whitehead, 2000: 4).

Where a serious threat to the safety of a witness emanating from an individual is credibly anticipated, the police do operate witness protection schemes, but the expense involved usually restricts their availability to only the most severe cases. Much more common and difficult to deal with are lower level threats such as intimidatory or abusive remarks and 'eyeballing' while in court, or even while giving evidence. The intimidation of witnesses, jurors and others (whether by actions or by threats) was made a criminal offence by s. 51 of the Criminal Justice and Public Order Act 1994, and is punishable by up to five years' custody, a fine or both.

Steps have also been taken to render the criminal justice process less intimidating, particularly in the case of child witnesses. For example, the Youth Justice and Criminal Evidence Act 1999 allows vulnerable or intimidated witnesses to be screened from the defendant while testifying in court, to be cross-examined by an intermediary or in camera, to give evidence by live video link or video recording (Ashworth, 2000: 190; Birch, 2000). The Act also increased the protection afforded to victims, both to guard against the threat of cross-examination in person by the accused where the latter is representing him/herself, and also to restrict the circumstances in which a victim may be cross-examined more generally with respect to their previous criminal history. Such measures go some way towards protecting witnesses from the more flagrant forms of secondary victimization on the part of the criminal justice system, though much will depend on the extent to which they elicit a change in culture and attitude on the part of criminal justice practitioners (Ashworth, 2000: 191). Moreover, there is a limit to what can be achieved by way of protecting witnesses from such forms of secondary victimization, at least within the context of an adversarial form of trial process (Doak, 2003: 31).

Measures relating to the role of victims in the decision-making process

As we have seen, even during the 'era of victim disenfranchisement' victims were accorded a role – albeit a limited one, as purveyors of evidence – in relation to the trial phase of the criminal process. The most visible manifestation of this role was the victim's presence in court, as a witness for the prosecution, in the minority of cases in which the defendant pleaded not guilty, thereby resulting in a formal trial. In addition to this highly visible but infrequently performed role, however, victims were (and still are) routinely called upon at an early stage in the investigation of an offence to provide witness statements that are taken by the police and signed by the victim. Quite apart from their evidential value with regard to the issue of guilt or innocence, these usually provide information about the known effects of the offence on the victim at the time the statement is taken, which may be relevant when sentencing an offender.[41] Where the consequences for the victim are serious, their statements may be supplemented by witness statements or experts' reports provided by doctors and other professionals. (It is also possible – though relatively unusual – for victims and other witnesses to be called to give evidence personally in court if the sentencer feels this is necessary in deciding what sentence is appropriate.) Such information is highly relevant to the court at the time of sentencing an offender, not only because of the duty to consider the issue of compensation (see below), but also because of the part it plays in assessing the 'seriousness' of an offence.[42] Under the Criminal Justice Act 1991 the principal aim of sentencing is the 'just deserts' based proportionality principle which requires the sentence imposed to be commensurate with the seriousness of the offence (see Cavadino and Dignan, 2002: ch. 4).

In recent years, however, several countries with adversarial legal systems have adopted measures that allow victims to engage more actively in the sentencing decision-making process.[43] This engagement can take a number of different forms, though the terminology which has been applied to these is confusing and far from consistent. Three principal variants may be identified, however. The first and most widely adopted is a written statement compiled by, or specifically on behalf of, the victim (as opposed to the prosecution or the court). Its contents are confined to factual statements about the effects (physical, financial or psychological) of an offence or its impact on the life of the victim.[44] These are frequently referred to as 'victim impact statements' (or VIS; see for example, Ashworth, 1993; Erez, 2000), though they are also known (particularly in an English context) as 'Victim Statements' or 'Victim Personal Statements' (see below) or even as 'victim effect statements' (JUSTICE, 1998: 94). A second variant allows victims to also state their views as to their preferred outcome with regard to sentencing or other decisions, though the format involving a written statement that is compiled by or on behalf of the victim is the same. These are often referred to as 'Victim Opinion Statements' (Sanders et al., 2001: 447; see also Sanders, 1999: chs. 3 and 5) and are allowed in certain state jurisdictions in the United States. The third and final variant resembles the latter but enables victims to express their views concerning sentencing outcome in the form of an oral statement in open court at the time of sentencing. This practice is usually referred to as 'victim allocution' (see Ashworth, 1993: 505).

The Seventh United Nations Congress on the Prevention of Crime and the Treatment of Offenders in 1985 expressed general support for the principle of victim participation initiatives. Indeed, it recommended that provision should be made 'allowing the views and concerns of victims to be presented and considered at appropriate stages of the proceedings where their personal interests are affected, without prejudice to the accused and consistent with the relevant national criminal justice system' (United Nations, 1985: para. 6b). However, the wording of this provision was a matter of considerable controversy at the time, and provoked an explicit reservation from the UK delegation when adopted, on the grounds that the rights of victims 'should not extend in any way to sentencing, case disposal or course of trial' (Joutsen, 1994: 58, quoting from the Seventh United Nations Congress on the Prevention of Crime and the Treatment of Offenders, 1985). These reservations were reflected in the publication of revised National Standards for the Supervision of Offenders in the Community (Home Office et al., 1995), which required the probation service (in the case of adult offenders)[45] to consider the impact of an offence on the victim when preparing pre-sentence reports. But as these assessments were based solely on information contained in the prosecution file rather than on direct input by the victim, they fell far short of the 'victim impact statements' that were being introduced at the time in several other common law jurisdictions.

When the Victim's Charter was revised in 1996, however, it revealed a significant change of attitude on the part of the government, since victims were informed that they could expect to be given the chance to explain how they had been affected by the crime. They were also assured that 'the police, Crown Prosecutor, magistrates and judges *will take this information into account when making their decisions*' (Home Office, 1996: 3, emphasis added). The first English victim impact statement initiative was introduced under the auspices of the Charter and involved the use of 'Victim Statements',[46] though these were intended to do no more than provide criminal justice decision-makers with an additional source of purely factual information. Contrary to the impression conveyed by the Victim's Charter, the latter were under no obligation to take it into account though they were, of course, free to do so if they wished. The Victim Statement initiative was piloted in the same areas as the other Victim Charter initiative, the so-called One Stop Shop (see above), and eligible victims in those areas were invited (by letter) to opt in to either or both schemes. Two different methods of compiling Victim Statements were piloted in different parts of the country. The first involved a form that was completed by the victims themselves; in the second, information provided by victims was recorded by a police officer, either using the same itemized form or by compiling a 'free-form' statement. The ambiguity surrounding the underlying purpose of the initiative was compounded by the fact that the scheme used the same stationery as for the regular victim's witness statements, making it difficult for decision-makers to identify the exact provenance of the information with which they were provided.

Both sets of Victim Charter initiatives were evaluated by the same team of researchers, who investigated five of the pilot sites. The Victim Statement initiative had two principal components: the first assessing victim satisfaction ratings at the start of the process and also at the end; the second investigating the use of Victim Statements by prosecutors and the courts. With regard to the victim's perspective, fewer than one-third of the victims who were eligible availed themselves of the opportunity to provide a statement (Hoyle et al., 1998: 25).[47] Those who did participate tended mainly to do so for a mixture of expressive reasons (to tell others, including the offender, how they had been affected) and instrumental reasons (because they wished to influence the relevant decision-makers, especially the court when passing sentence). Although the great majority of victims were pleased that they had made a statement,[48] the proportion of victims who felt 'neutral' about making it (43 per cent) was higher than the proportion who reported that it made them feel better (just over one-third). For a minority (18 per cent), however, it had been an upsetting experience. Another striking finding was that the proportion of offenders who felt that they had made the right decision in providing a statement declined from 77 per cent at the start of the process to 57 per cent by the final interview (Hoyle et al., 1998: 32). Conversely, the proportion who felt they had made the wrong decision increased from 2 per cent at the first interview to 20 per cent by the time of the final interview. One of the main reasons for this apparent disillusionment was that many victims felt their statements had been ignored. As with the One Stop Shop initiative, therefore, it appears that for a significant minority of victims, the scheme may have raised expectations only to dash them again when the anticipated benefits were felt not to have been delivered.

With regard to the user's perspective, most decision-makers appeared to welcome the use of Victim Statements in principle, but took very little notice of them in practice (Morgan and Sanders, 1999). With respect to bail/custody decisions or charge decisions their impact was virtually non-existent. With respect to sentencing decisions they seldom made any difference but, to the limited extent they did, they tended to increase the severity of the sentence. One reason for their extremely limited impact was that, as seen above, victims' statements duplicate information that is available from other sources and rarely contain additional information that is felt to be both relevant and reliable.[49] A second reason had to do with the timing of the statements since victims provide information that they perceive as relevant at the start of the case and very rarely update this information, whereas the courts are mainly guided by the information perceived to be relevant at the time of sentencing (Sanders et al., 2001: 455).

Despite the clearly articulated misgivings expressed by the evaluators of the pilot Victim Statement initiative, the government launched a slightly modified version of the scheme, which was renamed the 'Victim Personal Statement' scheme, in 2000. The new scheme is based on a two-stage process, the first of which allows victims who wish to to supplement their initial witness statement by making an additional statement explaining how the crime has affected them. The second stage enables victims to update their initial statement by describing any longer term effects that may not have been evident at the time of the initial impact. However, even the modified scheme still suffers from many of the defects associated with its predecessor, including ambiguity of purpose and the likelihood that in many cases victims' expectations will be raised without being met (Sanders et al., 2001: 458).[50] Although the category of crimes to which the revised scheme applies has been extended to cover *all* crimes prosecuted by the Crown Prosecution Service, it still excludes offences that fall outside the ambit of the Victim's Charter.[51] Yet, as Sanders (2002: 220) has observed, it is precisely with regard to these other offences that their impact will not normally be so evident, and where the provision of victim input into the decision-making process could provide an important missing dimension.

Measures relating to a victim's entitlement to redress from the offender

The most obvious form of redress to which victims may be entitled under the conventional criminal justice system takes the form of financial compensation that offenders may be ordered to pay on being sentenced by the court. Indeed, the introduction and strengthening of courts' powers to award compensation orders over the years represented the first tentative waves in what has become a torrent of victim-focused initiatives in recent years. Compensation from offenders was first introduced in the Criminal Justice Act 1972 as an ancillary penalty in cases where the victim had sustained injury, loss or damage. Ten years later, courts were given the power to award compensation in its own right, rather than simply as an addition to some other penalty, and were told to prioritize compensation for victims over fines when both were imposed at the same time (Criminal Justice Act 1982). Further encouragement came from the Criminal Justice Act 1988, which required courts to consider awarding compensation in all cases where there has been loss or damage to personal property or personal injury, and to give reasons for not doing so.

The principle of victim compensation appears to be favoured by victims (Shapland et al., 1985; Hamilton and Wisniewski, 1996), and the number of compensation orders imposed by the courts grew steadily for a number of years. Between 1990 and 2001, however, there was a sharp fall in both the number of compensation orders awarded,[52] and the proportionate use of the measure in both the magistrates' court and Crown Court. Consequently, the majority of victims receive nothing from the person who has committed an offence against them, even when the latter is convicted. In respect of violent offences the proportion of offenders who were ordered to pay compensation in the magistrates' court fell from 60 per cent to 35 per cent, and a similar decline was also recorded in the Crown Court, from 29 per cent in 1990 to 16 per cent in 2001.[53] In respect of minor property offences, the proportion of offenders who were ordered to pay compensation in the magistrates' court declined from 22 per cent to 14 per cent, and in the Crown Court it declined from 13 per cent in 1990 to 8 per cent in 2001. The reason for the apparent shift in attitude on the part of the courts is not immediately apparent and seems all the more surprising in view of the increasingly high profile that has been given to crime victims over the same period. A Home Office study found that one of the main reasons sentencers gave for not awarding compensation was that offenders lacked the means to pay, and some felt reluctant to impose an order if the amount that could be afforded would appear too derisory (Flood-Page and Mackie, 1998: 62, 111). But since unemployment levels were falling and overall living standards were rising during the same period, it seems probable that other factors may also have been at work. One distinct possibility is that the sharp increase in the proportionate use of custodial sentences during the same period may be partly to blame.[54]

ꭓ Whatever the reasons for their apparent decline in popularity among sentencers, the system of court-ordered compensation orders suffers from a number of serious defects as a means of providing redress for victims (see also Duff, 1988: 148ff; Miers, 1990b).[55] The first weakness is that, as we have seen, only a minority of convicted offenders are ordered to pay compensation, while victims whose offenders are cautioned are effectively 'disenfranchised' in respect of any entitlement to compensation (Walklate and Mawby, 1993). A second weakness from the victim's point of view is that the courts are obliged to take account of the offender's means when determining whether to award compensation and also in fixing the amount and the rate at which it has to be paid. Because most offenders have extremely limited means, victims are rarely compensated in full for their loss. The problem is exacerbated by a reluctance on the part of sentencers to give effect to their express statutory obligation to prioritize compensation for victims. For research has shown that they continue to impose fines and costs in many cases, even where the effect is to depress still further the amount that is available for compensating the victim (Moxon et al., 1992: 29; Flood-Page and Mackie, 1998: 127). It has been suggested that this failure by the courts to comply with the law affords evidence of a seemingly irreconcilable tension between the retributive impulses that are favoured within the conventional criminal justice approach and even this very limited attempt to incorporate an element of reparative justice (Dignan and Cavadino, 1996: 144). We shall come across further evidence of such tension in Chapter 5, when we examine attempts to integrate other restorative approaches within the conventional criminal justice process. A third problem relates to the fact that victims' expectations are likely to be raised when compensation is ordered, but may be dashed when payment is not forthcoming, or is received in small, irregular amounts over a considerable period of time.[56]

Even in those cases where compensation is ordered and paid on time, however, it affords a limited form of redress to the victims who receive it, since it only provides compensation for the material loss or damage that they have sustained. It does little to repair any harm that may have been done to the victim's mental or psychological sense of well-being, or to restore the social or moral relationships that may have been damaged by an offence (Watson et al., 1989: 214).[57] Moreover, neither victims nor offenders are likely to feel greatly empowered by an award of compensation since, as we have seen, they are not directly involved in the decision-making process and have no control over its outcome. Indeed, from the offender's point of view it is difficult to differentiate between a compensation order and other court-imposed financial penalties such as the fine or an order for costs. Consequently, the former is unlikely to succeed in making them feel personally accountable to the victim. Conversely, from a victim's point of view, there is no right of appeal against a failure to award compensation and, even if forthcoming, any money that is received appears to come from the court rather than from the offender in person. So, even though the sentencing decision may afford some means of redress to victims, its impact is likely to be limited at best, and may even be counterproductive if, as is often the case, expectations are raised, only to be dashed.[58]

Post-sentence victim-focused measures

Measures relating to the status of victims and their role in the decision-making process

For very many years, victims' involvement with the criminal justice system came to an abrupt end with the sentencing of the offender, subject to the possibility of receiving compensation if ordered by the court. However, the publication of the Victim's Charter in 1990 marked a new phase in the accommodation of a victim perspective within the criminal justice process. It did so by conferring on certain categories of victims an expectation that their 'wishes and interests' (or those of their family) would for the first time be taken into consideration during the decision-making process relating to the release of offenders from custody (Home Office, 1990: 25). This was backed by new obligations imposed on the probation service and by corresponding changes in the criteria to be applied by the Parole Board in reaching its decisions on the release of offenders.

Initially the new provisions applied only in respect of life-sentenced prisoners, and were thus restricted to those who had been most severely victimized as a result of extremely serious offences. Since then, however, their scope was extended in 1995 to embrace victims of serious sexual or violent offences where the term of imprisonment was four years or more,[59] and again in 2001 by reducing the sentence threshold to which they apply to prison sentences of one year or more.[60] When the Victim's Charter was first published in 1990, little thought appears to have been given to either the way it should be implemented or its profound – and indeed potentially revolutionary – implications for the probation service, whose orientation and responsibilities had after all hitherto been exclusively concerned with offenders. Nor was it based on any research into victims' views and preferences. This lack of detailed planning was compounded by a failure to provide any new or dedicated funding to support the additional victim contact responsibilities that were imposed on the service.[61] The failure to provide guidance and financial support fuelled suspicions that the changes were simply a sop to public opinion (Kosh and Williams, 1995: 20), and was roundly condemned by others (JUSTICE, 1998: 105). It also meant that it was several years before a system emerged that would give substance to the expectations set out in the original victim's charter.[62]

In order to assess the status and role of victims during the post-sentence phase, it is necessary to consider the responsibilities of both the probation service and the Parole Board. As far as the probation service is concerned, its victim contact responsibilities involve a two-stage process. The first stage obliges the probation service to initiate contact with eligible victims within two months of sentencing. The second stage, which is voluntary, involves further contact with victims who request it, at the time that an offender's release is being considered, towards the end of the sentence. The purpose of the initial contact is to provide victims with *information* about what happens during an offender's sentence and how any decision to release an offender is reached. The victim is also asked at this stage whether they would like to be kept informed of developments during an offender's sentence and whether they would like to receive *support*, which is available from Victim Support. The purpose of the second stage, for those victims who 'opt in', is to *consult* with them, to obtain information about any concerns they might have regarding an offender's release, which provides an opportunity for such concerns to be fed into the parole decision-making process, to which we now turn.

Although victims do not have any direct part to play in the release decision, the Parole Board is nevertheless required to take account of the interests of victims when considering whether an offender should be granted conditional or early release.[63] Factors that the Parole Board is expected to take into consideration include: the risk to the victim; the offender's attitude towards the victim; any concerns the victim (or victim's family in the case of an offender convicted of murder or manslaughter) might have with regard to intimidation or fears for their personal safety. One way of addressing such concerns is by imposing additional licence conditions in the form of exclusion zones or no contact provisions, in order to provide additional safeguards for the protection of victims. Where such conditions are requested on behalf of victims, the overwhelming majority are said to be accepted by the Parole Board (Falconer, 2003: para. 29).

An evaluation of the probation service's victim contact work found that the primary reason for opting in to the scheme (expressed by 49 per cent of victims) was in order to seek information and answers to questions (Crawford and Enterkin, 2001: 712).[64] Only 18 per cent of victims appeared to be motivated by the chance to influence decision-makers with regard to the imposition of conditions by contributing information that could be included in a report. Most victims (60 per cent) were satisfied with the information they received, though a significant minority (14 per cent) indicated that they felt traumatized as a result of their experience, suggesting that for some the attempt to address their concerns by talking things over may result in secondary victimization. There was also evidence that victim expectations may sometimes have been raised and then dashed since a third of victims felt they had been given too little information, particularly in relation to the prisoner's location, specific release dates and any treatment the offender might be receiving. Moreover, several victims expressed annoyance at what they perceived to be a 'one-way' flow of information since they were aware that any specific concerns they might raise would normally have to be relayed to the offender.[65] Although this is in line with natural justice requirements and the specific provisions of the European Convention on Human Rights, it seems likely to have a disempowering effect on victims by reminding them of their subordinate status.

Concerns have also been raised about the motives for involving victims during the post-sentencing phase of the criminal justice process. One fear is that information gathered from victims may be used without their consent in order to assist in the rehabilitation of offenders (JUSTICE, 1998: 106). Some evidence that victims might indeed on occasion be used 'in the service of offenders'[66] came to light in the evaluation of the probation service's victim contact work, which found that one prison had a policy of using non-confidential victim reports to confront prisoners with their offending behaviour. A second rather different concern is that victims might also be used 'in the service of severity' in order to justify more punitive measures directed at offenders. Until recently, such concerns have mainly been founded on the more punitive pitch being pursued within probation and criminal justice policy in general. However, there are signs that this may be about to change. In a speech to the Parole Board annual conference in April 2003, Lord Falconer (2003: 2), posed a much more specific question about what the government's aim of 'putting the victim at the heart of the criminal justice system . . . might mean in terms of the sentence served and the release process'. More particularly, he asked whether the Parole Board's current practice of considering victims' interests only in the determination of release conditions goes far enough. He went on to suggest that there might be a case for requiring the Parole Board to take the views of the victim into account as one of the factors (though not necessarily the decisive one) in reaching a decision on the substantive issue of whether to release an offender or not. Allowing victims' *views* on the subject of an offender's release to be admitted as relevant considerations in the decision-making process would greatly intensify concerns about victims being used in the interests of severity without regard to the need for adequate standards and safeguards to protect the interests of offenders. Such a move would also, somewhat illogically, confer on victims a far more decisive role with regard to the post-sentencing phase of the criminal justice process than has so far been conceded with regard to the sentencing decision itself.

Taking stock: accommodating a victim perspective within a conventional criminal justice framework[67]

In the course of this chapter we have observed what appears to have been a remarkable transformation in the relationship between victims and criminal justice agencies within a very short space of time. Not that long ago, all victims were almost completely disenfranchised with regard to the criminal justice process. Now, certain categories of victims at least can expect to be kept better informed, treated with greater respect and sensitivity, offered access to support and provided with a degree of protection against intimidation and secondary victimization. They have a greater opportunity to contribute to the decision-making process with regard to 'their' own cases, and are somewhat more likely to receive compensation for loss or injury.

Even for those victims who have benefitted from recent attempts to ensure that the criminal justice system provides a better service for victims, however, the changes we have examined so far constitute a partial enfranchisement at best. It is true that victims are better informed than they once were, but the information they receive tends to be incomplete, is often late in arriving, and fails to provide explanations for what has been decided and why. Very rarely is there an opportunity to discuss the decisions and their implications with those who are responsible for making them. Some steps have been taken to afford a degree of protection from intimidation and secondary victimization but, as we have seen, the safeguards are both partial and limited in scope. Moreover, many victims continue to experience secondary victimization, both with regard to the 'regular' criminal justice process and, for some also, ironically, as a result of the victim-focused reforms themselves.

Victims do now have some input into the decision-making process, but the communication channels established for this purpose tend to be one-way only, and to afford at best an indirect 'voice' that is only permitted to draw on a restricted repertoire of possible contributions. Once again, there is no opportunity to engage in dialogue or even an exchange of views either with criminal justice officials or, more crucially, with the other significant party, the offender. This feature represents one of the biggest differences between the criminal justice model and the variants of the restorative justice model that are depicted in Table I.1 (pp. 6–7). Moreover, even though there is now some scope for victims to obtain redress from the offender, neither victim nor offender is able to influence the form this takes or the amount that is appropriate, quite apart from the other defects to which it is subject. By restricting the scope for meaningful participation in this way, the victim (like the offender) is necessarily consigned to a limited, partisan and confrontational role within the criminal justice process. While this may be in keeping with the traditional adversarial ethos of the common law criminal process, it is unlikely to empower victims – or offenders – or make them feel less marginalized. Furthermore, by raising expectations that cannot be delivered, it may even increase the dangers of secondary victimization.

We have also observed in the course of this chapter how victims have come to assume a much higher profile in penal policy terms in recent years. This is another development that shows every sign of continuing and is also worthy of further reflection. Just as victim-focused reforms within the criminal justice system have assumed a particular form in recent years, the same could also be said of many recent victim-oriented policy initiatives.

First, the way victims (and offenders) have been conceptualized in recent years is highly *selective* inasmuch as it encompasses certain victims – those who are victimized by conventional 'predatory' offenders – but not others, who have been victimized by various kinds of regulatory offences. By differentiating between them, penal policymakers seem to imply that the threat to victims posed by predatory offenders – most of whom are relatively young, impoverished and powerless – is far more 'real' and serious than that posed by corporate offenders, most of whom will be relatively mature, wealthy and powerful. Mathiesen (1974) has suggested that one of the social functions performed by penal policies (including the use of imprisonment) in advanced capitalist societies is to divert attention away from socially harmful acts that are committed by those engaged in the process of production. Perhaps the same could be said of selective victim-focused penal policies of the kind we have been examining.

Second, there has been a tendency for politicians to formulate victim-focused initiatives on the basis of their own stereotypical assumptions about what victims might want rather than asking victims themselves. This is true of virtually all the victim-focused reforms associated with the introduction of the Victim's Charter, including the introduction of the One-Stop-Shop and Victim Statement initiative and also the imposition of victim contact responsibilities on the probation service.

Third, victims and offenders have typically been portrayed by penal policy-makers in highly dichotomized terms as two completely separate social groupings, even though as we have seen this is based on an empirically false premise (see Chapter 1). Moreover, the interests of victims are routinely assumed to be diametrically and automatically opposed to those of offenders (Williams, 1999a: 81). Thus, references to the need to 'rebalance the criminal justice system in favour of the victim' (Home Office et al., 2002a) entail an implicit corollary that this will necessarily and inevitably be at the expense of the offender. David Garland (2001: 142) has suggested that the discovery of the victim by penal policymakers needs to be understood in the context of other recent penal policy developments. The most important of these consists of a decisive shift in the treatment of offenders towards a much more repressive and exclusionary approach, to which he gives the name 'punitive segregation'. Paraphrasing Garland, the adoption of more overtly partisan victim-focused policies (like the switch to more repressive ways of dealing with offenders) serves both instrumentalist and expressive purposes. Thus, they help to deflect demands by those campaigning for better safeguards for offenders and improvements in the treatment of prisoners by suggesting that innocent victims are worthier and more deserving recipients of their concerns and compassion than culpable offenders (Garland, 2001: 180). At the same time they serve to demonstrate that 'something is being done'[68] about the consequences of crime to allay the concerns of those who fear they might be victimized.

Much of what Garland says about contemporary developments in penal policy and concomitant victim-focused policy initiatives is true –

particularly with regard to their increasingly exclusionary nature – though not all of it. Certainly there are examples of stereotypical images of victims being invoked to fuel increasingly polarized penal policies that are based on the assumption of an irreconcilable dichotomy between the interests of victims and offenders. But there are also other victim-focused measures, such as those associated with various restorative justice initiatives, to which we will turn in the remaining chapters of the book, that appear to be based on a very different set of assumptions. Nevertheless, it is important to keep in mind this broader penal context within which recent restorative justice developments have been introduced because of the question it raises about the extent to which it is possible to integrate a restorative justice approach within the regular criminal justice system. This is a question to which we will return in Chapter 6.

Notes

1 A criminal justice audit conducted in Milton Keynes showed that spending on victims accounted for only around 1 per cent of the resources available to all criminal justice agencies including Victim Support (Shapland et al., 1995).

2 Assuming they had sufficient resources, and were knowledgeable and powerful enough to do so.

3 In practice, of course, the prospects of mounting a successful prosecution may often be fatally undermined if the victim is unwilling to testify. However, the victim has much less leverage in cases where the prosecuting authorities decide not to institute proceedings since, under the common law 'expediency' or 'opportunity' principle, there is no obligation to prosecute.

4 Sentencing policy and recent proposals for reform are discussed in more detail in Cavadino and Dignan (2002, ch. 4).

5 They include a Convention on State Compensation for victims of violent crime in 1983 and a Recommendation providing for measures to safeguard intimidated witnesses in 1997. Interestingly, the European Convention on Human Rights (ECHR), which was incorporated into English law by the Human Rights Act 1998, lacks any specific reference to victims' rights, though the fair trial provisions under Article 6 may impact indirectly on victims inasmuch as their rights will need to be balanced against those of the defendant (Ashworth, 2000: 188; Whittaker, 2001: 264).

6 In the USA see, for example, the Federal Victim and Witness Protection Act 1982 and the Federal Crime Act 1984; and in Germany see the Victim Protection Act 1986. See Brienen and Hoegen (2000) for a comprehensive treatise on the position of crime victims with regard to legislative provisions and criminal justice practice in 22 European jurisdictions.

7 The introduction of state compensation for victims of violent crime operates independently of the criminal justice system and was discussed in Chapter 2 in connection with the Welfare Model.

8 The Victim's Charter was one of a series of similar initiatives published around the same time. They included the Citizen's Charter and the Court's Charter, both published in 1992. See Williams (1999b) for further discussion.

9 The charter has also been criticized for its length, obscurity and for the inaccessible language in which it is written; see, for example, Williams' (1999b: 387) comments on the second edition.

10 A third edition was said to be in preparation in 2001, following a Home Office review of the charter (Home Office, 2001b) but, as we shall see, this was superseded by a decision to publish a statutory code of practice for crime victims, as stipulated in the Domestic Violence, Crime and Victims Bill, published in December 2003. The Code of Practice is likely to come into effect in 2005–6.

11 The review simply acknowledged that the charter did not apply to corporate *victims* but was completely silent on the subject of those who are victimized by corporate *offenders*.

12 The rebalancing metaphor has been criticized by some on the ground that it likens criminal justice to a 'zero-sum' game in which the need to increase rights for victims entails (and justifies) a reduction in rights for offenders (see, e.g. Capes, 2004a, 2004b).

13 Although the government seems to have assumed that measures designed to improve the effectiveness of the system in bringing offenders to justice will also help to rebalance the criminal justice system in favour of victims, it by no means follows that the interests of the prosecution are necessarily synonymous with those of the victim (see Sanders, 2002: 200 for further discussion on this point).

14 It is intended that this will be binding on all criminal justice agencies, which will be obliged to provide specific services on issues such as the provision of information, support and protection, within challenging deadlines (Falconer, 2003: 3).

15 As provided for in Clause 24 and Schedule 4 of the aforementioned Bill.

16 Outlined in Clauses 25–8 of the Domestic Violence, Crime and Victims Bill.

17 The Panel is chaired by the Minister for Criminal Justice, and comprises ten voluntary lay members with experience of victims' issues, plus three co-opted members.

18 As we saw earlier, the Victim's Charter does not apply to victims of non-predatory crimes that are dealt with by agencies other than the police. This important omission relates to every aspect of the charter and needs to be borne in mind throughout the following discussion.

19 In addition, the relatives of homicide victims are provided with a specifically adapted information pack – 'Information for Families of Homicide Victims' – that was prepared with the assistance of victims' organizations including Justice for Victims, Support after Murder and Manslaughter and Victim Support. Other victims, however, whose offences are prosecuted by agencies other than the police, are not entitled to any such information.

20 A second, closely associated pilot initiative known as the Victim Statement Project was also introduced under the auspices of the Victim's Charter at the same time. This was intended to give victims a chance to describe the financial and emotional effects of their offence upon themselves. Because this latter initiative also has important implications for the role of victims at both the pre-trial and court-based stages of a case, it will be considered separately in the next section, though the two measures are similar in many respects, and are often dealt with together for this reason.

21 The scheme only applied to offences involving criminal damage in excess of £5000, domestic burglary, domestic violence, sexual assault, other physical assault (apart from common assault) and racially motivated offences.

22 The findings were summarized in Hoyle et al. (1999). See also Sanders et al. (2001).

23 Just under half (45 per cent) who had opted into the scheme felt better about having been a victim of crime at the end of the case than they had at the beginning, compared with only 13 per cent of those who had not opted in.

24 Information about bail and remand decisions was not provided, nor were the police able, for understandable reasons, to provide reasons for decisions taken by other agencies such as the Crown Prosecution Service.

25 Andrew Ashworth (1993, 1994, 2000) is the most prominent opponent. He has drawn a distinction to which much of the early literature on the subject refers, between participatory or 'procedural rights', which in general he opposes, and substantive or 'service' rights, such as the right to information, protection and compensation, which he favours. Even he is prepared to concede that there may be a case for allowing victims to furnish relevant factual information – for example detailing the precise harm suffered – though he insists that this should be subject to proper safeguards in the form of appropriate evidential requirements.

26 See, for example, JUSTICE (1998: 38), Sanders (2002: 218). See also the reference to victims' rights on Victim Support's website www.victimsupport.org.uk/about/awareness/rights.html

27 But also because it is believed to inject irrelevant considerations into the sentencing process that are unrelated to the public interest; and because (like the victim impact statement) it may unfairly raise victims' expectations since there can be no guarantee that they will be met (see Ashworth, 1998: 36).

28 In relation to adult offenders. With regard to young offenders cautions were replaced by a statutory system of reprimands and final warnings introduced by the Crime and Disorder Act 1998. These initiatives, which are to some extent inspired by restorative justice precepts, are discussed further in Chapter 4.

29 Though research evidence suggests that, in practice, it remains the case that victims' preferences are likely to prevail (Hoyle, 1998; Hoyle and Sanders, 2000).

30 These are available online at: www.lslo.gov.uk/pdf/agplea.pdf.

31 With the exception of mentally vulnerable victims (JUSTICE, 1998: 54–5).

32 Other important decisions – for example those relating to bail or remand – are not affected by the changes. But here also the government has recently proposed that the police should have the power to impose conditions on a suspect's bail during the period before charge; for example, if they consider it necessary to protect victims and witnesses (Home Office et al., 2002a: para. 3.37).

33 Redress for victims may also be forthcoming from sources other than the offender, including voluntary agencies such as Victim Support (see above, Chapter 2), and also professional sources. However, assistance in the form of counselling has in the past sometimes been withheld from victims prior to a court appearance in the belief that it might 'taint the evidence' – a practice that has been condemned as another form of secondary victimization by the criminal justice system (JUSTICE, 1998: 37).

34 At least in the case of adult offenders. As noted above (see note 28), the position is different in cases involving juveniles, following the Crime and Disorder Act 1998. See Chapter 4, for details.

35 Almost three-quarters of witnesses who were questioned in the first national witness satisfaction survey recalled receiving information either in the form of the *Witness in Court* leaflet or another similar leaflet (Whitehead, 2000: 2).

36 Victim Support and the Crown Prosecution Service have concluded a national agreement whereby the latter will, at least in the case of Crown Court hearings, notify the Witness Support service of all prosecution witnesses who are required to attend court.

37 In a survey conducted in 1996 by Shapland and Bell (1998), 75 per cent of responding Crown Courts and 60 per cent of magistrates' courts said they had information points, leaving a substantial minority without such provision.

38 The first national witness satisfaction survey showed that 17 per cent of witnesses had to wait longer than four hours before giving evidence, though the problem was less acute for victims (9 per cent of whom had to wait that long) than for defence witnesses (Whitehead, 2000: 3). The survey also showed that as many as 40 per cent of those who attended court with the expectation of giving evidence were not called upon to do so, usually because the defendant decided to plead guilty.

39 In addition, Shapland and Bell (1998: 541) report that 20 per cent of Crown Courts were able to make special arrangements if required.

40 Victims, females and children were most likely to report feeling intimidated by an individual (Whitehead, 2000: 4). Overall levels of intimidation were higher than those recorded by the British Crime Survey, which reported that only 8 per cent of victims and witnesses had experienced some form of intimidation (Tarling et al., 2000: 1). However, a higher proportion of BCS victims (15 per cent) reported intimidation in cases where the victim had some knowledge of the offender, thereby increasing the scope for intimidation.

41 A form (known as MG19) has been produced by the Home Office for the police to give victims to complete, which details any loss, damage or injury that may have been sustained. This is passed on to the Crown Prosecution Service and, ultimately, to the court, where it may be taken into consideration when deciding whether to order an offender to pay compensation to the victim, as described below (JUSTICE, 1998: 89).

42 Quite apart from any information that is provided directly by victims themselves, probation officers are also required, when preparing pre-sentence reports, to assess the consequences of an offence including its impact on the victim, and to comment on the offender's attitude towards the offence and the victim. Spalek (2003: 220–2), has argued that, because of the inadequate guidance they are given, probation officers are apt to perpetuate stereotypical notions of 'the ideal victim' in discharging their responsibilities.

43 And also, in some instances, in other criminal decisions including, inter alia, bail, prosecution, charge and arrangements relating to an offender's release from custody including the date of release itself. This discussion is confined to the sentencing issue. But see above – p. 71 – on pre-trial decisions and below – p. 83 – on post-conviction decisions.

44 See Chapter 1, for further discussion of the distinction between effects and impact.

45 The responsible agency in the case of juvenile offenders was at that time social services, but following the Crime and Disorder Act 1998 responsibility now rests with Youth Offending Teams.

46 The term was said to have been adopted in order to distance the more restrictive English scheme from those in other common law jurisdictions in which victims are either promised or given much more explicit procedural participation rights (Hoyle et al., 1998: 6; Morgan and Sanders, 1999: 1).

47 Compared with just under half (46 per cent) of those invited to participate in the 'One-Stop-Shop' scheme. Somewhat higher rates were recorded in areas that sent out forms with the initial information about the two schemes, however (Hoyle et al., 1998: 14, 25).

48 Three-quarters in the case of those who completed the statement by themselves and two-thirds in the case of victims whose statement was compiled on their behalf by police officers (Hoyle et al., 1998: 30).

49 In part this is because there is a tendency for victims to *understate* rather than overstate the impact of the offence (Hoyle et al., 1998: 28) and, in cases where the damage or suffering is portrayed as being unusually severe, sentencers are reluctant to act on such information in the absence of independent verification (Morgan and Sanders, 1999: 25).

50 N.B. Shortly after the introduction of the revised scheme, on 16 October 2001, the Lord Chief Justice, Lord Wooy, issued a Practice Direction in which he stressed that the opinions of victims and their close relatives with regard to the sentence itself are not relevant and should *not* be taken into account by the court. Consequently there is now even less likelihood of victims' expectations being met in the future.

51 Victims of white-collar offences, for example, as discussed in Spalek (2001).

52 In 1990 around 117,200 offenders were ordered to pay compensation in the magistrates' court, and around 12,400 in the Crown Court. By 2001, the numbers had fallen to 97,100 and 5,200 respectively (Home Office, 2001d: Table 7.20; 2002: Table 7.20).

53 One reason why fewer compensation orders are imposed by the Crown Court is because of its greater proportionate use of custody, and the fact that compensation orders are not normally combined with custodial sentences. Paradoxically, of course, this normally means that the more serious an offence, the less likely is the victim to receive compensation from the offender (Duff, 1998: 150).

54 The proportionate use of custody in magistrates' courts was 15 per cent in 2001, which is more than twice the level recorded in the early 1990s, while in the Crown Court the proportionate use was 64 per cent, which compares with 43–44 per cent in the early 1990s (Home Office 2002: 85, 87).

55 N.B. A consultation paper published in 2004 contained proposals to increase the proportion of offenders who are required to pay compensation to their victims, including the introduction of a surcharge on those who are convicted or who are issued with a fixed penalty notice (Home Office, 2004).

56 Early research showed that the compliance rate for compensation was comparable with that for the fine, with around three-quarters of orders being paid within 18 months. However, the compliance rate varies in different parts of the country, one study showing that the completion rate within one year ranged from 56 to 86 per cent (Moxon et al., 1992). A more recent Scottish study, where the compensation provisions are virtually identical, showed that 87 per cent were paid in full, though only half were paid on time and, in 6 per cent of cases, no payment at all was made (Hamilton and Wisniewski, 1996).

57 Watson et al. (1989: 217) argue that whether or not offenders knew one another at the time of the offence, they are involved in a moral relationship by virtue of a mutual presumption of respect for one another's security. The relationship is violated by any unlawful action on the part of an offender since this involves a deliberate denial of respect for the victim's security (see also Dignan and Cavadino, 1996: n.13).

58 The Scottish study by Hamilton and Wisniewski (1996) showed that victims were dissatisfied with the amount of compensation, the time it took for offenders to pay, and the lack of information they were given.

59 See the 1995 National Standards for the Supervision of Offenders in the Community (Home Office et al., 1995) and Probation Circular No. 61/1995.

60 See Home Office/National Probation Service Circular 62/2001.

61 Ironically, the financial constraints this imposed on the probation service had an adverse impact on certain offender-focused initiatives, and resulted in the closure of a number of bail information schemes, for example (see Williams, 1999a: 82). It also led to a withdrawal of funding from other existing victim-focused initiatives such as the pioneering Victim Offender Mediation Schemes in West Yorkshire and the West Midlands (Tudor, 2002: 137–8).

62 Significant milestones included three sets of government guidance (Home Office, 1991, 1995, 2001c), two statements issued by the Association of Chief Probation Officers (ACOP, 1993, 1994) and a joint statement issued by ACOP and Victim Support (1996). See also HM Inspectorate of Probation (2000) for an overview.

63 'Conditional release' is the term used for prisoners who are serving fixed-term sentences while the term 'early release' is used in respect of life sentenced prisoners.

64 In interviews, victims indicated that they were interested in factual information relating to the offender's custody; contextual information that would enable them to understand the conditions experienced by the offender; and explanations of criminal justice terminology and procedures (Crawford and Enterkin, 2001: 712; see also Crawford and Enterkin, 1999).

65 Thereby increasing the risk of intimidation. It may be possible to reduce the risk by incorporating the victim's concerns in the probation officers' report, but if attempts to disguise or 'downplay' victims' concerns are taken too far, they may simply be ignored in the release decision, thereby dashing any expectations that might have been raised by consulting with victims in the first place.

66 A phrase coined by Ashworth (2000: 186), as was the phrase 'victims in the service of severity', discussed below. He regards both as forms of 'victim prostitution' (Miers, 1992) that need to be exposed and opposed.

67 As in the case of the welfare model, which was discussed in the previous chapter, readers may find it helpful in reading this concluding section to briefly refer once again to Table I.1 in the Introduction and, in particular, to the column headed 'Criminal Justice Model'. In view of the scale and pace of the changes that have been examined in this chapter, however, it is important to note that the typology itself is only able to depict the principal features that are associated with this model.

68 Garland's reference to the state's propensity to engage in impulsive and reflective retaliatory action directed against offenders as a form of 'acting out' finds its counterpart in some of the victim-focused policy initiatives we have been examining (see especially the reference to Falconer, 2003, on p. 84). In a somewhat different context, Mathiesen (1990: 178) has coined the term 'action function' to refer to measures that are taken to reassure people that steps are being taken in response to the problem of law and order and the social threats that they are persuaded to take most seriously.

Further reading

Capes, E. (2004) Overview: is reconciliation possible?, in E. Capes *Reconciling Rights in Criminal Justice: Analysing the Tension between Victims and Defendants*. London: Legal Action.

Crawford, A. and Enterkin, J. (2001) Victim contact work in the probation service: paradigm shift or Pandora's box, *British Journal of Criminology*, 41: 707–25.

Hoyle, C., Cape, E., Morgan, R. and Sanders, A. (1998) *Evaluation of the One Stop Shop and Victim Pilot Statement Projects*. London: Home Office.

Jackson, J. (2004) Putting victims at the heart of criminal justice: the gap between rhetoric and reality, in E. Capes *Reconciling Rights in Criminal Justice: Analysing the Tension between Victims and Defendants*. London: Legal Action.

JUSTICE (1998) *Victims in Criminal Justice: Report of the JUSTICE Committee on the Role of the Victim in Criminal Justice*. London: JUSTICE.

Sanders, A. (2002) Victim participation in an exclusionary criminal justice system, in C. Hoyle and R. Young (eds) *New Visions of Crime Victims*. Oxford: Hart.

Restorative justice and what it might mean for victims

Intellectual foundations of the restorative justice movement
Policy implications for victims and the criminal justice system
Types of restorative justice approaches
Conclusion
Notes
Further reading

The term 'restorative justice' is usually attributed to Albert Eglash (1977), who sought to differentiate between what he saw as three distinct forms of criminal justice. The first is concerned with retributive justice, in which the primary emphasis is on punishing offenders for what they have done. The second relates to what he called 'distributive justice', in which the primary emphasis is on the rehabilitation of offenders.[1] The third is concerned with 'restorative justice', which he broadly equated with the principle of restitution. He was probably the first person to link the term with an approach that attempts to address the harmful consequences of an offender's actions by seeking to actively involve both victim and offender in a process aimed at securing reparation for victims and the rehabilitation of offenders (Van Ness and Strong, 1997).

Many subsequent advocates of restorative justice have sought to portray it as a revival of an older tradition that predates the contemporary criminal justice approach towards wrongdoing rather than a newly discovered alternative.[2] In seeking to bolster the historical pedigree of restorative justice, however, those who claim that analogous principles and practices were universally adopted throughout pre-modern societies have been justifiably taken to task for overstating and selectively interpreting the available anthropological evidence (see in particular Daly, 2002a: 61–4; Johnstone 2002: ch. 3; Bottoms, 2003). For while it is true that processes based on securing reconciliation or restitution are commonly found in many pre-modern societies, it is by no means true of all of them (Roberts, 1979). In those societies where they do occur they are not necessarily the only or even the dominant method of resolving conflict or maintaining order. Moreover, both the form they take and the context in which they operate may contrast sharply with contemporary understandings of restorative justice processes, particularly with regard to the issue of coercion and the role played by sanctions of various kinds. So although historical and anthropological accounts of restorative justice type processes may be interesting in their own right, they provide little or no normative support for contemporary RJ practices. Nor do they help to account for the tremendous diversity of restorative justice initiatives that have sprung up in recent years.

In order to make sense of this latter phenomenon, this chapter will begin by charting the intellectual and philosophical roots that have helped to nurture the modern restorative justice movement.[3] Three principal strands will be identified – the 'civilization' thesis,[4] the 'communitarian' thesis and what I will refer to as the 'moral discourse' thesis[5] – and their broad implications for both victims and the wider criminal justice system will then be considered. The principal restorative justice manifestations or variants that have been inspired and shaped by these intellectual sources will be considered next, and their putative benefits for victims identified, before going on to consider their main operational features and the context in which they have been implemented. Chapter 5 will attempt to summarize the performance of restorative justice processes principally, but not exclusively, from a victim's perspective, in the light of the available empirical evidence. Finally, Chapter 6 will return to some of the main concerns that have been identified in the victimological literature and will consider their implications for restorative justice.

Intellectual foundations of the restorative justice movement

The 'civilization' thesis

The 'civilization' thesis is linked to a long-standing critique of our contemporary criminal justice system: that it is excessively preoccupied with the punishment of offenders, the treatment of whom is often unduly harsh if not barbaric, while neglecting the interests of the victim who has been harmed by the offence. One of the earliest and most uncompromising exponents of this thesis was Gilbert Cantor, for whom the obvious solution was to 'civilize' – in both senses of the term – the way in which offences are dealt with (Cantor, 1976: 107). This would involve a reconceptualization of the offence as a civil wrong and a substitution of civil for criminal proceedings, the outcome of which would in his view be far more 'civilized' (in the sense of being more humane and enlightened) than the barbaric 'game of crime and punishment'. Even those 'savage few' who are incapable of being civilized would be dealt with in the same way, though imprisonment would be retained as a last resort for those whose refusal to comply with court orders could amount to contempt of court.

The 'civilization' thesis also finds echoes in the work of other penal reformers who advocated the adoption of reparation or restitution by the offender for the victim as a more constructive alternative to conventional forms of punishment. They include, most notably, Marjory Fry (1951, 1959; see also Chapter 1) in England, Louk Hulsman (1981, 1982, 1986) in the Netherlands and, in the United States, Randy Barnett (1977, 1980; Barnett and Hagel, 1977) and Charles Abel and Frank Marsh (1984). For most of these, the principal attraction of a 'civilian' approach was that it provided a means of ameliorating the plight of offenders, and the fact that it might also help repair the harm done to the victim was seen as a useful spin-off.[6] However, other supporters of the 'civilization thesis' (see for example Stephen Schafer, 1960, 1968, 1970; Martin Wright, 1982) did place greater emphasis on the importance of meeting victims' needs.

In its original guise the 'civilization thesis' entailed two significant restrictions. The first concerned the institutional framework, since it was assumed that crime was best dealt with in the ordinary civil courts, with all the formality (in terms of procedures and rules of evidence) that this entails. The second related to the range of permissible outcomes which, for the most part, were confined to physical restitution (repair or return of stolen property where possible) or financial compensation.

Another distinct but complementary development that can be seen as a broader variant of the 'civilization thesis', however, has its roots in the Christian Mennonite movement,[7] with its emphasis on the values of healing and reconciliation. Instead of reconceptualizing crime simply as a civil wrong, which still pits 'victims' and 'offenders' *against* one another within a formal adversarial set of proceedings, many within the Mennonite movement have emphasized the importance of *bringing victims and offenders together* to talk about the offence. This philosophy underpinned some of the earliest attempts to develop informal methods of offence resolution and several of the earliest and best known advocates of restorative justice, including Howard Zehr and Ron Classen are themselves Mennonites. They were prominent in the development of victim–offender mediation programmes[8] in which victim and offender are encouraged, with the aid of a mediator, to discuss the harm that has been caused by an offence, and what can be done to repair the damage and put things right between them. Because they call for greater involvement by the parties themselves, they potentially offer greater scope for their empowerment than either civil or criminal court proceedings would. Moreover, the absence of formal procedural rules provides an opportunity for both parties to address the issues that matter most to them. Furthermore, since they are not restricted to outcomes prescribed by law, they provide scope for the parties to formulate reparative outcomes that go beyond the provision of material restitution.

The 'communitarian' thesis

Communitarianism is a political philosophy in its own right,[9] which can be seen as advocating a third way between extreme collectivism and extreme individualism.[10] Within a restorative justice context, however, the 'communitarian' thesis has a more specific focus comprising a number of loosely related elements. It takes as its starting point a critique of the criminal justice system – particularly with regard to its conceptualization of crime as an offence committed 'against the state' and its neglect of victims – that is similar in many respects to the one associated with the 'civilization thesis'. Where it parts company from the latter is in its insistence that the interests of the community, as well as those of victims, need to be accommodated in devising alternative ways of dealing with crime. The problem with victim–offender mediation, according to this perspective, is that in concentrating solely on the interpersonal relationships of victims and offenders it fails to take sufficiently into account the social and moral implications that crime has, not just for the victim but also for the whole community (Marshall, 1994; Dignan and Cavadino, 1996: 169).[11]

One of the earliest and most influential exponents of the 'communitarian thesis' was Nils Christie (1977), whose now classic article, 'Conflicts as Property' combined an assault on the 'non-happening'[12] that is characterized by conventional criminal trial proceedings with an alternative vision based on a 'model of neighbourhood courts'. Although the case he cited in order to illustrate his argument involved a civil dispute, the forum in which the matter was deliberated bore little resemblance to the formal civil courts of law favoured by supporters of the 'civilization thesis'. The dispute itself took place in the province of Arusha in Tanzania and concerned the recovery of property to which the 'suitor' believed he was entitled following the breaking off of an engagement. A number of features set the 'sort of happening' described by Christie apart from the conventional western court process, whether civil or criminal. One was that the parties themselves were not only 'centre stage' but took the leading roles in the drama that unfolded. However, they were not the only actors since they were accompanied by family and friends who also had a 'supporting role' in the proceedings, though they did not take over from the principal actors. Also present were 'members of the community', in the form of most of the grown-ups from the village and several from adjoining villages. They too had a subordinate but important role since the performance involved a degree of audience participation that included short questions, information or jokes and also, rather more importantly, 'crystallization and clarification' of the norms to be applied in resolving the matter. The only people who were not actively engaged in the process were three local party secretaries. Although nominally judges, they were 'obviously ignorant with regard to village matters', the implication being that they were dependent upon, and would take their cue from, the local experts who were present in abundance. Finally, conspicuous by their absence were any other professional experts since they were not required and since there would, in any event, be no part for them to play in an amateur dramatic performance of such intensity.

A number of features in Christie's seminal account can be discerned in the 'communitarian thesis' that has become increasingly influential[13] since its original airing though – as Bottoms (2003: 80) has observed – few would have foreseen the extent of this influence at the time. The two most obvious of these include: first, the active participation of both the disputants themselves and also 'the community', who are often referred to as the principal 'stakeholders'; second, an 'anti-professional' ethos that is reflected in a suspicion of lawyers and other experts because of their propensity for taking over conflict and sidelining the true protagonists.[14] A third distinctive feature of Christie's account is its 'anti-statist' ethos since the state, in the form of the Crown, is also criticized for appropriating the limelight, the opportunity to engage with the offender and also the compensation (in the form of a fine) that is more properly due to the victim of an offence (Christie, 1977: 4). A fourth and final aspect of Christie's account that has continued to resonate in the unfolding 'communitarian thesis' is its preference for the kind of informal dispute settlement processes that were developed by pre-modern societies. Indeed, this preference is closely linked with a growing sensitivity towards the cultural values of indigenous peoples, who form a significant minority of the population in countries such as New Zealand and Canada. As Bottoms (2003: 106) has astutely suggested, this greater willingness to acknowledge that the imposition of western-based criminal justice systems by settling colonists has alienated these communities and lacks legitimacy in their eyes may also have helped to strengthen the appeal of restorative justice (RJ) for policymakers in such countries.

For Christie and his communitarian followers, however, such processes are esteemed not simply as a better means of dealing with interpersonal disputes but, equally importantly, as a means of reviving communities themselves and reinvigorating their capacity to exert informal social control over their members. Thus, as Crawford (2000: 290) has perceptively noted, communities are prized not only as a means to an end but also as an end in themselves. Instrumentally they are valued by virtue of the part they are capable of playing in informal justice processes. But they are also valued intrinsically since the restoration of a strong communal moral order is seen as a way of preventing crime and thus reducing the incidence of victimization.

Influential as the 'communitarian thesis' has undoubtedly become, however, it raises a number of important questions that for the most part have not been adequately addressed within the RJ literature:[15]

1 What is the meaning of 'the community' and how is the concept to be understood in the absence of the kind of communities that exist in pre-modern societies, particularly since it is the latter which provided Christie with the inspiration for his 'neighbourhood court model'?[16]

2 Assuming that the term 'community' can be satisfactorily defined, how might the concept be operationalized when deciding who, precisely, from 'the community' should participate in restorative justice processes?

3 In what capacities might 'the community' or its representatives participate in RJ processes (as observers, victims, decision-makers or other)?

4 Assuming that 'the community' might, on occasion, appear in the capacity of a victim (whether direct or indirect) to what redress, if any, might it be entitled?

5 What role should be accorded to 'the community' or its representatives, and is this (or should it be) affected by the capacity in which it participates in the process?

6 What should happen when the interests or wishes of 'the community' and the victim do not coincide; which takes precedence, and who should decide?

7 What assumptions are made about 'the community' when designing restorative justice processes that allow for some form of community participation, and what if these assumptions are not matched by the empirical reality?[17]

8 What safeguards are required to ensure that the interests of victims and offenders are not prejudiced by the possibility of such conflict?

It is not possible to do justice to all of these questions at this point, and what follows are a few preliminary remarks directed in the main towards questions 1, 3 and 5 (relating to the identity, capacity and role of 'the community' respectively).[18]

Very few of those who advocate a 'communitarian thesis' have attempted to say precisely what they mean by 'the community', though some have acknowledged the difficulties involved in seeking to define it. Walgrave (2000b: 267), for example,[19] has very colourfully likened the all-too-easy reference to the term to a kind of *fata Morgana*, which he describes as 'a mirage of what may exist somewhere deep in our memories, but which we cannot really make concrete'. McCold (1996: 91) has pointed out that there are many different levels of community from 'the human community' down to local communities, but even the latter term lacks practical specificity when it comes to determining who might take part in restorative justice processes on behalf of 'the community'.[20] Others, perhaps mindful of Christie's recognition that there are too few neighbourhoods in today's industrialized societies, have sought to define community without reference to geographical or spatial parameters. Braithwaite[21] (1989: 172–3), for example, refers to 'communities of interest', that may be based on workplace, occupational and leisure activities. Finally, McCold (1996: 91) makes reference to personal communities, such as family and friends and also (though he does not refer to them as such) to social communities such as schools, churches and community organizations.

The notion of 'personal communities' is also related to the concept of 'communities of care', which is a term used by some restorative justice advocates (see, for example, Braithwaite, 1999: 17; Braithwaite and Roche, 2001) as a means of identifying those who might be invited to participate in restorative conferencing processes (see below).[22] 'Communities of care' have been defined as the 'group of people who are committed to care for, protect, support and encourage an individual' (Van Ness and Crocker, 2003), and are often referred to as supporters of either the victim or the offender.[23] This is still a fairly narrow definition, however, since it is simply an extension of the 'bilateral' approach that is associated with supporters of the 'civilization thesis' (see also Dignan, 2002a: 177), and does not extend to 'the community at large'.

Other restorative justice advocates maintain that the wider community may also have an interest in, or concern about, at least certain types of offences. McCold (1996: 91), for example, has suggested that the way we define 'community' in any given instance will depend in part on the nature of the conflict including 'the level of harm inflicted, the relationship of the disputants, and the aggregation represented'. Where the offence is a relatively minor one, involving two people who know one another, any community involvement is likely to be restricted to their respective 'communities of care'. But this may not be the case where the harm is more serious, the victim a stranger, and the offence is of a type giving rise to widespread public concern. Although McCold himself does not indicate how this wider community interest may be represented in restorative justice procedures, others have suggested that the interests of the 'community at large' may be represented in such cases by those acting in an official capacity. Take the case of a restorative justice conference where the offence involves a breach of social norms that is not adequately addressed by whatever outcome may have been negotiated by the participants and their respective communities of care. Some (Braithwaite and Mugford, 1994: 147; Moore, 1993: 30), have argued that the facilitator of such a conference has a duty to consider the wider public interest, and to ensure that this is also addressed in any resulting plan of action. Thus, in the absence of any satisfactory mechanism for determining who might represent the wider community in restorative justice processes, one response has been to cast the facilitator in the role of a symbolic representative of the community at large, or 'moral community'.

Even less thought has been given by those who advocate a 'communitarian thesis' to a distinct but related set of questions relating to the capacity in which 'the community', however it is defined, might participate in restorative justice processes. One obvious capacity that we have already come across is that of indirect stakeholder when the direct protagonists call upon their respective 'communities of care' to act as supporters. However, this does not exhaust the possibilities since 'the community' might also be considered to be the direct victim with regard to certain types of offences such as vandalism directed against community facilities such as parks, 'street furniture', civic buildings and even local community schools and hospitals. Often it may be possible for someone to 'represent' the interests of the community organization in question as a direct stakeholder in any restorative justice process, though it may not always be obvious who is the most appropriate person to take on this function.[24] In many restorative justice initiatives, as we shall see, 'the community' is also frequently invoked as a kind of surrogate or proxy victim, even in relatively minor cases, particularly where the actual victim does not wish to take part in a restorative justice process, or has no wish to receive any direct reparation. In more serious cases, as we have seen, some restorative justice advocates also conceive of 'the wider community' as having an interest in the outcome of a restorative justice process that extends beyond the interests and wishes of the direct stakeholders. It might be helpful to refer to this additional capacity as that of a 'vicarious stakeholder', in order to differentiate it from those of direct or indirect stakeholder. However, the concept of vicarious stakeholder raises further difficult questions relating not just to the capacity of any community representative in such cases, but more specifically to the role they are expected to perform.

Where 'the community' is involved in a restorative justice process as a *direct* 'stakeholder', the role of any representative is arguably no more contentious[25] than it would be in the case of a personal victim, even if it involves contributing to discussions about what needs to be done to put matters right between offender and victim. Where 'the community' is involved as a *vicarious* stakeholder, however, much would depend on the precise nature of the community representative's capacity and role. One possibility is that the community representative merely attends the restorative justice process in the capacity of a 'witness' or 'bystander',[26] in which case their role would be entirely passive and uncontroversial. Where the community representative is considered to 'stand for' the wider public interest, and has the authority to propose or veto outcomes from this standpoint, however, this raises much more serious concerns over the proportionality of any response (Ashworth, 2002: 585). Such concerns are likely to prompt calls for adequate safeguards to protect the interests of both offenders and direct victims.[27] However, it also raises wider concerns over the nature and identity of 'the communities' whose interests may be represented in such processes and the means by which their representatives are selected.

There is a presumption in much of the restorative justice literature that communities in general are reasonably benign, tolerant, likely to espouse broadly progressive values and that communitarianism is therefore 'a good thing'. John Braithwaite, who argues (2000: 122) that contemporary restorative justice is founded on what he calls an 'individual-centred communitarianism', may have helped to reinforce such attitudes through his writings on the principles that underlie his political theory of republican justice (see, for example, Braithwaite and Pettit, 1990; Braithwaite and Parker 1999). But while Braithwaite himself is at pains to portray this as an ideal normative theory, he and others have cautioned that some of the real world communities into which restorative justice practices are being introduced would not subscribe to his republican ideals (Braithwaite and

Pettit, 1990: 107; Crawford, 1997, 2000: 290–1; Dignan and Lowey, 2000: 18–19). Many communities are intolerant, illiberal, coercive, engage in socially exclusionary practices and espouse a form of communitarianism that is not at all 'individual centred' but authoritarian and repressive. Where such communities claim to be adopting restorative justice practices, there are understandable concerns about the extent to which the demands of 'the community' may ride roughshod over the rights and interests of individual offenders or victims, particularly if they belong to 'dissident' or minority groups.[28] Such concerns are accentuated where the ostensibly restorative justice processes are intended to, or do in practice, operate in the absence of any effective judicial safeguards.[29]

The 'moral discourse' thesis

For much of recent western penological history, the formal punishment system has tended to rely almost exclusively on the application of 'external' sanctions that are directed *against* an offender as opposed to 'internal' sanctions which operate on the basis of an offender's conscience (see Cavadino and Dignan, 2002: 167).[30] During the last few years, however, an alternative response has emerged, which can be thought of as the 'moral discourse' thesis. This stems from an acknowledgement that conscience is generally a much more powerful weapon to control misbehaviour than punishment (Braithwaite, 1989: 71) and seeks to build on this insight by engaging in normative or moralizing dialogue with an offender as part of the response to an offence. One of the best-known exponents of this 'moral discourse thesis' is John Braithwaite (1989, 1999), whose theory of 'reintegrative shaming' has been particularly influential.

The theory of reintegrative shaming is predicated on the assertion that crime should be confronted rather than simply ignored or tolerated, but argues that the way this is done makes a great deal of difference to its effectiveness. The problem with conventional criminal justice responses, according to the theory, is that they involve a destructive or disintegrative process of publicly shaming offenders in a way that is likely to result in their near-permanent stigmatization. Because the shame is both indelible and open ended it is extremely difficult to shake off, and this makes it difficult if not impossible for offenders to resume ordinary law-abiding lives even after their formal punishment has come to an end. This makes it more likely that offenders will behave in the way that labelling theorists predict, by adopting a deviant self-image. It is also more likely that they will become permanent outcasts from society and thus helps to explain why such negative labelling may be counterproductive.

One way of avoiding this vicious cycle is for offenders to be shamed for what they have done, not in the formal, exclusionary and alienating setting of a criminal trial, but in the presence of the victim and also those who mean a lot to them, while continuing to show respect for them as individuals. According to the theory of reintegrative shaming, the presence and active participation of the victim makes it more likely that the offender will be obliged to confront the offence and less likely that they will be able to neutralize their responsibility for the harm they have caused. Where the offender is shamed in the presence of 'significant others' it is more likely to have an impact than where the shame is induced by an impersonal judge. Most importantly, however, the shaming itself should be finite in duration and, once it has occurred, should formally[31] be brought to an end so that the focus can switch to what needs to be done in order to repair the harm and reintegrate the offender into the law-abiding community. Once again the presence of 'significant others' including those drawn from the offender's community of care (see above) is important, both in countering the disintegrative effects associated with stigmatization and in identifying and taking the steps that might be needed to prevent reoffending.

Braithwaite's theory of reintegrative shaming has been augmented and supplemented by other scholars who have drawn on psychological under-standings derived from 'affect theory'[32] to elucidate the emotion of shame which, as Braithwaite himself concedes (1999: 42, 2002: 79), was under-theorized in his earlier work on reintegrative shaming. Although shame is a normal emotion that can play an important part in maintaining social relationships provided shameful consequences are acknowledged and con-fronted, it can also have destructive consequences when they are not, and shame itself is denied or by-passed (Scheff and Retzinger, 1991; Nathanson, 1992). If shame is not acknowledged and confronted it may result in a person showing aggression either towards themselves or towards others, or engaging in denial or avoidance strategies; these four responses constitut-ing Nathanson's (1992) 'compass of shame'. Although restorative justice processes – and particularly conferences (see below) – are acknowledged by some working within this tradition to have the potential to help offenders confront the consequences of their behaviour and respond to shame in a constructive manner, this is by no means inevitable. Both Moore with Forsythe (1995) and Retzinger and Scheff (1996) have sought to iden-tify the mechanisms and strategies that may enable shame to be utilized in forging constructive social bonds while avoiding responses that may accentuate the scope for conflict. The most successful processes are those that successfully elicit what Retzinger and Scheff (1996: 316) refer to as the 'core sequence', which consists of two sequential steps. First the offender expresses genuine shame and remorse over his or her actions, in the form of an apology. This is then followed by the victim taking at least the first steps towards forgiving the offender for the offence. The whole process is referred to as 'symbolic reparation', though Retzinger and Scheff are by no means the only ones to use this term.

Other important contributors to the 'moral discourse thesis' include Anthony Duff and Nicholas Tavuchis. Duff (1986) was one of the first people to articulate a 'communicative theory' of punishment, which he sees as an attempt to engage in moral dialogue with offenders, censuring them for their attitudes and hoping to secure their contrition as a prelude to mending their ways. Although he is not normally thought of as a 'mainstream' restorative justice exponent, Cavadino and Dignan (2002: 44) point out that his early work contains elements of reintegrative shaming[33] and thus prefigures some of the themes that Braithwaite later articulated. Moreover, his more recent work (Duff, 2001, 2002, 2003) has focused on the common ground that he identifies between proponents of restorative and retributive justice theories.

Tavuchis's contribution to the 'moral discourse thesis' consists of a sociological analysis of the apology, which is the social mechanism that helps to elicit the core sequence of a successful restorative justice process (Retzinger and Scheff, 1996: 321). Tavuchis's account has recently been very fully and perceptively analysed by Tony Bottoms (2003: 94), who points out that Tavuchis offers an ideal-typical account of a successful apology from two different but complementary perspectives. The first relates to the social structural context within which such an apology takes place, which assumes some kind of relationship between the parties, however tenuous and indirect this may be at a personal level. At the very least it assumes that they belong to the same social/moral community. It also assumes a form of discourse between the parties that is 'essentially dyadic in its nature' (Bottoms, 2003: 95). The second perspective relates to the 'experiential dynamics' of an apology which Tavuchis (1991: vii) himself characterizes as a 'delicate and precarious transaction' because it depends on the negotiation of a series of emotionally fraught moves by each of the parties. The first of these moves consists of a call for an apology by the person who has been wronged, or someone acting on their behalf; the second is the apology itself; the third is an expression of forgiveness by the victim to the wrongdoer. Bottoms (2003: 96) draws attention to Tavuchis's observation that if these moves are successfully accomplished they can have the 'miraculous quality' of bringing about a social transformation that may result in reunion and reconciliation between the parties. Tavuchis's own account of this miraculous quality notes that: 'no matter how sincere or effective, [an apology] does not and cannot *undo* what has been done. And yet, in a mysterious way and according to its own logic, this is precisely what it manages to do' (Tavuchis, 1991: 5; also cited by Bottoms, 2003: 95).

The 'moral discourse thesis' has had a significant impact on the development of restorative justice practices, most notably in connection with police-led conferencing initiatives that have been directly influenced by Braithwaite's notion of reintegrative shaming (see below). But most restorative justice commentators also place great emphasis on the importance of the apology, which is almost universally presented as a natural and almost essential prerequisite of any meaningful attempt to resolve an offence, whatever restorative justice process it involves. The centrality of the apology within most restorative justice writings raises a number of important questions, however. For, as Bottoms (2003: 97) has perceptively noted, the archetypal form of apology, to which Tavuchis, Duff and others refer, is dyadic in nature whereas restorative justice processes almost invariably involve at least one third party and, in the case of conferencing initiatives, often very many more than one. The involvement of third parties need not inhibit the 'delicate and precarious transaction' to which Tavuchis refers, and might even assist in negotiating the series of emotionally fraught moves that an apology entails. But their involvement will certainly affect the dynamics of the encounter and could also, as Tavuchis (1991: 52) himself notes, cause complications. An even more important question, however, is whether the tendering of genuine apologies with their potentially miraculous healing qualities can be facilitated by restorative justice processes in contemporary societies where the social context of the encounter may be very different from the one assumed in Tavuchis's account (Bottoms, 2003: 98). How successful are restorative justice processes in orchestrating encounters that result in meaningful and restorative apologies where the protagonists do not know one another or even where they do not belong to the same moral or social communities? Indeed, how successful are they in circumstances where the parties *do* know one another and may well have been involved in ongoing personal or social relationships? These are questions to which we will return in Chapter 6.

Policy implications for victims and the criminal justice system

Before going on to examine the variety of restorative justice initiatives that have been nurtured by these three distinct philosophical and intellectual traditions, it is worth reflecting briefly on their policy implications with regard both to victims and also the regular criminal justice system.

From a victim's perspective the most notable feature of all three intellectual precursors is their profound ambivalence in relation to victims. With regard to the 'civilization thesis', we have already noted that many of its earliest advocates were chiefly motivated by a desire to ameliorate the harsh treatment meted out to offenders. Even their support for victim-oriented penalties such as restitution and reparation was prompted in part by a perception that this was likely to be the most effective way of promoting humane reform of the wider penal system. With regard to the 'communitarian thesis', we noted earlier the potential tension between the interests of victims and those of the community, and the uncertainty as to which set of interests should prevail where they are in conflict. As for the moral discourse thesis, both Braithwaite's theory of reintegrative shaming and Duff's 'communicative theory' of punishment were primarily offender focused and both were originally conceptualized as providing a more effective way of controlling crime rather than a means of meeting the needs of victims.[34] Indeed, victims hardly featured at all in Braithwaite's groundbreaking work on *Crime, Shame and Reintegration*, and were not even mentioned in a passage setting out a restorative justice conference style process for dealing with criminal offenders, though reference was made to participation by those known to the offender (Braithwaite, 1989: 173–4). It was only as the theory of reintegrative shaming came to be elaborated in the light of practice developments in New Zealand and Australia (see below) and was assimilated with the emerging body of literature on restorative justice that its potential relevance for victims was spelt out (see, for example, Dignan, 1992: 469, 1994; and in the USA Van Ness, 1993). This ambivalence with regard to victims within the three main intellectual traditions that have helped to nurture the restorative justice movement does not necessarily mean that the resulting restorative justice initiatives are detrimental to the interests of victims. But it does mean that they cannot automatically be assumed to be beneficial without a careful assessment of the available empirical evidence (see Chapter 5).

With regard to the relationship between restorative justice and the conventional criminal justice system, the intellectual precursors of the restorative justice movement contain some very mixed messages and at least three broad policy strands can be discerned which, for the sake of convenience, I will refer to as: 'abolitionism', 'separatism' and 'reformism' (see also Dignan, 2002a: 178ff). We noted earlier that many proponents of the 'civilization thesis' were inspired by a radical critique of the conventional criminal justice and penal systems, and some aligned themselves with critical criminologists such as Hermann Bianchi (1994) and Willem de Haan (1990) in advocating a policy of total *abolitionism*. Some within the restorative justice movement have adopted a similar position, either explicitly in the case of Hulsman (1991) and van Swaaningen (1997) (see also Bianchi and van Swaaningen, 1986) or implicitly (see Fattah, 1995, 1998; Zehr, 1990) by presenting restorative justice as an alternative paradigm that has little or nothing in common with the conventional criminal justice system.

Some restorative justice advocates take a more pragmatic view and, while they agree that restorative justice and conventional criminal justice are fundamentally incompatible, accept that there is very little prospect that the regular criminal justice system will be overthrown or displaced in the foreseeable future (see, for example, Marshall, 1990; Marshall and Merry, 1990; Wright, 1991; Davis et al., 1992). Their solution is based on a '*separatist*' approach in which restorative justice programmes should operate completely outside the criminal justice system in a supplementary capacity, because their objectives and practices are so different. There is also a concern that the distinctive aims and values of such programmes will be 'contaminated' if they are required to co-exist with and operate within a criminal justice system whose values are inimical· to those of restorative justice.

Finally, a third group of restorative justice proponents have advocated a '*reformist*' approach with regard to the criminal justice system, whereby the system itself is modified in line with restorative justice principles, values, outcomes or processes. The reformist approach encompasses a wide range of possibilities, however, that vary considerably in terms of their scale and ambition. The most modest approaches are associated with some of the early exponents of the 'civilian thesis', such as Marjory Fry, who campaigned for the introduction of restitutive or reparative penalties which they favoured as a more constructive and humane way of dealing with offenders. It is clearly possible to incorporate minor concessions of this kind (and the same is true of other potentially reparative penalties such as the compensation order, reparation order and community service order) into the criminal justice system though their overall effect on the system as a whole is likely to be limited.

A slightly more radical possibility is to try to integrate restorative justice principles and practices within the criminal justice system itself; an approach that is often referred to as 'mainstreaming', though again there are various ways in which this might be attempted. One option is to enable criminal justice decision makers to specify restorative justice interventions as an alternative to more conventional ways of dealing with offenders (and their victims) in cases that come before them.[35] Another is to 'prescribe' restorative justice processes such as conferencing as the standard way of dealing with certain categories of offences or offenders, as New Zealand has done with respect to juvenile offenders (see below). Finally, the most ambitious of the reformist approaches favours a more thoroughgoing transformation of current criminal justice practices so that they all conform, as far as possible, to restorative justice principles and values (see, for example, Dignan, 1994, 2002a; Walgrave and Aertsen, 1996). It may be helpful to bear these different policy strategies in mind when examining the different kinds of restorative justice approaches that are described in more detail in the next section.

Types of restorative justice approaches

Now that we have considered the main philosophical and theoretical roots of the restorative justice movement, it is easier to appreciate the variety of practice-based initiatives that have borne fruit in recent years and to understand why the attribution of the 'restorative justice' label remains a matter of controversy. In keeping with the analytical framework set out in the Introduction, I will now examine a range of broadly restorative approaches that between them represent five distinct categories or models. The aim of this review[36] is to relate each approach back to the intellectual/philosophical tradition with which it is associated; consider its aims (principally but not exclusively from a victim perspective); comment on its main operational features; and examine the context in which it has been implemented (with particular reference to the United Kingdom). The five main categories of restorative justice approaches are as follows:

1 Court-based restitutive and reparative measures.
2 Victim–offender mediation programmes.
3 Conferencing initiatives.
4 Community reparation boards and panels.
5 Healing or sentencing circles.

Court-based restitutive and reparative measures

Overview: origins and aims

Some of the earliest victim-oriented reforms of the criminal justice system involved offenders being required to provide financial restitution or other forms of reparation to their victims. Although they lack many of the attributes commonly associated with a restorative justice approach, such reforms nevertheless have some affinity with and are closely allied to it. Indeed they are often very closely interrelated in practice with restorative justice initiatives, particularly in England but also elsewhere, which is why they are included in this chapter. As we have seen, the introduction of restitutive and reparative measures was advocated by proponents of a version of the 'civilization thesis'. Although their motives might have been primarily influenced by a desire to ameliorate the harsh treatment meted out to offenders, such reforms were also intended to address one of the main shortcomings of the conventional criminal justice system, which is its failure adequately to acknowledge or redress the personal harm that is experienced by victims of an offence (see Chapter 3).

Operational features

Three main sets of restitutive or reparative measures have been introduced in England and Wales (in common with a number of other common law countries including New Zealand) in recent years. The first involves a progressive strengthening of victims' entitlement to financial compensation from their offender in a series of Acts passed between 1972 and 1988.[37] As a result, offenders can now be ordered to pay compensation for any injury, loss or damage resulting from an offence, either as a penalty in its own right or as an ancillary order in addition to the main sentence without the victim having to apply for it. Moreover, courts have been directed to give precedence to the payment of compensation rather than fines in cases where an offender is unable to afford both, and to give reasons for not awarding compensation. This means that, in theory at least, they are obliged to consider the award of compensation in every case where an offence has resulted in personal injury, loss or damage to personal property. Although financial compensation may also be an outcome of restorative justice processes, one important difference is that it is then the product of a discussion involving the offender and victim (or victim's representative), and will thus be something that the offender has agreed to undertake, rather than being imposed and enforced by court orders.

The second potentially reparative measure was the introduction of the community service order in 1972,[38] though this is of less direct relevance to personal victims since it involves the imposition of unpaid work in (and usually for the benefit of) the community. Community service is seen as a form of restorative justice by some people (for example Walgrave, 1999, 2000b), though not everyone agrees with this formulation. Community service may involve 'the community' in determining the work that should be performed by offenders (since the projects themselves are frequently demand led and respond to local need), and may often benefit the community against whom the offences may have been committed. It can also be 'tailored' to the requirements of an individual offender (by relating the project to the offender's particular skills or interests, for example). All of these elements are consistent with restorative justice principles of repairing the harm caused by an offence, engendering a sense of accountability on the part of offenders and seeking their 'reintegration' into the law-abiding community where possible. However, community service (like a compensation order) is still a coercive sanction that is imposed irrespective of the wishes of the offender. Although it may embody reparative and rehabilitative aspects, it can also (as we shall see) incorporate more straightforwardly punitive elements that sit uncomfortably with a restorative justice approach.

The third set of reparative measures was introduced as part of a wide-ranging programme of reforms to the youth justice system by the Labour government that was elected in 1997, following a long period (almost two decades) out of office. Elements of a restorative justice approach informed some of these reforms, but they were also shaped by a variety of other influences, by no means all of which were compatible with restorative justice principles or philosophy. Only those reforms that have been influenced, at least in part, by restorative justice thinking will be considered here, and readers are referred to other sources for more detailed accounts of the full 'new youth justice' reform programme, as it has come to be known[39] (see, for example, Cavadino and Dignan, 2002: ch. 9; Crawford and Newburn, 2003: ch. 1; Bottoms and Dignan, 2004). The Labour government's interest in restorative justice philosophy was initially signalled in a White Paper entitled *No More Excuses* (Home Office, 1997). This proclaimed three restorative justice principles in terms of the 'three Rs' of:

- 'responsibility', on the part of young offenders and their parents
- 'restoration', involving young offenders apologizing to victims and making amends for what they have done
- 'reintegration', whereby young offenders rejoin the law-abiding community having paid their debt to society by putting their crime behind them (see also NACRO, 1997; Dignan, 1999).

The implementation of these principles was most evident in three related sets of initiatives that were contained in the Crime and Disorder Act 1998.[40] They comprised a reform of the system of cautioning for young offenders; the introduction of a new 'entry-level' penalty for young offenders, known as the 'reparation order'; and the addition of a new middle-ranking penalty[41] known as the 'action plan order'.

Reform of the cautioning system comprised, initially,[42] a replacement of the old permissive non-statutory cautioning scheme that had been condemned for allowing offenders to be repeatedly cautioned (even though this was relatively rarely done in practice) with a much more restrictive statutory scheme. Under the reformed scheme, minor young offenders could normally be expect to be diverted from prosecution no more than twice, the first involving a warning or 'reprimand' that is somewhat akin to the old-style formal police caution, and the second involving a 'final warning' that involves more than just a 'telling off'. Offenders who are to be warned are also assessed with regard to their suitability or need for a 'rehabilitation programme' (also known as a 'change programme'), which may include a variety of components including offenders apologizing to victims and/or undertaking reparation either for the victim or the community.

The reparation order was largely envisaged as a low-level tariff for young offenders intended largely to replace a purely admonitory court-ordered penalty known as the 'conditional discharge'. A reparation order requires an offender to undertake some sort of reparation either to the victim (provided s/he consents) or for the community. The kind of reparation that it entails is principally reparation 'in kind' rather than financial compensation (though it can be combined with a compensation order), but it can also include a letter of apology or even the possibility of mediation between victim and offender (see below), provided the victim agrees to this. Courts are able to prescribe a maximum aggregate period of 24 hours of reparative activities within a period of three months, and are obliged to consider such a penalty[43] where they have the power to do so and are not minded to impose a more severe penalty since the reparation order cannot be combined with other such disposals.

The 'action plan order' was envisaged as a short (three months maximum), intensive intervention suitable for young offenders the first time they commit an offence that is serious enough to be dealt with by means of an intermediate level 'community sentence'. This highly focused intervention also has a reparative dimension and is intended to combine 'punishment, rehabilitation and reparation' with a view to changing offending behaviour and preventing further crime (Home Office, 1997: para. 5.18).

All three initiatives require consultation with victims before offenders may be required to undertake any direct reparation for them (including an apology), and all place very strong emphasis on the desirability of reparation as a key element in each of the three types of intervention. Indeed, the same types of reparative activities are permissible for each type of intervention, and the evaluation of the pilot Crime and Disorder Act initiatives found that it was common in practice for standard programmes to be developed to give effect to the reparative components irrespective of the type of intervention concerned (Holdaway et al., 2001: 42). Compared with the compensation order and community service order, these Crime and Disorder Act initiatives embody a somewhat fuller restorative approach by virtue of their victim consultation requirements. However, they are still not fully restorative in the sense that, at least in formal terms, 'the outcome' takes the form of a coercive sanction that is imposed by a court, rather than an undertaking that is voluntarily assumed by an offender following some kind of dialogue or communication with the victim (Wallis, 2003). These (and other) limitations led me to conclude in 1999 that, even if they were to be fully and successfully implemented, 'the reforms hardly amount to a "restorative justice revolution", let alone the "paradigm shift" that some restorative justice advocates have called for' (Dignan, 1999: 58).

Implementational context

All three sets of restitutive and reparative measures – compensation orders, community service and reparative initiatives – have been introduced on a statutory basis and, to this extent at least, have been incorporated as part of the 'mainstream' criminal justice response to youth offending. Moreover, both the compensation order and reparation order contain mandatory elements that oblige the court to give consideration to their imposition in certain circumstances, at least, rather than leaving it to the sentencer's complete discretion. Despite these 'entrenching provisions', however, all three sets of measures have proved problematic from a restorative justice perspective, as we shall see in Chapter 5.

Victim–offender mediation programmes

Overview: origins and aims

Victim–offender mediation is the longest established of the main restorative justice approaches, and originated in 1974 in Kitchener, Ontario, where a major source of influence was the Christian Mennonite movement, with its emphasis on the value of personal 'reconciliation' between victims and offenders. The writings of Howard Zehr (1985, 1990, 2002), himself a Mennonite, have done much to promote and popularize the practice of mediation and also the concept of restorative justice with which, in his earlier writings, he equated it in the days before conferencing was widely known about. As the oldest type of restorative justice programme operating in North America, victim–offender mediation is still the most prevalent form of restorative justice practice in the United States. Here, it accounts for over one-half of all programmes (51 per cent) according to a wide-ranging recent survey of restorative justice practice (Schiff et al., 2001; Schiff and Bazemore, 2002: 182). The growth of mediation in continental Europe, where it is likewise still the dominant form of restorative justice practice (Miers, 2001) almost certainly owes less to the faith-based version of the 'civilization thesis' and more to the influence of Nils Christie's writing.

Here, his graphic imagery of the theft of interpersonal conflict by the state and its officials and his alternative vision of justice in which the disputants themselves are placed centre stage (as opposed to his support for the wider 'communitarian thesis') has been particularly influential. In addition, widespread dissatisfaction on the part of practitioners with the perceived inadequacies of the criminal justice system and its response to young offenders in particular appear to have been contributory factors in a number of European countries, including Belgium, Finland and Norway (Miers, 2001: 79). Five principal goals of victim–offender mediation[44] are as follows:

1 To support the healing process for victims by providing an opportunity – on a strictly voluntary basis – to meet and speak with their offender and participate in discussions about the way the offence should be resolved.
2 To encourage offenders to take direct responsibility for their actions by requiring them to hear about the impact of their offence on the victim, and by providing an opportunity for them to participate in discussions about the way the offence should be resolved.
3 To facilitate and encourage a process that is empowering and emotionally satisfying for both parties.
4 To 'redress the balance' by switching the emphasis from the 'public interest' (as insisted upon by the conventional criminal justice system) to the interpersonal interests of those most directly affected by an offence.
5 Where desired, to enable the parties to agree on an outcome that addresses the harm caused by an offence in an appropriate and mutually acceptable manner.

Operational features

Victim–offender mediation involves an opportunity for victims and offenders who wish to avail themselves of it to engage in a process of dialogue relating to the offence. It is facilitated by a neutral third party, who is normally a trained mediator, and whose role is to act as an intermediary or sometimes a channel for communication, but not to propose or impose a decision on the parties. Mediation is intended to provide a safe and structured setting in which both parties are able to discuss the crime, the harm it may have caused, and ways of putting matters right between them.

Most victim–offender mediation programmes (unlike some forms of conferencing, see below) emphasize the importance of initial preparation which often involves one or more meetings with each of the parties prior to the face-to-face encounter. The purpose of these preparatory sessions is to explain what is involved, allay concerns, identify some of the issues and expectations of each party and maximize the prospects for a direct and meaningful exchange between them (Umbreit, 1994, 1997).

Often the mediation process does not get as far as a face-to-face encounter (which is commonly referred to as 'direct mediation'), however, but takes the form of a more restricted kind of dialogue. Here, the role of the mediator is limited to acting as a go-between and communicating information, views and feelings between the parties. This variant is often referred to as 'indirect' or 'shuttle' mediation and is the commonest approach in some jurisdictions including the Netherlands (Miers, 2001: 80) and England and Wales, but not in North America where direct mediation is the norm (Umbreit and Roberts, 1996). One of the problems with indirect mediation (see Introduction) is in determining what degree of participation is required in order for it to count as a restorative justice intervention, whether for the purposes of auditing or evaluating restorative justice processes (Miers et al., 2001: 25).

Although victim–offender mediation schemes, as the name suggests, are primarily concerned with the resolution of criminal offences, they do also have some affinity with other broader conflict resolution initiatives and with community mediation services[45] in particular. Community mediation services provide a more general mediation service in respect of a wide variety of disputes ranging from various kinds of neighbour disputes to those involving anti-social behaviour or low-level criminal incidents, particularly where there has been a history of conflict between the parties. Such disputes are often highly complex and frequently involve allegations of wrongdoing or inconsiderate behaviour by both parties. Consequently, one of the main differences between the two approaches is that community mediation services tend to adopt a very strict 'no-blame' approach, and to place greater emphasis on the need to avoid further conflict in the future rather than attempting to apportion responsibility or encourage reparation for past wrongdoing. However, the position is complicated by the fact that some schemes offer both community mediation and victim–offender mediation services.[46] Another parallel development relates to the growth of schools-based conflict resolution services, including the use of 'peer mediation' to enable pupils to develop the skills needed to resolve playground disputes and conflict such as bullying.

Implementational context

Unlike the reparative initiatives discussed earlier, victim–offender mediation initiatives in England and Wales have not been systematically incorporated into the criminal justice process as has happened, in theory at least, in a number of other continental European jurisdictions.[47] Instead, English victim–offender mediation schemes have tended to operate on an ad hoc, stand-alone basis, without any specific statutory authorization (see Dignan and Lowey, 2000: 47). This has had important implications for their size, geographical distribution, organizational basis, operational and financial viability. Most schemes have been relatively small scale and local in character with a restricted geographical coverage, resulting in uneven and inconsistent provision in different parts of the country. Some schemes have been developed within one or more of the statutory criminal justice agencies such as the probation service or the police, often working in conjunction with the relevant local authority.[48] Other schemes are community based, depend heavily on the commitment and enthusiasm of 'a few key charismatic individuals' (Miers, 2001: 28), and rely on disparate sources of funding. Because they are not integrated into the regular criminal justice process, all victim–offender mediation schemes have depended for their operational viability on the need to cultivate good working relations with all the relevant criminal justice agencies on which they depend for their referrals. Nevertheless, almost all have found it difficult to secure sufficient numbers of appropriate referrals (Marshall and Merry, 1990: 240; Dignan and Lowey, 2000: 48). Moreover, virtually all English victim–offender mediation schemes, including those located within statutory organizations, have suffered from acute resource constraints and uncertainties over future funding (Miers et al., 2001: 26), which raises very serious questions about the long term financial viability of this mode of implementation. More generally, it seems inevitable that if mediation schemes (or indeed other forms of restorative justice) continue to operate in this ad hoc, stand-alone manner, they 'will in practice be doomed to a precarious and marginal existence at the periphery of the criminal justice system' (Dignan and Lowey, 2000: 48).

Victim–offender mediation schemes have also varied widely in terms of the stage of the criminal justice process at which they are intended to operate. In the early days (from around 1980 until the implementation of the Crime and Disorder Act 1998), most schemes operated at the pre-court stage and were intended to be used in connection with a caution as part of a diversionary process. Often referred to as 'caution plus' schemes, most were aimed at relatively minor juvenile offenders, but one of the best known and most successful[49] also catered for adult offenders, not all of whose offences were trivial. Other schemes tended to operate at the sentencing stage following an offender's conviction, though some accepted referrals at virtually all stages of the criminal justice process, and one[50] focused on serious offenders including those sentenced to imprisonment by the Crown Court.

Official attitudes towards victim–offender mediation in England and Wales have waxed and waned over the years. In 1985 the Home Office funded a number of pilot mediation and reparation schemes (based in Coventry, Cumbria, Leeds, Wolverhampton), and also contributed to the evaluation of these and a number of other schemes. However, funding was not continued beyond the pilot phase, publication of the official evaluation report (Marshall and Merry, 1990) was significantly delayed, and government interest ebbed away. According to one informed commentator (who was himself involved in some of the evaluations), this was not because the evaluation findings were negative, but because of a difference of opinion between policymakers and practitioners regarding the way mediation and reparation should develop in the future (Davis, 1992: 34–40).

The prospects for any significant extension of victim–offender mediation remained bleak until the introduction of the initiatives dealt with in the previous section which, in principle at least, created much greater scope for mediation to be developed as one of the reparative interventions available when dealing with young offenders. Moreover, significant additional funding was also made available by the Youth Justice Board[51] to stimulate the development of various restorative justice approaches including victim–offender mediation. In practice, however, the development of mediation has been relatively modest, and the evaluation of the youth justice pilot schemes (see previous section) found that only 9 per cent of cases dealt with by means of a reparation order resulted in mediation between victim and offender, almost certainly as a result of the implementational difficulties referred to earlier (Holdaway et al., 2001: 89). Finally, in 2001 the government launched an evaluation of three restorative justice schemes focused on adult offenders, one of which (Remedi, in South Yorkshire), is mainly involved in the provision of mediation services, both direct and indirect (Shapland et al., 2002). However, as Crawford and Newburn (2003: 27) have observed, in many ways victim–offender mediation has been eclipsed by recent developments in 'conferencing', which represents an alternative restorative justice model.

Restorative conferencing initiatives

Overview: origins and aims

The term 'conferencing' is applied in this book to a third, quite distinct, form of restorative justice approach, though in some of the restorative justice literature[52] the term has also been used, rather confusingly, as a generic label almost as a synonym for the entire range of restorative justice processes. Moreover, the position is further confused by the fact that the conferencing model itself encompasses two principal variants, which are referred to in this book as 'family group conferencing' on the one hand, and 'police-led community conferencing' on the other. As we shall see, there are important differences between them regarding their origins and theoretical foundations, certain elements of their operational practice including the role of victims and also the institutional framework within which they have been implemented. These differences are important when it comes to assessing empirical evaluation of restorative justice practices, as we shall see in Chapter 5.

Family group conferencing originated in New Zealand where it was inspired by a constellation of factors that culminated in the passage of the Children, Young Persons and their Families Act 1989. One of the most important was a perceived legitimacy deficit on the part of the criminal justice and family welfare system with regard to its treatment of minority group offenders, notably those from the Maori community but also Pacific Island Polynesians (Maxwell and Morris, 1993; Daly, 2001, 2002a). To the extent that it represents a conscious attempt to develop a more culturally sensitive and appropriate way of responding to offending behaviour, the family group conferencing variant draws on an important strand in the communitarian thesis outlined above, even though, as we shall see, it consciously disavows other aspects of this thesis. A second factor that helped to inspire the development of family group conferencing was a 'welfare-based' commitment to empowering the families of young people who are referred to professional agencies and the courts either because an offence has been committed or on 'child protection' grounds (Masters, 2002: 45).[53] The third factor that contributed to the development of family group conferencing in New Zealand was the growing influence of the victim's movement, which by 1989 had already inspired a number of reforms albeit not specifically with regard to the youth justice system itself (Morris and Maxwell, 2000: 221, n.7). All three sets of factors are reflected in the operation of family group conferencing, as we shall see.

Police-led community conferencing originated in Australia in the early 1990s and differs from most other restorative justice approaches including family group conferencing in terms of both its intellectual and institutional origins. Unlike family group conferencing, the police-led community conferencing model has consciously drawn almost from the outset on Braithwaite's theory of reintegrative shaming,[54] which as we have seen forms part of the 'moral discourse thesis'. As elaborated by Braithwaite himself, however, the theory of reintegrative shaming also incorporates strands of communitarian thinking, particularly with regard to his and Pettit's (1990) normative theory of 'republican justice'. As we shall see, these communitarian elements are likewise strongly reflected in the practice of this particular model.[55] The police-led community conferencing model also differs from family group conferencing inasmuch as it was pioneered by mid-level professionals and administrators, particularly within the police, initially in the small New South Wales town of Wagga Wagga (Daly, 2001: 61). This inception process is quite different from the combination of 'top-down' and 'bottom-up' activism (on the part of state officials and professional workers and Maori groups respectively) that contributed to the New Zealand family group conferencing approach (Ministerial Advisory Committee, 1988).

Operational features

In terms of their operational features, one of the biggest differences between the two conferencing variants relates to the identity of key 'stakeholders' (see Introduction) within the process and, in particular, to the scope for involvement on the part of the wider community. Within family group conferencing, a restrictive line is taken with regard to both sets of issues. Thus, the only people who are able to attend conferences and play an active part, as of right, are the offenders and direct victims themselves (Morris and Maxwell, 2000: 215). Supporters of both parties, who form part of their 'community of care' or 'community of interest'[56] are also acknowledged as indirect stakeholders though their role is described as a 'supporting' one.[57] This 'offence community' concept is much narrower in scope than the interpretation of 'community' within the police-led community conferencing model (see also Dignan, 2002a: 177).

Here, members of the wider community may be invited to participate, at least in some police-led schemes, even though they may not form part of the 'offence community' as defined above. In RISE[58] conferences in Canberra, for example, community members may be invited to participate in conferences for offences that do not involve a direct victim as such, such as drink driving offences (see Sherman et al., 2000). This difference of attitude with regard to the role of 'the community' in conferencing is matched by a difference in the way victims themselves are conceptualized. Thus, proponents of police-led community conferencing are more likely to acknowledge that offences can have 'multiple victims' (Young, 2000; see also Masters, 2002). In addition to 'the wider community', they also include members of the offender's family and even offenders themselves, many of whom may well have experienced forms of victimization during their lives, whether or not they have contributed to the present offence. This acknowledgement of the wider impact that offending may have on others including the community at large forms part of the normative assertion that those who are affected or concerned by an offence in their neighbour-hood should be represented in the forum for determining the outcome of such an offence (Schiff, 2003: 32).

Another important and closely related difference between the two con-ferencing variants concerns the role of the victim in the conferencing process.[59] In the family group conferencing model Morris and Maxwell (2000: 211) describe their role, and that of the offender, as being to 'participate in the decision about how best to deal with, and make amends for, the offending'. One of the main aims of the process is described in terms of meeting victims' needs, and a number of benefits are identified including: making victims feel better about what has happened to them as a result of their participation; fostering reconciliation between the parties; facilitating agreements as to reparative outcomes (whether symbolic or actual); and reconnecting both parties with their communities.

In the case of the police-led community conferencing model, all parties including victims are said to have a part to play in the 'reintegrative shaming' process, though this is criticized by supporters of family group conferencing as well as those more sceptical of restorative justice in general. The former (e.g. Morris and Maxwell, 2000: 216; see also Young, 2001: 201) object to victims being cast in the role of 'shamers', and suggest that where this happens it is less likely to result in reconciliation. Sceptics such as Ashworth (2000: 186) object that it amounts to a form of 'victim prostitution' in which victims are effectively 'used' in order to bring about certain effects on offenders with a view to reducing the incidence of reoffending.

Procedurally also, there are important differences between the two conferencing models. One of the biggest differences, which flows directly from their link with Braithwaite's theory of reintegrative shaming, is that police-led community conferences adopt a 'scripted' format in the sense that the co-ordinator is expected to ask similar questions of each of the participants in a certain order. The aim of the 'script' is first to elicit shaming of the offender's 'deeds' – by questioning the offender, direct victim and supporters of each – without shaming the offender as a person. A second aim is to facilitate the reintegration of the offender back into the law-abiding community while avoiding the negative consequences associated with 'stigmatic shaming' (Braithwaite and Mugford, 1994). One way of attempting this is to invite participants (usually the offender's supporters) to identify the strengths and positive aspects of the offender's character instead of concentrating exclusively on the offending behaviour. Family group conferences, in contrast, are much less heavily 'choreographed' by the co-ordinator. Consequently, what has been described as the 'offence resolution' phase of the process (Masters, 2002: 49) may vary both in terms of the order of proceedings (Morris and Maxwell, 2000: 209) and also, presumably[60] the nature of the exchanges themselves.

A second important procedural difference between the two variants is that New Zealand style family group conferencing places a much greater emphasis on the need for and value of pre-conference preparation of the parties than does the police-led conferencing model. Ostensibly the latter places a greater emphasis on the value of spontaneity, though the use of a script presumably could also make for a more routinized and predictable encounter between the parties. A third such difference between them is that family group conferences include an additional phase, which has been described as the 'action planning stage' (Masters, 2002: 49). During this period, any professionals and victims who may have been present in the preceding offence resolution stage leave the young person and their family to discuss in private the plans and recommendations they wish to propose. Once this is completed the full conference reconvenes so that all may discuss the proposals and, provided they are acceptable to everyone,[61] the details of the agreement can be formally recorded. Police-led community conferences lack this private planning or 'family time', which reflects the welfare-based commitment to family empowerment that, as noted above, was one of the distinctive motivating factors behind the New Zealand approach.

Implementational context
The implementational context of both sets of conferencing variants has varied widely as they have spread, with remarkable speed, beyond their original birthplaces. One of the most distinctive aspects of family group conferencing in New Zealand is that it has not only been 'mainstreamed' but forms a fully integrated and indeed central element within a radically reformed youth justice system.[62] Not all young offenders are conferenced by any means, since the great majority are diverted from prosecution by the police and dealt with either by means of a straightforward caution or by informal offence resolution action co-ordinated by police youth aid.[63]

Figures relating to the proportion of young offenders who are dealt with by means of family group conferencing vary somewhat, ranging from 15 to 20 per cent (Morris, 2002: 602) to between 20 and 30 per cent (Daly, 2001: 70). However, the really important aspect is that within the statutory framework introduced by the 1989 Children, Young Persons and their Families Act, young people cannot be prosecuted unless they have been arrested by the police or referred to a family group conference which then recommends prosecution. Moreover, even if the young person is prosecuted, judges are unable to dispose of an offence in most cases without taking into account the recommendations of a family group conference (Morris and Maxwell, 2000: 208). Consequently, in New Zealand family group conferences are in practice used for all medium-level and serious offending with the exception of murder and manslaughter, whereas most other jurisdictions have used conferencing (and indeed other forms of restorative justice) mainly for less serious offenders. Another distinctive feature of New Zealand style family group conferencing is that co-ordinators are employed by the Department of Social Welfare, which is mainly responsible for child care and protection issues, though there have been calls for responsibility to be transferred to an independent department dealing with youth justice issues (Maxwell, 1998: 2).

Family group conferences have also been mainstreamed with statutory backing in five Australian states, and three of these (New South Wales, South Australia, Western Australia) conference high volumes of young offenders each year (Daly, 2001: 62–4). Unlike New Zealand, however, the approach tends to be used for low-level offending as an alternative to prosecution. In most other jurisdictions family group conferencing has so far been introduced on a very small scale ad hoc basis with no specific statutory backing. In England and Wales, for example, family group conferencing has so far been used very tentatively in a criminal justice context, with a few pilot projects catering mostly for small numbers of young offenders (Dignan and Marsh, 2001).[64] This state of affairs is unsurprising since, as Morris (1999) has pointed out, conferencing is based on an alternative form of decision-making process rather than the courts. So despite the financial and other support it has received from the Youth Justice Board, there seems little prospect of any significant expansion of family group conferencing in the absence of a supportive statutory framework setting up a new decision-making structure. Family group conferencing has secured a somewhat surer foothold within the child welfare sphere, however, where many key decisions are taken in a non-judicial forum, and where it has benefited from the stronger institutional support provided by social service departments (Dignan and Marsh, 2001). Indeed, Challiner et al. (2000), note that around half of these have some experience of conferencing.

Another interesting exception to the general tendency for family group conferencing outside New Zealand to be confined to small-scale non statutory initiatives relates to Northern Ireland which, although constitutionally part of the United Kingdom, has its own separate legal system. The introduction of family group conferencing into Northern Ireland draws heavily on New Zealand experience, notably with regard to the decision to mainstream a restorative justice approach as part of a systemic reform of the youth justice system. Moreover, as Bottoms (2003: 106) has pointed out, there is also a parallel between the two jurisdictions concerning the context in which the adoption of a restorative justice approach has taken place. For Northern Ireland, like New Zealand, also has a sizeable minority group that has become increasingly alienated from the official criminal justice system which is seen as a product of a colonialist or quasi-colonialist past. Here also, restorative justice reforms are seen by policymakers as one way of seeking to enhance the legitimacy of the youth justice system by showing greater awareness of different cultural attitudes towards criminal justice institutions.

In Northern Ireland, the reforms have emerged from a formal review of the criminal justice system undertaken in connection with the 'Peace Process' that was set in train by the Good Friday Agreement of 1998 (Criminal Justice Review Commission, 2000). The review itself was an attempt to establish a system that is acceptable to both the main political/religious communities (Republican/Catholic and Unionist/Protestant in Northern Ireland). Proposals to reform the criminal justice system in accordance with restorative justice precepts[65] were accepted by the British government (Northern Ireland Office, 2001) and most have subsequently been incorporated in the Justice (Northern Ireland) Act 2002.

The most important provision in the present context (envisaged by the Criminal Justice Review Commission as the first phase in a radical but progressive reform programme) consists of a post-conviction, court-ordered conferencing process.[66] This will apply to all young offenders who plead guilty or are convicted in the youth court except for those charged with offences that are triable only on indictment, or terrorist offences.[67] Even these will be eligible for referral to a youth conference at the discretion of the court, with the sole exception of murder (section 59 Justice (Northern Ireland) Act 2002). A key feature of the new youth conference system is that no one (child, parents or victim) can be forced to take part in it (unlike the nearest English equivalent, the referral order system). A second key feature of the Northern Ireland system is that the youth conference co-ordinator has to be employed as a civil servant within a government department, which rules out both the police or community representatives acting as co-ordinators.[68]

Turning now to the police-led community conferencing model, we have already noted that this originated as a very small-scale experimental initiative in Wagga Wagga in New South Wales. Although this particular initiative was discontinued, a very similar approach formed the basis of the Re-integrative Shaming Experiments (RISE) in Canberra (Australian Capital Territory), and is currently used, albeit on a small scale, in two other jurisdictions: Tasmania and Northern Territory (Daly, 2001: 64). The latter is currently the only Australian police-led statutory scheme. Ironically, the police-led conferencing model has flourished much more successfully outside Australia, in parts of the United States,[69] Canada and, most notably, in England and Wales. Here, the 'scripted conferencing' approach was adopted initially by Thames Valley police in 1998 as an alternative to the old-style police caution,[70] rather than as an alternative to prosecution, as in the case of New Zealand's family group conferencing model or indeed the Australian RISE initiative (see Pollard, 2000; Young, 2001). The approach is now used across the force in three different contexts: when administering 'restorative cautions' (which are attended by the offender and, usually, his or her parents); in 'restorative conferences' (at which victims and possibly their supporters may also be present); in 'community conferences' (which are attended by members of the wider public).

Following the election of the Labour government in 1997, the Thames Valley approach attracted the interest of the then Home Secretary, Jack Straw, and has subsequently influenced the development of new-style reprimands and final warnings (see above). The most important change, for present purposes, took the form of new and much more detailed guidance, which was issued in April 2000 (Home Office, 2000c; see also Bottoms and Dignan, 2004: 157). The aim of the revised guidance was explicitly to encourage the wider use of restorative justice principles and practice in the delivery of both reprimands and final warnings by all forces, drawing directly on the Thames Valley approach. Since then, the Youth Justice Board has made available training for police officers, YOT workers and others to facilitate restorative warnings and conferences. Further guidance was issued in November 2002, which largely consolidated the original version, though it also included further encouragement to adopt a restorative approach 'to make final warnings more effective and meaningful' (Home Office/Youth Justice Board, 2002: 6). It is too soon to say what effect the revised guidance may have, since it is still open to forces to deliver 'standard' reprimands and final warnings. But there can be no doubt that the police-led conferencing approach has received strong official endorsement.

Community reparation boards and citizens' panels

Overview: origins and aims
Citizen panels and community boards have a history that predates the restorative justice movement and by no means all of the contemporary examples espouse restorative justice values and principles. Similar bodies with a variety of names were introduced in various parts of the United States as long ago as the early 1920s as a means of stimulating community involvement in the sanctioning of young people convicted of minor offences (Bazemore and Umbreit, 2001; Schiff, 2003: 322). Another well-known variant operating within a rather different context is the explicitly

welfare-oriented Children's Hearings system in Scotland in which panels of lay people drawn from the local community decide how to deal with children who have broken the law and those in need of care and protection as an alternative to judicial forms of decision making.[71]

Within a restorative justice context, one of the earliest and best known contemporary adaptations of the approach is the Vermont Community Reparative Board (see Dooley, 1995, 1996; Karp and Walther, 2001), though there are similar initiatives albeit with different names in San Jose, California (Neighbourhood Accountability Boards), Chicago, Illinois (Community Panels) and Denver, Colorado (Community Accountability Boards). Indeed, reparative boards constitute the second most prevalent type of restorative justice programme in the United States, accounting for just under one-third of the total (Schiff and Bazemore, 2002: 182). In terms of their intellectual and philosophical origins, such initiatives draw in part on the civilization thesis, with its emphasis on reparation as a more constructive response to youth offending, and also on the community empowerment element within the communitarian thesis. Despite the reparative ethos, however, Vermont's reparative boards have placed a lower priority on the value of victim participation than most other restorative justice approaches and, at least in the early days, made much less effort to involve victims in the process. Likewise, the scope for offenders to participate in the decision-making process itself appears to be much more limited than in most other restorative justice processes. For although they are expected to attend and talk about the offence and its consequences, Bazemore and Umbreit (2001) point out that the board itself typically draws up the programme of reparative sanctions, often in private, which is then presented to the offender for consultation as opposed to involving the offender directly in determining the nature of the response.[72] As such, the process is much less participatory and empowering for the parties than either mediation or conferencing, and much more closely resembles court-ordered reparative sanctions except for the fact that a lay tribunal determines the sanction that is imposed.

Somewhat closer to home, a slightly different variant of the citizen panel model has been developed as part of the English government's wide-ranging youth justice reform programme, and this has also been influenced by restorative justice precepts. Following on from the introduction of youth offender teams, reparation orders and the increased support for victim consultation and involvement in other restorative justice processes, the government has established a new decision-making forum for determining how certain categories of young offender should be dealt with following a conviction. Under the Youth Justice and Criminal Evidence Act 1999, a new semi-mandatory sentencing disposal was introduced for young offenders pleading guilty who are convicted for the first time.[73] Such offenders are referred to a 'youth offender panel' comprising two lay members of the community who are drawn from an approved list, and a member of the local youth offending team (see above). The panel's role is to provide an informal forum within which the young offender, family and panel members and, where appropriate, the victim, can discuss the offence and its impact and reach an agreed outcome in the form of a 'contract'.[74]

In terms of its aims, the youth offender panel is expected to be guided in its task by the three principles that were felt by the Home Office (1997: 31–2) to underlie the concept of restorative justice: 'responsibility, restoration and reintegration'. Compared with Vermont's reparative boards, the policy documents leading up to the referral order appeared to place much greater emphasis – at least in principle – on the value and importance of victim participation, which was expressly provided for in the 1999 Act. As for the intended outcomes, these comprise a mixture of 'restorative outcomes' – including financial or other kinds of reparation for the benefit of the victim of an offence, mediation or community reparation – and also 'rehabilitative' or 'preventive' outcomes designed to reduce the likelihood of further offending. This ambivalence is explained by the particular policy context in which all recent English restorative justice initiatives have been conceived, which prioritizes the aim of preventing youth offending above all others. Consequently, other restorative justice aims including those intended to benefit victims can only be pursued to the extent that they are compatible with the newly introduced principal aim of the youth justice system. This tension between two potentially conflicting sets of objectives places England and Wales apart from most other jurisdictions that have sought to introduce restorative justice measures and is likely to significantly limit its potential, particularly from a victim's perspective.

Operational features

The Vermont reparative boards cater for both juveniles and adults, unlike the English youth offender panels which, as we have seen, are restricted to young offenders (aged 10–17) only. Both processes are instigated by a court referral following a conviction and, in effect, delegate the normal sentencing function to a lay tribunal, though technically the sentence that is imposed by the court consists in Vermont of a probation order and in England of a referral order. However, attendance at the relevant board or panel is a requirement of both sanctions. In Vermont the 'operational period' during which the meetings take place and the reparative tasks have to be conducted is 90 days, which is the normal probationary period. In England the referral order is somewhat more flexible since the length of the order is specified by the court at the time of the referral, and can last from 3 to 12 months depending on the seriousness of the offence. Another difference between them relates to the greater degree of judicial oversight in Vermont, which derives from the fact that only the court is empowered to formally require the payment of compensation or making of restitution. However, in both jurisdictions the lay forum is responsible for monitoring compliance with the agreement, which it does with the aid of review meetings, and the offender is liable to be returned to the court in the event of non-compliance.

Implementational context

The main difference in implementational context between the two sets of processes relates to the lead agency that bears the primary responsibility for managing the process. In Vermont this responsibility rests with the probation service whose staff are employed by the Department of Social and Rehabilitation Services, whereas in England the responsibility for recruiting, training and co-ordinating the work of youth offender panels rests with the multi-agency youth offending teams. Although the referral order appears to have a stronger restorative justice ethos, in certain respects both sets of initiatives, as we have seen, are constrained to a considerable extent by the implementational context in which they operate.

Healing and sentencing circles

Overview: origins and aims

Finally, and for the sake of completeness, brief mention should also be made of a fifth type of restorative justice approach known as healing or sentencing circles. These are just two of the better known representatives of a variety of initiatives that are mainly associated with the indigenous peoples of Canada (Assembly of Manitoba Chiefs, 1989; Roberts and Roach, 2003: 240). Philosophically, these initiatives have much in common with several aspects of Christie's version of communitarianism (see above), though his 'anti-statist' ethos is much less in evidence with regard to circle sentencing, which takes place in the context of a regular criminal trial and thus relies upon judicial discretion. Whatever form they take, most forms of circle-based restorative justice initiatives combine psychological and spiritual dimensions that operate at both an individual and communal level. For the individuals involved, the main goals are expressed in terms of 'healing' the affected parties, whereas the communal goals are expressed in terms of invoking and reinforcing the community's values as a means of reintegrating those who have violated them back into the group to which they belong. As such, they may be viewed as mechanisms for community building and community empowerment, both of which are goals that are strongly associated with Christie's writing.

Operational features

Procedurally, circle-based restorative justice initiatives share some aspects of a family conferencing approach, but draw more directly on traditional ritual processes. These often include the use of a symbolic 'talking piece' such as an eagle's feather that is passed around the circle, entitling each recipient to speak in turn. They also tend to embody a much broader notion of community participation than family group conferencing (LaPrairie, 1995), including community elders, kinship groups and those with whom the offender may share other social obligations. Many accounts stress the complexity and intensity of the process that can involve a series of separate but interrelated proceedings (see, for example, Bazemore and Umbreit, 2001; Schiff 2003: 322). They include:

1 A circle that is convened to consider an application by an offender to invoke the circle process.
2 A healing circle specifically for the victim.
3 A healing circle specifically for the offender.
4 A sentencing circle to formulate a consensus as to what happened, to identify the harm caused by an offence and to devise an appropriate sentencing plan.
5 One or more follow-up circles to monitor the agreement and support the offender's compliance.

Implementational context

Circle-based restorative justice initiatives are unusual inasmuch as they have largely remained confined to aboriginal communities in North America, unlike other restorative justice initiatives that have been adopted much more widely.[75] The main implementational difference between the two sets of processes is that healing circles tend to operate outwith the criminal justice system,[76] whereas sentencing circles operate within the context of a regular criminal trial, may sometimes take place in the courtroom and also involve the judge (Stuart, 1996). Although the role of the judge is somewhat uncertain and variable within the sentencing circle process itself, the judge alone is authorized to pronounce the actual sentence and thus, in effect, retains at least a formal power of veto (Lilles, 2001: 175). Partly because of the time and expense they entail, circle sentences have mainly been used for more serious offences, in respect of both youth and adult offenders,[77] though they have also been used in connection with community disputes, child protection cases and in disciplinary cases in schools (Schiff, 2003: 322).

Conclusion

In this chapter we have examined the intellectual and philosophical roots that have helped to nurture the modern restorative justice movement, and have identified the efflorescence of practices and processes with which they are associated. Although some commonalities have been identified, the overwhelming impression is one of diversity. The two features that are shared by all five approaches relate to the goal of putting right the harm that has been caused by an offence and a focus on the personal accountability of the offender towards those who may have been harmed by the offence (see Introduction). Those practices that are generally thought of as 'most restorative'[78] (mediation, conferencing and circle-based initiatives) also share a commitment to an informal, inclusive and non-coercive decision-making process, though this is not true of reparative boards or most other court-based reparative interventions. Beyond that, however, the approaches vary considerably with regard to each of the main dimensions we have considered: theoretical foundations, operational practice and implementational context including their relationship to the formal criminal justice system. Moreover, they also differ greatly with regard to the significance they accord to victims and the role (if any) they prescribe for them within the decision-making process. For obvious reasons it will be important to keep in mind these various differences when evaluating restorative justice approaches from a victim perspective, which is the subject of the next chapter.

Notes

1 This is normally referred to as the 'treatment' or 'welfare' model.

2 See, in particular, Braithwaite (1999: 2), who memorably claimed that 'restorative justice has been the dominant model of criminal justice throughout most of criminal justice for all the world's peoples'. See also Strang (2002: 3–5), Van Ness (1993), Van Ness and Strong (1997: 7–9), Weitekamp (1999), Zehr (1990).

3 While it is true that restorative justice practice has frequently run ahead of restorative justice theorizing it is equally true that these practice developments have not occurred in a philosophical or theoretical vacuum. So although some have suggested that restorative justice is 'a practice in search of a theory' (see, for example, Crawford and Newburn, 2003: 19), it would perhaps be more correct to say that neither practice nor theoretical developments have occurred in complete isolation.

4 This will draw on and develop ideas initially set out in Dignan and Cavadino (1996); see also Bottoms (2003).

5 John Braithwaite's work on reintegrative shaming forms a major part of this thesis, and has had a profound effect on the subsequent development of restorative justice, as we shall see (Braithwaite, 1989). However, the concept of reintegrative shaming itself has proved somewhat controversial (see, for example, Toews and Zehr, 2001). Braithwaite (1999: 9 and 2002: 17) himself has subsequently used the term 'dialogic regulation'. And others – notably Tavuchis (1991) and Duff (2002) – have also contributed valuable insights to this thesis, which is why I have adopted a more general term.

6 Or 'salubrious by-product' in Cantor's own words (1976: 113).

7 The Mennonites are not the only ones to find fault with the adversarial model, with its formality, its strict rules of procedure and its 'winner-takes-all' style of adjudication. Indeed, there is much common ground between their critique and a more secular variant associated with the growth of the informal justice movement of the 1970s and 1980s, which also questioned the suitability of contemporary western courts for handling the kind of interpersonal quarrels likely to arise in the course of ongoing social relationships (See e.g. Abel, 1982; Merry, 1982; Matthews, 1988.)

8 Originally known as Victim Offender Reconciliation Programmes, or VORPs. See Peachey (1989).

9 See in particular Etzioni (1995) and, within a criminal justice context see also Cavadino et al. (1999: 48ff, 97ff), Hughes (1996) and Jordan and Arnold (1995).

10 To put it very simply, extreme collectivism would prioritize the claims and

interests of the community or collective over the rights of individuals. Extreme individualists, on the other hand, would be more likely to echo Margaret Thatcher's famous dictum that there is no such thing as society and to deny that individuals have any responsibility to moderate their own rights and interests for the benefit of the common good.

11 On the tension *between* the 'civilian' and 'communitarian' tendencies within restorative justice (see also Dignan, 2002a: 175ff).

12 Christie used this term to contrast the highly participatory drama of a civil court case in Tanzania with its tedious, dull and non-participatory counterparts in Britain and Scandinavia.

13 Indeed, Braithwaite (1999: 5) has described it as 'the most influential text of the [contemporary] restorative tradition'.

14 Though this scarcely does justice to Christie's own much more pejorative formulation, which characterizes lawyers as 'professional thieves', who go around stealing other people's conflicts. This suspicion of lawyers has sometimes featured prominently in proposals to develop restorative justice style processes, most notably with regard to the introduction of referral orders into the English juvenile justice system (see Bottoms and Dignan, 2004: 143).

15 But see Crawford and Clear (2001) and see also Crawford (1997) for a more general discussion of the various meanings and roles of communities in local criminal justice areas.

16 Braithwaite (1989: 85) describes traditional communitarian societies as those that combine 'a dense network of individual interdependencies with strong cultural commitments to mutuality of obligation'. Paraphrasing Braithwaite, these are societies in which behaviour is likely to be influenced by expectations relating to close kinship links, indebtedness associated with economic or social relationships, tradition and shared moral values.

17 Crawford (1997, 2000: 290), and Ashworth (2002: 583) have both voiced concerns over this issue.

18 Questions 2 and 4 will be addressed when discussing the various victim-focused manifestations that have been associated with the restorative justice movement in recent years later in this chapter. The remaining questions will be addressed in Chapter 6.

19 See also Schiff's (2003: 329) reference to 'the ambiguity of community'.

20 Thus, McCold simply refers to a dictionary definition, which defines the term 'local community' as 'a social group *of any size* whose members reside in a specific locality, share government, and have a common cultural and historical heritage' (emphasis added).

21 Drawing on the ideas of Stein (1960), Keller (1968) and Webber (1970).

22 Although the communitarian dimension is most evident in relation to conferencing initiatives, it is not entirely absent from the more bilateral approach that is associated with certain forms of mediation, particularly 'community mediation projects' (see below). Moreover, Bottoms (2003: 86) has pointed out that even within victim-offender mediation there is often support for the principle that mediators should be representative of 'the communities' from which they are recruited, since this is felt to have the potential to reinvigorate those communities. In practice, however, mediators tend to be drawn from a fairly restricted sector of the community and, in the case of some types of programmes (notably victim offender reconciliation projects) the great majority are members of a particular 'faith community'.

23 When deciding who they might wish to invite to a restorative justice conference as a 'supporter', parties are sometimes asked to consider who they might wish to attend an important event in their life. Thus, supporters often include family members and/or friends, but could also include teachers, counsellors or others who have concern for their well-being.

24 In a school, for example, the cleaner who discovers and has to clean up following a break-in may make for a more meaningful encounter with an intruder than either the head teacher or a governor of the school.

25 Subject to any concerns there may be about a possible power imbalance and no doubts concerning the type (and amount) of reparation to which 'the community' may be entitled.

26 One justification that is sometimes put forward for restorative justice processes is that they provide a means of vindicating the victim's entitlement not to be harmed in the way that they have been. And for their right to redress to be acknowledged, not just by the offender and the 'offence community' comprising those who have been directly affected by the offence, but by the community in general also.

27 See also discussion in Chapter 6.

28 Dirk van Zyl Smit (1999) points out that it is too easy to assume 'that individuals in a particular area share, or can be brought to see that they share, ideals which the community is deemed to have'. Clifford Shearing (1994: 5), who also writes in a South African context, has likewise warned that 'we should stop thinking of communities as homogeneous neighbourhoods and start recognising them as comprised of interest groups that are often in conflict'. Similar concerns have also been raised in a Northern Irish context (see Dignan with Lowey, 2000: 18).

29 This is not to deny that the introduction of 'state-sponsored' forms of restorative justice may also be contested in some jurisdictions. One example is Northern Ireland, which has experienced a pronounced legitimacy deficit in respect of legal and political institutions including the courts, police and security services because they are deemed to be insufficiently responsive to the concerns of a particular sector of the community (see Dignan with Lowey, 2000: 15; McEvoy and Mika, 2002: 534–62; see also Shapland, 2003: 213).

30 Though there have been limited exceptions in the past; for example probation, at least in its early 'police court missionary' phase, and also the silent penitentiary system (see Cavadino and Dignan, 2002: 175, n.131).

31 Braithwaite (2002: 74) himself favours the adoption of appropriate gestures, rituals or even 'reintegration ceremonies' (see also Braithwaite and Mugford, 1994) to bring the shaming process to an end and certify the readmission of the offender back into the moral community.

32 'Affect theory' has to do with the study of emotions (including that of shame) that lie behind action and that may predispose people to behave in certain ways. One of the pioneers in this field was Sylvan Tomkins (1962), whose ideas have been developed by Donald Nathanson (1992).

33 As well as elements of denunciation and reform.

34 This is not to suggest that the two are mutually exclusive. For victims may also be thought to have an interest in developing more effective ways of reducing the risk that they or others will be victimized again in the future.

35 We will consider examples drawn from both the youth justice and adult criminal justice systems in England and Wales later in the chapter.

36 For other reviews see Braithwaite (1999), Dignan with Lowey (2000), Miers (2001), Schiff (2003) and Crawford and Newburn (2003).

37 For details see Chapter 3; see also Cavadino and Dignan (2002: 132ff), Miers (1990b), Zedner (1994).

38 Following a trial period in six pilot areas, the order was made available nationwide in 1975.

39 The term 'New Youth Justice' was coined and popularized in a book by that name which was edited by Goldson (2000).

40 In addition, an existing sentencing disposal available for young offenders, known as the supervision order, was augmented by the insertion of a possible additional requirement that the offender make reparation either to the direct victim of the offence or to the community.

41 Sentencing disposals for both adult and young offenders in England have since 1991 been ranked according to their severity into three principal bands: custodial penalties; 'community sentences'; and other sentences including fines, warning penalties and, now, reparation. Courts are required to ensure that the sentence that is imposed is appropriate (proportionate) to the seriousness of the offence according to statutory 'threshold criteria'. See Cavadino and Dignan (2002) for further details.

42 The system has subsequently been modified further, as we shall see, in line with a police-led restorative conferencing approach based on an Australian initiative and pioneered in England and Wales by the Thames Valley police force.

43 And to give reasons for not imposing such an order.

44 These goals are slightly adapted from those set out in Dignan with Lowey (2000: 24).

45 See generally Dignan et al. (1996), Dignan (1998) and Liebmann (1998) for community and neighbour dispute mediation in England and Wales.

46 For example, Sandwell Mediation Service in the West Midlands.

47 Notably Austria, Germany, Norway and Slovenia (Miers, 2001).

48 Thus, probation is the 'lead agency' in the case of the West Midlands Probation Service Victim Unit and the Leeds Victim/Offender Unit based in West Yorkshire. Other schemes such as Northamptonshire's Adult Diversion Unit have been based on multi-agency partnerships involving the police, probation and local authority departments such as education.

49 This began life as the Kettering Adult Reparation Bureau during the 1980s, and subsequently changed its name to the Northamptonshire Adult Diversion Unit when its remit was extended across the whole county (see Dignan, 1990, 1992).

50 The Leeds Victim/Offender Unit. See Wynne (1996).

51 The Youth Justice Board was established by the Crime and Disorder Act as a 'non departmental public body' with strategic responsibility for the youth justice system as a whole, including extensive grant-making powers to promote the development and evaluation of new and innovative practice initiatives.

52 See, in particular, Bazemore and Umbreit (2001) and Schiff and Bazemore (2002).

53 Indeed, Daly (2001: 61) reports that the application of conferencing in the youth justice (as opposed to child protection) arena was described by Maxwell (in a personal communication) as an 'afterthought'.

54 Moore and O'Connell (1993) explicitly acknowledge the influence that Braithwaite's theory of reintegrative shaming had on the first police-led community conferencing initiative, known as the Wagga Wagga approach. See also O'Connell (1992). However, Daly (2001: 63) points out that the 'Wagga

model' was originally inspired following a visit to New Zealand in 1990 by two New South Wales police officers, and that the connection with Braithwaite's theory was only established in 1991, the year that the pilot project commenced.

55 Unlike family group conferencing, however, police-led conferencing has not been influenced by political considerations based on racial or ethnic sensitivities, which reflect a rather different kind of communitarian influence.

56 Morris and Young (2000: 14) explain that 'By "community of interest" we do not mean elected, appointed or self-appointed community representatives but rather the collection of people with shared concerns about the offender, the victim, the offence and its consequences, and with the ability to contribute towards a solution to the problem which the crime presents or represents'.

57 Members of the wider community may also be invited to conferences by the offender's family, in order to provide information or support (Morris and Maxwell, 2000: 215).

58 The acronym stands for *Re-Integrative Shaming Experiments*.

59 Assuming the victim is present. One important difference between conferencing (of either variant) and victim–offender mediation is that the former may still proceed even in the absence of victims, whereas victim–offender mediation, as we have seen, requires at least some degree of participation by victims, even if this is only indirect.

60 In the absence of a predetermined shaming 'agenda'. Whether or not the nature of the exchanges is different, however, is a matter of speculation since the two sets of processes have not as yet been subjected to detailed comparative empirical analysis.

61 Both victim and the police are thus able to 'veto' the plan if they are unhappy with it.

62 Some moves are also being made to extend restorative justice to adult offenders in New Zealand, at both pre-prosecution and pre-sentencing stages, and three recent Acts – the Sentencing Act 2002, the Parole Act 2002 and the Victims' Rights Act 2002 – all contain restorative principles and provide for restorative processes in respect of adults as well as juveniles (Boyack, 2004).

63 Somewhat akin to 'caution plus' schemes referred to above; see p. 114.

64 Though the government's pilot restorative justice schemes for adult offenders, referred to above, provide an opportunity for family group conferences to be trialled for older offenders also.

65 The Criminal Justice Review Commission (2000) commissioned a comparative review of restorative justice options for Northern Ireland (Dignan with Lowey, 2000) which informed its own detailed recommendations. See also Shapland (2003).

66 Though the Act itself also provides for a system of pre-court diversionary conferences.

67 Also excepted are those with whom the court proposes to deal by making either an absolute or conditional discharge.

68 The Review Commission had recommended that the youth conference co-ordinator in Northern Ireland should be based in a department that would be seen by the public as embracing justice values, and it recommended the creation of a Department of Justice for this reason (Criminal Justice Review Group, 2000: Recommendation 159, 257), but this proposal was not included in the Act.

69 The best known of these is Bethlehem, Pennsylvania (McCold and Wachtel, 1998).

70 As a result, the approach is largely confined to less serious offenders and the lower reaches of the disposals 'tariff' which, as Crawford and Newburn (2003: 31) have observed, increases concerns over the risk of 'net widening'.

71 The origins, role and performance of the Scottish Children's Hearing system are described in much greater detail in Bottoms and Dignan (2004).

72 In this, as in other respects, practice may vary from board to board, which makes it difficult to generalize too categorically.

73 Initially, the mandatory referral principle applied to all young offenders except those who intended to plead not guilty and those who, in the opinion of the court, should be dealt with by means of a custodial sentence, a hospital order or an absolute discharge (the first two of which are rare for first-time defendants). This meant that many very minor offenders were given referral orders, despite concerns that such a response might be disproportionate and counter-productive. Subsequently, the government amended the scope of the referral order by making it discretionary in the case of non-imprisonable offences (SI 2003/1605). This should alleviate the problem but is unlikely to eliminate it entirely, since very many extremely minor offences (for example, theft of a Mars bar) are still imprisonable.

74 A flow chart depicting the referral order process is set out at Annex D in the guidance produced by the Home Office (Home Office et al., 2002d).

75 Though the Community Peace Committee Programmes (referred to by Crawford and Newburn, 2003: 35) that have developed since 1997 in some South African townships show some affinity with healing circles.

76 Some are explicitly diversionary, as in the case of the Toronto Community Council Project described by Roberts and Roach (2003: 241).

77 Unlike family group conferencing, they have mainly been used in respect of Aboriginal offenders, but not exclusively so (Lilles, 2001: 163).

78 McCold and Wachtel (2002: 115) have devised a typology that purports to differentiate between practices and processes with regard to their 'degree of restorativeness'.

Further reading

Bottoms, A.E. (2003) Some sociological reflections on restorative justice, in A. von Hirsch, J. Roberts, A.E. Bottoms, K. Roach and M. Schiff (eds) *Restorative Justice and Penal Justice: Competing or Reconcilable Paradigms?* Oxford: Hart.

Braithwaite, J. (1989) *Crime, Shame and Reintegration.* Cambridge: Cambridge University Press.

Christie, N. (1977) Conflicts as property, *British Journal of Criminology*, 17: 1–15.

Daly, K. (2001) Conferencing in Australia and New Zealand: variations, research findings and prospects, in A.M. Morris and G. Maxwell (eds) *Restorative Justice for Juveniles: Conferencing, Mediation and Circles.* Oxford: Hart.

Schiff, M. (2003) Models, challenges and the promise of restorative conferencing strategies, in A. von Hirsch, J. Roberts, A.E. Bottoms, K. Roach and M. Schiff (eds) *Restorative Justice and Penal Justice: Competing or Reconcilable Paradigms?* Oxford: Hart.

chapter five

Evaluating restorative justice from a victim perspective: empirical evidence

Restorative justice and victims: overview of research findings
Conclusions
Notes
Further reading

The evaluation of restorative justice initiatives is still in its infancy and any assessment of their efficacy consequently presents a number of major challenges. One challenge relates to the sheer variety of restorative justice initiatives, as we saw in Chapter 4, which makes it difficult to draw blanket conclusions about the extent to which 'restorative justice in general' may or may not be beneficial for victims. Some approaches, as we shall see, may be intrinsically more victim oriented and sensitive to the needs and wishes of victims than others. A second challenge relates to the wide diversity of contexts in which restorative justice approaches have been implemented in different jurisdictions, whether in terms of their relationship to the regular criminal justice system, or the types of offences, offenders and victims for which they are intended to cater. It is just as important to be mindful of the significance of *context* in relation to apparently successful restorative justice evaluation findings as it is with other kinds of criminological research.[1] Conversely, when confronted with apparently negative findings it is equally important to be sensitive to possibility that these might be the result of 'implementation failure' as opposed to inherent defects in the approach itself.

A third challenge relates to the criteria by which restorative justice initiatives should be evaluated, even when (as in this book) the focus is mainly restricted to a 'victim's perspective'. Even the most enthusiastic restorative justice advocates (see, for example, Braithwaite, 1999: 20) have acknowledged the problems involved: whether to 'stipulate' criteria on the basis of known or presumed effects of criminal victimization (see Chapter 1); whether to ask victims specifically what kind of restoration they sought at the outset and then to report on the extent to which their 'wish list' was fulfilled; or whether to use more general 'proxy' measures such as overall retrospective satisfaction with either process or outcome. As we shall see, the latter approach is the commonest, even though it glosses over the complexities involved in assessing what restoration might mean for victims and how successful different approaches might be in achieving it. A fourth challenge relates to the methodology by which restorative justice initiatives might most appropriately be evaluated. Should restorative justice processes be assessed purely on the basis of their own aims and objectives and the extent to which they are realized? Or should their performance be assessed in relative terms, for example, in comparison with the performance of regular criminal justice processes? If the latter, what techniques are used to ensure comparability between the two sets of processes? Finally, a fifth challenge relates to the interpretation of the findings and, in particular, in setting the 'benchmark' for determining whether a particular restorative justice initiative has been 'successful' or not in relation to a given set of criteria (see also Morris, 2002: 601). Also on the subject of where the benchmark should be set, Kathleen Daly (2003a: 234) has drawn an important distinction between what it may be *possible* for restorative justice to achieve[2] – which she refers to as the 'nirvana story of restorative justice' – and what attainments are routinely practicable and achievable on a regular basis.

It is clearly important to bear these challenges in mind when attempting to assess the actual and potential benefits of restorative justice from a victim's perspective in the light of the empirical evidence that is currently available. This chapter will attempt to provide an overview[3] of the victim-oriented findings relating to each of the main restorative justice approaches as outlined in Chapter 4. With respect to court-based restitutive and reparative measures, the main emphasis is on some of the implementational problems that have been encountered. Thereafter, the overview will comment, where applicable, on the following sets of issues: the extent to which each approach specifically aims to provide restorative outcomes for victims, the type of research that has been undertaken, findings relating to its performance in meeting its victim-oriented aims, and also any contextual factors (including implementational context) that may affect its potential scope in benefiting victims more generally. The overview will also comment more thematically, where appropriate, on our current state of knowledge (or lack of it) concerning victims and restorative justice, including the extent to which victims appear to want to participate in restorative justice processes.

Restorative justice and victims: overview of research findings

Court-based restitutive and reparative measures

Such measures are hybrid in nature, incorporating some features that are associated with restorative justice processes and some that are more closely associated with conventional criminal justice processes and outcomes (see Introduction). It is for this reason that compensation orders were examined more extensively in the context of the criminal justice model in Chapter 3. The community service order has been extensively evaluated (see, for example, Pease et al., 1977; Pease, 1985; McIvor, 1992; Howard League, 1997) and is, in any event, of relatively limited relevance for individual victims, so only a brief overview will be provided here. Of greatest interest in this context are the reparative measures that were introduced in England and Wales in 1998, as part of a wide-ranging programme of youth justice reforms, which will thus merit slightly fuller consideration.

One serious problem with the compensation order is that courts continue to be reluctant[4] to give effect to the clear statutory requirement that they should take account of victims' interests when passing sentence.[5] Indeed, the use of compensation orders has declined in both sets of criminal courts between 1990 and 2001 even though living standards were rising and unemployment levels falling during this period (Cavadino and Dignan, 2002: 133). Another shortcoming is that compensation is unlikely to be forthcoming (in England and Wales at any rate) where an offender is diverted from prosecution, for example by being cautioned;[6] nor is it likely to be awarded where an offender is sentenced to imprisonment. Moreover, even where compensation is awarded and paid in full, it is only capable of providing for material needs. As we have seen, however, victims may also experience psychological or emotional difficulties as a result of an offence, quite apart from the damage that is likely to have been caused to any relationship between them, at least where the parties are known to one another (see Watson et al., 1989: 214; Dignan and Cavadino, 1996: 158). Furthermore, neither victim nor offender are likely to have been empowered by any award of compensation since they are not involved in the decision-making process.

As far as community service is concerned it is, of course, true – as suggested above, and as Walgrave (1999, 2000b) has argued – that this can be implemented in a manner that is broadly consistent with restorative justice principles even though it may not emanate from a restorative justice process. However, it is equally true that it can be made to serve other objectives, whether rehabilitative or straightforwardly retributive. For example, offenders may be required to undertake unpleasant, degrading or pointless tasks that are unrelated either to the offence they have committed, the wishes of the victim, the needs of the community or their own interests and aptitudes. It is a matter of regret that the tendency in England and Wales in recent years has been to strengthen the explicitly punitive aspect of the community service order, for example by requiring those who are subjected to an order of more than 60 hours to perform at least 21 of those hours working in a group placement on work of a manual nature.[7] This tendency is also reflected in the decision in 2001 to officially change the name of the community service order to the '*community punishment order*', which symbolically distances the measure still further from a restorative justice approach. The English experience highlights one of the main problems associated with restorative justice initiatives that are introduced as part of the regular criminal justice system, which is that they are all too likely to be made to serve other sentencing objectives, however incompatible these may be with restorative justice ideals and principles.

With regard to the reparative initiatives introduced by the Crime and Disorder Act, these formed part of a wider ranging programme of youth justice reforms that were evaluated by Holdaway et al. (2001; see also Dignan, 2002b). They too were beset by implementational difficulties, despite concerted attempts to promote the practice of reparation and to ensure that victims were more involved in consultation about the form that this should take. One problem was that the goal of victim consultation was in tension with another objective of the youth justice reforms, which was to speed up the processing of young offenders through the courts. Because magistrates were keen to meet the targets they had been set to reduce the average time it took to bring young recidivist offenders to court, they were often reluctant to adjourn cases to enable victims to be consulted before sentencing the offender. Those responsible for evaluating the pilot schemes felt that this could explain why the great majority of reparation orders involved community reparation, since the Act required victims to have consented *before* an offender could be ordered to make reparation to a direct victim (Holdaway et al., 2001: 88; Dignan, 2002b: 79).[8]

A second problem was that the communication of victim contact details by the police to reparation workers was believed to infringe the requirements of the Data Protection Act 1998 (which was also the year of the Crime and Disorder Act). This meant that in order to comply with a strict interpretation of the Act, consultation could only be undertaken after the police (as 'authorized data holders') had elicited consent from the victims to disclosure of their contact details, thereby increasing the time required to complete the consultation process. It also meant that the issue of reparation was first raised with victims by police officers, who are not trained as reparation workers and for whom it may not be the highest priority, rather than reparation workers, which could conceivably make a difference to take-up rates.

A third implementational problem related to the framework adopted for the delivery of reparative interventions. One of the most distinctive and radical features of the Crime and Disorder Act was that it created a new multi-agency structure of local youth offending teams (commonly known as YOTs) comprising probation officers, social workers, police, health and education workers. Youth offending teams were given primary operational responsibility for delivering the government's youth justice reform programme, though they had considerable discretion with regard to the way this was done. Some YOTs undertook all assessment and intervention work themselves (referred to as the 'in-house model'), whereas others contracted with specialist external providers, including those from the voluntary or not-for-profit sector (referred to as the 'outsourced' model; Holdaway et al., 2001: 82).[9] A problem experienced by some of the pilot YOTs that had adopted an in-house structure was that some staff who were recruited from 'traditional' criminal justice agencies such as probation were reluctant to undertake victim contact and consultation work because they did not consider it to form part of their responsibilities (Holdaway et al., 2001: 87). Even before they were introduced, the restorative potential of these reparative initiatives had been assessed in very modest terms, as we have seen. But as a result of the implementational problems we have discussed, it is clear that even this limited potential was not fully realized.

Victim–offender mediation programmes

Victim-oriented aims

The general aims of victim–offender mediation programmes were set out in Chapter 4. From a victim's perspective, such programmes ostensibly[10] offer a number of benefits (see also Dignan and Cavadino, 1996). First, they claim to provide an opportunity to participate in the decision-making process, which could potentially have an empowering effect. Second, they offer a range of reparative outcomes that is potentially far wider and more flexible than those associated with court-based sanctions, including not only financial compensation and restitution but various other forms of direct and indirect reparation and also symbolic forms of reparation such as an apology. A third potential benefit related to both of the above is that the process may have a 'healing effect', at an emotional or psychological level, particularly if the victim feels less anxious or fearful as a result of meeting and speaking with the offender. Indeed, where the victim receives a genuine apology and feels able to reciprocate by expressing a willingness to forgive the offender, it is frequently claimed that this may bring about a sense of 'closure', enabling the victim to put the offence behind them and get on with their life. Of all the different restorative justice approaches, victim–offender mediation is sometimes portrayed as according the highest priority to meeting the specific needs of victims (see, for example, Bazemore and Umbreit, 2001).

Evaluating victim–offender mediation: an overview

As the oldest form of restorative justice it is not surprising that victim–offender mediation is also the most intensively evaluated, though the quality of the research has been somewhat variable, and has frequently lacked the methodological rigour associated with some of the more recent forms of conferencing in particular. Much of the early research was largely descriptive and exploratory in nature, and even the more elaborate studies have tended to focus on a relatively limited range of evaluative criteria that have included some restorative outcome measures but with a particular emphasis on participant satisfaction ratings. Consequently, the validity of the findings is often adversely affected by the methodological shortcomings to which most studies have been subject.

General evaluation findings

In general, evaluation studies show that a majority of victims are satisfied with the mediation process in terms of its fairness, the way they have been treated and also in terms of its outcomes. A number of studies have used quasi-experimental methods in which the experiences and perceptions of those who have taken part in mediation (either direct or indirect) are compared with those of a sample group. The latter usually consists of cases that are considered eligible for mediation but not actually assigned to a meeting. Some studies also incorporate a cross-national perspective since common data collection instruments and analytical techniques have been used in evaluating victim–offender mediation schemes in the United States (Umbreit and Coates, 1993), Canada (Umbreit, 1996) and England (Umbreit and Roberts, 1996). Most of these evaluations reported positive findings. In the US schemes, the most important issues for victims were the opportunity to tell offenders about the effects of the crime, to question them about it, and to reach agreement on restitution. In the Canadian schemes, victims who met their offenders were more likely than those in the comparison group to have received answers to their questions (87 per cent and 51 per cent respectively), more likely to value apologies by offenders (74 per cent and 40 per cent respectively), and less likely to remain upset about the crime and the offender (53 per cent and 66 per cent respectively). In the English schemes, victims and offenders were more likely to express satisfaction in the justice system's response to their case, and to feel that the response had been fair than those who were referred to mediation projects but did not participate in them. However, the latter evaluation (in common with many others) found that the proportion of victims who participated in direct as opposed to indirect mediation was much lower in England than elsewhere. It also found that victims who had engaged in direct mediation expressed higher levels of satisfaction for programme outcomes than those who had taken part in indirect mediation. All three sets of evaluations reported a reduction in the victim's fear of being revictimized by the same offender following mediation.[11]

As for their impact on recidivism levels,[12] the findings have been somewhat variable and inconclusive to date.[13] In general the majority of findings do not show statistically significant reductions in reoffending levels, though there are exceptions. For example, in a recent evaluation of seven English restorative justice schemes, four were found to have had no effect on future offending whereas one victim–offender mediation scheme which dealt with more serious adult offenders did show a significantly lower rate of reconvictions than a control group (Miers et al., 2001).[14] One possible explanation for the disappointing reconviction findings relates to the relatively small size of the samples dealt with, which means that the effect has to be greater to reach levels of statistical significance. Indeed, when 'aggregate' data are examined – either by combining the original data from individual studies (as in Nugent et al., 2001) or by using the technique of statistical meta analysis (as in Latimer et al., 2001) – significant reductions in reoffending levels have been reported.

Despite the generally positive findings, virtually all victim–offender mediation evaluations are subject to methodological shortcomings that raise questions regarding their validity. The main weakness relates to the absence of adequate control groups, the most reliable of which involves the use of random allocation to either treatment (mediation) or control (e.g. conventional trial and punishment) samples. Most evaluations of victim–offender mediation projects have either not used controls at all or have relied on matched comparison groups involving cases that are referred to mediation but fail to participate. Sometimes this is because one of the parties refuses to take part, or it may be because of problems in contacting them. Either way, there is a risk that the findings may be subject to a 'self-selection' effect whereby those cases that proceed to mediation involve parties who are more sympathetically disposed towards it at the outset. Moreover, the techniques that have been used mainly involve interview data or self-administered questionnaires as opposed to structured observations. Consequently, few attempts have been made to relate 'process variables' – relating for example to the way the parties felt they were treated, their attitudes towards one another or the perceived 'sincerity' of an apology – with the outcome, whether in terms of reconvictions or victim satisfaction ratings. This makes it more difficult to determine which features of the mediation process might be associated with more and less positive outcomes, in contrast to some of the conferencing studies which have set out to investigate these issues (see below).

Contextual factors

Since most victim–offender mediation initiatives in the common law world[15] operate on a 'stand-alone' basis (see Chapter 4) as opposed to being 'mainstreamed' as part of the regular criminal justice system, it is especially important to have regard to the 'contextual factors' that may affect their overall performance. As the 'first generation' of restorative justice initiatives, victim–offender mediation schemes have often faced a particularly tough challenge in gaining recognition and acceptance from more established criminal justice agencies such as the police, courts and probation service. Joanna Shapland (1988) has perceptively likened these to feudal fiefdoms, each jealously guarding its own preserve, independence and methods of working.

Some of the early English mediation and reparation schemes experienced acute difficulties since they were launched during an era of 'minimum interventionism',[16] which favoured where possible the diversion of young offenders from courts and from custody. Perhaps not surprisingly, a number of early mediation and reparation schemes were criticized for subordinating the interests of victims where these were in conflict with the then paramount aims of diversion of offenders from prosecution and mitigation of sentence (Davis et al., 1988, 1989; Davis, 1992). This was not true of all such schemes, however, and a number of subsequent evaluations were more favourable (Marshall and Merry, 1990). Indeed, an evaluation of a scheme aimed at adult and young adult offenders suggested that it was possible to develop a more even-handed approach, enabling offenders to be diverted from prosecution with the support of criminal justice agencies and without necessarily sacrificing the interests of victims in the process (Dignan, 1990, 1992).

Implementational problems have continued to dog British mediation and reparation schemes, however, many of which continued to experience problems with regard to both funding and referral levels until the turn of the century. Some short term government funding was provided to a number of pilot projects during the mid-1980s, but was not renewed. Other projects that had received support from local probation services subsequently lost this support as a result of government initiated changes in probation service priorities.[17] Ironically, this niggardliness came back to haunt the government when the study it commissioned to retrospectively study the effectiveness of restorative justice schemes identified a lack of adequate funding for the schemes as a major obstacle in carrying out the research (Miers et al., 2001: 1). More specifically, resource problems were blamed for the relatively low rate of interventions, particularly those involving the more resource-intensive approaches such as direct mediation. Even among those schemes that have managed to keep going, concerns have been raised in some quarters that mediators may sometimes be overprotective, only allowing victims and offenders to participate in respect of whom there is felt to be a high chance of success (Hagley, 2003). Despite protestations that this is done to prevent 'secondary victimization', such blanket paternalism is difficult to reconcile with the aim of 'victim empowerment'. One final implementational obstacle in England and Wales has been the 'new youth justice' reform programme introduced since the Crime and Disorder Act 1998, which has largely favoured the adoption of other broadly restorative justice measures as opposed to victim–offender mediation (Holdaway et al., 2001; Dignan, 2002b: 80).

Family group conferencing initiatives

Victim-oriented aims

The general aims of family group conferencing were spelt out in Chapter 4, which noted that although the approach was originally devised within a child welfare context its subsequent adaptation for use in a youth offending context has resulted in the adoption of a number of victim-oriented aims. As with victim–offender mediation, victims are given an opportunity to participate in a forum in which decisions are made about the best way of dealing with an offence, including any reparation.[18] More specifically, prospective benefits include making victims feel better about what has happened to them, fostering reconciliation between the parties, facilitating agreements as to reparative outcomes (whether symbolic or actual) and reconnecting both parties with their communities.

Evaluating family group conferencing: an overview

Although there have been fewer evaluations of family group conferencing, those studies that have been conducted have generally been more intensive, both in terms of their methods and also their duration. Thus, they have generally involved detailed observations and recording of the conference process itself, together with interviews and self-administered survey forms. The two most important large-scale family group conference evaluations[19] have been conducted in New Zealand (Maxwell and Morris, 1993; Morris and Maxwell, 1998) and South Australia (Daly, 2001, 2003a). The former has entailed follow-up monitoring since the initial evaluation was reported in 1993. Because conferencing has been legislatively mandated as a 'mainstream' response for certain categories of offenders in both jurisdictions, this has precluded the use of fully controlled evaluations using random allocation methods. However, the detailed recording of conference observations and statistical analysis of the resulting data have made it possible to identify a number of process-related factors that appear to be associated with reductions in reoffending.

General evaluation findings

Family group conferences in New Zealand were initially not all that well attended by victims, with a participation rate of approximately only 50 per cent (Maxwell and Morris, 1993). However, this was attributed to poor implementational practice rather than resistance on the part of victims, since only 6 per cent, when asked, said that they did not wish to meet the offender. Among the factors inhibiting victim participation were a failure to invite them, lack of adequate notice and unsuitable timing. These findings prompted a number of legislative and other changes in 1995 that were intended to increase victim satisfaction rates, but so far evidence of their effectiveness is somewhat limited and inconclusive.[20]

Most of those who did attend (60 per cent) found it a positive, helpful and rewarding experience (Morris et al., 1993: 311). They appeared to appreciate being involved in the offence resolution process and also the increased understanding brought by meeting the offender and their family face to face. Not all victims found it a positive experience, however, and about a quarter of victims reported that they felt worse as a result of attending the conference. Morris et al. (1993: 315) suggested that victims' negative experiences were again attributable to implementational weaknesses rather than inherent failings in the conferencing approach itself, and this is supported by some, though not all of the factors they cite. Where victim disappointment related to communication difficulties or a feeling that they received less attention, sympathy or support than other participants, these may well be factors that could be addressed by better training of co-ordinators or improved briefing of victims. However, it is more difficult to see how improvements in training and practice could address the feeling that the offender and/or their family were not truly sorry, which was the commonest reason cited; or the fact that the young person and their family were unable to make reparation, which was another factor.

With regard to outcomes – most of which took the form of apologies or community work – the proportion of victims expressing satisfaction[21] was just under 50 per cent. This is much lower than the satisfaction rates recorded for young people, their families and professional staff. Around one-third of victims were dissatisfied with the outcome, either because it was perceived to be too soft or too harsh, or (more frequently) because the promised outcome never materialized or they were simply not informed about the outcome. Where the cause of dissatisfaction relates to failings on the part of professional staff (as in the case of the latter factor), it should again be possible to address them by improvements in training and practice. But where there is a mismatch between expectation and end result it may be more difficult to guard against disappointment, though better preparatory briefings could obviously help.

Turning to the other major evaluation of family group conferencing,[22] Daly's (2001, 2003a) research on South Australia Juvenile Justice (SAJJ) conferencing project reports that the level of victim participation is much the same as in New Zealand.[23] But perhaps this is not surprising since both the South Australian approach to conferencing and its enabling legislation were strongly influenced by the New Zealand model. Daly found that close to 80 per cent of victim attenders felt that the conference had been worthwhile, and an overwhelming majority (between 80 and 95 per cent) rated the process highly with regard to 'procedural justice' variables such as whether they were treated fairly, with respect[24] and had a say in the outcome. However, she found relatively less evidence that conferencing was achieving 'restoration', particularly with regard to victims.

Among the more positive findings, many victims reported that they were less frightened of and angry towards the offender[25] following the conference than they had been previously. However, she also found that there were limits on the extent to which victims were willing to see offenders in a positive light. Thus, most victims appeared to doubt the sincerity of their offender in apologizing, and only 27 per cent believed that the main reason why they had apologized was because they really were sorry.[26] For their part, a majority of offenders (61 per cent) insisted that the main reason for saying sorry was that they really were sorry. However, their responses to other questions suggested that more felt sorry for what they had done (74 per cent) than felt sorry for the victim (56 per cent before the conference and 47 per cent afterwards). As for the effects of a conference in aiding a victim's recovery, 60 per cent of victims thought that they had 'fully recovered' and had managed to put the offence behind them.

The findings were rather more equivocal regarding the part played by conferencing – as opposed to victim resilience, support from family and friends or simply passage of time – in contributing to any recovery. When victim recovery was cross-tabulated with completion of any agreement, however, the recovery rate was higher with regard to cases with completed agreements (69 per cent) than those without (42 per cent). This suggests that, whatever factors victims themselves may believe have contributed to it,[27] the prospects for recovery do appear to be assisted by the successful attainment of a reparative outcome.

One of the most important factors for victims attending conferences was a desire for reassurance that the offender would not reoffend (32 per cent). As to the effect of family group conferencing on reoffending, both the New Zealand and South Australian findings are remarkably similar. Both studies found – by subjecting reoffending data to statistical analysis – that two conference-related variables appeared to be associated with lower rates of reoffending. They were remorse on the part of offenders and when the decision-making process was based in a genuine consensus in which the young person agreed with the conference outcome. Another important factor for victims was the wish to be able to tell the offender how the offence had affected them (30 per cent). Contrary to the impression conveyed by some of the restorative justice literature, however, not all victims in the SAJJ study were motivated by curiosity as to what an offender who is not known to them is really like, or to find out why they had been victimized. Daly (2003a: 223) found that a substantial minority of victims (approximately one-third) were not at all curious about such matters.

Contextual factors

The two studies show that – at least where there is adequate legislative support – it is possible for family group conferencing to be adopted as a mainstream response when dealing with high volumes of young offenders whose offences are of a more serious variety. Both sets of studies show that conferencing can have some beneficial effects on victims. With regard to the gap between restorative justice theory and restorative justice practice, however, different conclusions have been drawn. Maxwell and Morris are more optimistic in pinning much of the responsibility for the gap on 'implementational failings' as opposed to inherent shortcomings in the restorative justice approach itself. Kathy Daly, on the other hand, is arguably more realistic in acknowledging that, even if these implementational weaknesses were remedied, there are still likely to be *'limits* on offenders' interest in repairing the harm' and *'limits* on victims' capacity to see offenders in a positive light' (2001: 76). If she is right, then this raises important questions about how a criminal justice system should deal with cases in which these limits are transcended.

Research on family group conferencing has also been conducted in jurisdictions that have not adopted conferencing as a mainstream response to offending, as in England and Wales, for example (see Dignan and Marsh, 2001: 87ff for a summary). Here, the experience of conferencing has followed a very similar pattern to the one outlined for victim-offender mediation, with a limited number of small-scale projects operating on the margins of the regular criminal justice system. Almost all have experienced acute developmental problems, including difficulties in attracting referrals, tensions between projects and mainstream criminal justice agencies and, in some cases, difficulties securing participation on the part of victims. Only in the context of child welfare decision making, where conferencing has enjoyed the advantage of stronger institutional and professional support, has it gained a surer foothold, though even here progress has been relatively slow to date.

Police-led conferencing initiatives

Victim-oriented aims

The general aims of police-led conferencing were discussed in Chapter 4, which also identified a number of concerns that have been raised from within a victim-oriented perspective. The most important of these relates to the fact that the theory of reintegrative shaming, which has strongly influenced the development of the approach, was primarily offender focused and, initially at least, placed greater emphasis on its 'crime control' potential than its ability to meet the needs of victims. This 'crime control' agenda is also reflected in the fact that police-led conferencing has often been actively promoted in cases where there may not be an individual victim; for example, in dealing with public order or drink driving offences[28] or those in which the primary offence was drugs related.[29] This does not mean that the aims of police-led conferencing necessarily exclude or downgrade the meeting of victims' needs, and indeed most of the studies seeking to evaluate this approach have attempted to investigate the extent to which victims' needs have been addressed. It would nevertheless be fair to say, however, that the overall design of these evaluations has been more strongly influenced by offender-related criteria than victim-related considerations, as we shall see in the next section.

Evaluating police-led conferencing: an overview

The evaluation of police-led conferencing initiatives has a much shorter history than either of the other two restorative justice approaches we have been considered so far, though in several respects their research design and methods have been more rigorous. In this section we will examine two of the best-known and most authoritative evaluations of police-led conferencing:[30] the Reintegrative Shaming Experiments (RISE) in Canberra, Australia (Strang, 2002) and the Thames Valley Police Restorative Cautioning initiative in England (Hoyle et al., 2002).

The RISE evaluation prides itself on the adoption of a rigorous experimental research design[31] involving the use of random allocation of subjects to either treatment or control groups. The advantage that is claimed for this approach is that it minimizes the likelihood that any differences between the groups are the product of variables relating to the members of the group and increases confidence that they are produced by the treatment itself. It is important to note, however, that the primary objective of the RISE project is to measure the effect of conferencing on repeat offending rates, and that in order to do so, the unit of random allocation relates to the offender and not the victim. From a pure victim perspective, therefore, the approach does not technically constitute a randomized controlled trial, and is more accurately described as a 'quasi-experimental comparison of victims whose offenders were randomly assigned to court or conference' (Strang, 2002: 74).[32] The principal source of data involved the use of statements taken from victims before and after their involvement in conferencing and is much the same as has been used in studies of other restorative justice approaches including victim–offender mediation and also family group conferencing.

The evaluation of the Thames Valley Police Restorative Cautioning initiative presents an interesting contrast in research design and methodology insofar as it eschews the random assignment approach in favour of a more qualitative strategy (Hoyle et al., 2002: 1). Here, the aim was to collect as much data as possible by means of observations as well as interviews in order better to illustrate the mechanisms that might account for changes which may have occurred after the conference has taken place. The study was also distinctive in adopting a strong action research component that was designed to measure and improve police compliance with the restorative justice approach insofar as this can be encapsulated within the context of a scripted model of working (see Chapter 4). This 'process evaluation' formed the basis of the more conventional 'outcome evaluation' that was conducted in the final phase of the research.

General evaluation findings

The victim participation rates for RISE cases involving an identified victim was around 80 per cent (Strang, 2002: 121). An interim report (Strang et al., 1999, as cited by Masters, 2002: 60) suggested that the victim participation rate was higher in respect of violent offences involving offenders under the age of 30 than for less serious property offences involving individual victims[33] committed by offenders under the age of 18 (90 per cent and 73 per cent respectively). These figures are far higher than for many other forms of restorative justice. However, they involved offences of middle-ranking seriousness where the police were satisfied that they could appropriately be dealt with by means of conferencing as opposed to prosecution, and where the offender was also willing for this to happen. In the Bethlehem Pennsylvania police-led conferencing project, where cases were initially selected without regard to the parties' willingness to take part, the victim participation rate was much lower at only 42 per cent (McCold and Wachtel, 1998: 95; see also Dignan with Lowey, 2000: 36).

RISE victims were also asked a series of questions designed to elicit their views with regard to 'process satisfaction' issues.[34] Some questions were put both to victims whose cases had been assigned to conferencing and those whose cases had been assigned to court, enabling comparisons to be drawn between them. But some questions were only meaningful to victims who had actually participated in the process, and these were put to conferencing victims but not those whose cases had been assigned to court since very few would have attended. In terms of overall satisfaction with the way their case had been dealt with by the justice system, a significantly higher proportion of victims whose cases had been dealt with by a conference expressed satisfaction than those whose cases had gone to court (70 per cent and 42 per cent respectively).[35] Victims whose cases were assigned to conferencing reported that they had been treated fairly and with respect regardless of offence type and irrespective of gender (Strang, 2002: 128), though little quantitative information was available regarding the perceptions of victims whose cases had gone to court. Not all victims were satisfied, however, and a significant minority of both court and conference victims expressed dissatisfaction with the way their case had been dealt with (27 per cent and 25 per cent respectively; Strang, 2002: 139). Moreover, the degree of dissatisfaction was higher among victims of violence in both groups (around one in three victims, compared with one in five victims of property offences who were dissatisfied).

In terms of outcomes, neither conferences nor courts were very effective in securing material reparation for victims. With regard to financial restitution there was virtually no difference between them. There was a slightly higher chance of victims benefiting from other kinds of material reparation including work from the offender, but even so only 25 per cent of conference victims received any form of material reparation, compared with just 12 per cent of victims whose case went to court (Strang, 2002: 92). However, there was some evidence that conference victims were somewhat less interested in receiving financial compensation from their offender than those whose cases had gone to court.[36] With regard to symbolic or emotional reparation, when asked specifically whether they felt they were entitled to an apology from their offender the great majority of victims (around 90 per cent) agreed with this proposition,[37] irrespective of how their case was dealt with. However, nearly four times as many conference victims actually received an apology (Strang, 2002: 115). Moreover, conference victims were significantly more likely to believe that the apology they received was sincere in comparison with court victims. Conference victims were significantly less likely than court victims to fear revictimization at the hands of their offender (Strang, 2002: 97), an effect that was even more pronounced among victims of violence. Conversely, conference victims were significantly less likely to express retaliatory sentiments towards their offender and once again this difference was particularly pronounced in respect of victims of violence (Strang, 2002: 138).[38] On a variety of other 'restoration measures' – including reductions in anxiety levels and experiencing a sense of closure – there were signs that conferencing could play a part in helping victims to get over their offence, though there is no comparable data relating to court victims (Strang, 2002: 107, 112).

With regard to its impact on reoffending rates, the RISE evaluation has produced some mixed findings, suggesting that the effects of conferencing may be offence specific. Thus, offenders under the age of 30 who were involved in violent offences were substantially less likely to offend (80 per cent less repeat offending) during the following three years after arrest if assigned to a conference than if assigned to court (Sherman and Strang, 2004: 19). No such reductions were observed for any of the other three offence categories, however. Indeed, those charged with property offences who were assigned to conferences had three times the number of repeat offences compared with those who were sent to court (Sherman and Strang, 2004: 19).[39]

Turning now to the Thames Valley Police initiative, one of the biggest contrasts in findings across the two sets of evaluations relates to the victim participation rate. The final Thames Valley evaluation report disclosed that victims only attended 14 per cent of cautioning sessions that were carried out according to restorative justice principles[40] (Hoyle, 2002: 103; Hoyle et al., 2002: Table 1). A small sample of 'absent victims' was separately analysed to investigate reasons for non-attendance (Hill, 2002). In most cases (52 per cent), the victim had been invited to attend the caution but did not wish to do so. A substantial minority of victims (30 per cent) were invited and would have wanted to attend the session but were unable to. Only a small minority of victims indicated that either they had not been invited to attend (15 per cent) or had not been informed about the caution (4 per cent). Although some victims expressed a variety of concerns about meeting their offender and others, their perceptions were found to be based on a poor understanding of restorative justice, which in turn was attributed to poor communication on the part of facilitators (Hill, 2002: 281). Moreover, as Hill also points out, even victims who decline to attend a conference might still benefit from indirect participation; for example, by having questions answered, providing a statement to the session (which could include 'a say' on the subject of reparation), and receiving feedback from it. The great majority of 'absent victims' did express an interest in communicating something – usually a summary of the harm they had experienced – to the offender. However, there was little evidence that the police facilitators actively sought to promote such benefits on behalf of absent victims.

In common with other studies, the Thames Valley evaluation found very high levels of satisfaction on the part of participating victims and their supporters with the restorative process, including the fairness of their treatment and the quality of the facilitation. However, the evaluators themselves suggested that this might in part have reflected low initial expectations stemming from inadequate preparation of participants, as a result of which the consideration they were shown during the conference itself could have come as a pleasant surprise (Hoyle et al., 2002: 29). Nevertheless, virtually all victims felt that the meeting had been a good idea and most (71 per cent) felt better as a result (p. 40). In terms of outcomes, the study found that during the observed cases 40 per cent of offenders apologized verbally at the appropriate point in 'the script', though only half of the victims felt that the apology was probably or definitely genuine (Hoyle et al., 2002: 35). A further third of offenders apologized, or offered to write an apology to someone not present at the meeting.[41] Most victims (almost two-thirds) who attended meetings felt differently about their offender as a result of the meeting, suggesting that it may have helped to break down stereotypes (Hoyle et al., 2002: 36). Just under 60 per cent of victims felt that they had been able to put the offence behind them. As for its longer term impact, there was evidence that most victim respondents who had attended a conference experienced a positive impact (which was sometimes substantial) several months later, while none reported any significant negative long-term feelings (Hoyle et al., 2002: 45). These beneficial effects were far less likely to be shared by non-participating victims, however, who were much more likely to report longer term negative feelings.

Finally, with regard to its impact on reoffending rates, the report tentatively suggested – based on detailed analysis of a relatively small-scale self-report study – that the restorative cautioning initiative was significantly more effective in reducing the likelihood of reoffending than traditional cautioning (Hoyle et al., 2002: 48ff). The study also concluded that the restorative process itself may have helped about a quarter of offenders to either stop or reduce their offending behaviour.

Contextual factors

Even though they derive from common theoretical and practice 'roots', there are some important differences between the Canberra/RISE and the Thames Valley versions of police-led conferencing, and the same is equally true of the evaluation studies themselves. The former is aimed at 'moderately serious' offenders who would otherwise have gone to court *provided* they satisfy a range of selection criteria, and is 'selective' inasmuch as only a small minority of potentially eligible cases[42] were referred into the RISE experiments. The latter has adopted a 'default position' whereby '*any* matter to be disposed of by a caution should be handled in a restorative manner' (Young and Hoyle, 2003: 280; emphasis added). Although the overall level of offence seriousness may be lower than in Canberra, there are no excluded categories, whether in terms of offences or age and type of offenders. The significance of the Thames Valley initiative is that it seeks to integrate a restorative justice approach as a mainstream response within a regular criminal justice agency that might not be thought of as an automatic proponent of such a radically different response. These contextual differences between the two schemes (as well as those based on nationality and culture) clearly need to be borne in mind when comparing research findings, for example, in relation to victim participation rates.

With regard to the evaluation studies themselves, although the RISE evaluation is better known, the authors of the Thames Valley study are undoubtedly correct when they stress the need for the critical lessons of their own process evaluation to reach a wider audience. After all, in addition to ascertaining what this or any other form of restorative justice may be capable of achieving, it is equally important to know *how* it can be implemented and how to avoid the pitfalls to which it may be prone. Although the detailed findings of the Thames Valley process evaluation are beyond the scope of this chapter, one cautionary lesson that is of relevance from a victim-oriented perspective concerns the risk of secondary victimization when offenders who do not fully admit responsibility for an offence are brought face to face with their alleged victims in a conference (Hoyle et al., 2002: 32).

Community reparation boards and citizen's panel initiatives

Victim-oriented aims
Of the two main variants we examined in Chapter 4, the Vermont Community Reparative Boards have tended to prioritize the value of community involvement over that of victim participation, whereas the recently introduced English youth offender panel system has sought to promote both sets of objectives. The aim of the youth offender panel system is 'to provide a less formal context than court for the offender, his or her parents, the victim, supporters of the victim and/or offender and members of the community to discuss the crime and its consequences' (Crawford and Newburn, 2003: 107). The panel system adopts a conference-type approach to decision making and, at least in principle, accords a high priority to the active and voluntary involvement of victims. Crawford and Newburn (2003: 184) cite four main rationales for promoting victim involvement in panel meetings. First, they provide an appropriate forum in which to consider the views of victims, enabling victims to relay these views directly if they choose. They also provide an opportunity for the harm that victims have experienced to be acknowledged. Second, it enhances the impact of the referral order process on offenders by obliging them to

confront and acknowledge their own responsibility for the harmful consequences of their actions. Third, it provides an opportunity for victims to raise any specific concerns or questions they might have with the offender and his or her family, and to form a better understanding of their attitudes, the reasons for the offence and the likelihood of its recurrence. Finally, it provides an opportunity for victims to experience some form of emotional reparation and/or to negotiate a mutually acceptable form of material reparation.

Evaluating community reparation board and citizen panel initiatives: an overview

There has been relatively little published research on North American Community Reparative Boards to date,[43] whereas the English youth offender panel system was the subject of an intensive 'pilot' evaluation of 11 areas that were selected to trial the new referral order prior to national implementation. Consequently, most of the discussion in this chapter will concentrate on the English variant, the evaluation of which involved a range of methods including observation of panel meetings, analysis of records, surveys and interviews. There was no random allocation element of the kind associated with the RISE conferencing experiments, but since the evaluation team was obliged to feed back its ongoing findings[44] to the pilot sites the research did play an important developmental role of the kind associated with action research projects.

General evaluation findings

In view of the relatively low priority accorded to victim involvement by the Vermont Community Reparative Boards, it is not surprising that victim participation is described as 'infrequent and inconsistent' (Karp and Walther, 2001: 211) and that recorded participation rates are low. Thus, in 1998 only 15 per cent of victims (62 out of 424) attended board meetings.

Rather more surprising at first glance is the finding that the direct victim participation rate was no better than this in the pilot English youth offender panels, even though they appear to place a much greater emphasis on the value of victim participation. Thus, the victim attendance rate for initial panel meetings where there was known to be an identifiable victim was only 13 per cent (Crawford and Newburn, 2003: 185). A number of factors help to account for this lower than anticipated attendance rate, including the fact that contact information was not always available (though this only applied to 10 per cent of cases with identifiable victims); victims were not always contacted even when contact details were available (applied to 22 per cent of cases); and victims who were contacted decided for various reasons not to attend (applied to 78 per cent of victims who were contacted). In addition to those who attended panel meetings, a further 15 per cent made some other input into the panels – for example by providing a statement, or by consenting to personal reparation – making a total of 28 per cent of the cases in which there was potential for victim involvement.

The minority of victims who chose to attend panel meetings were motivated by various factors including a desire to express their feelings directly to the offender (85 per cent);[45] to have a say in how the problem was resolved (71 per cent); out of curiosity (60 per cent); to help the offender (54 per cent); to ensure that they were repaid for their harm or loss (50 per cent); out of a sense of duty (35 per cent); or to ensure the penalty 'was appropriate for the offence' (35 per cent). Those who attended the meetings rated their experiences extremely positively with regard to various procedural justice measures, but somewhat less effusively with regard to restorative justice measures, both of which findings are in line with those for other restorative justice processes. In respect of the restorative justice measures, 69 per cent of victims felt that by the end of the panel meeting the offender had a proper understanding of the harm they had caused, though less than half (48 per cent) felt that the offender had expressed remorse or felt that the harm done to them had been repaired (Crawford and Newburn, 2003: 203). Likewise, less than one-third (30 per cent) felt that their experience had enabled them to put the whole thing behind them. When asked to compare their emotional feelings with regard to the offence and the offender before and after panel meetings, victim responses indicated a significant reduction in adverse reactions. For example, they were less likely to express sentiments of hurt, fear, anger or concerns over their future safety with regard to the offender following the meeting, suggesting that the meeting may have been helpful in overcoming some of the negative consequences of victimization (Crawford and Newburn, 2003: 207). In the absence of comparable data for victims whose cases were dealt with by the courts, however, it is impossible to be sure that such changes are the result of the panel process itself or indeed to compare the two sets of processes in terms of their beneficial impact on victims.

Participating victims did not approve of all aspects of the panel process, however, and many were strongly resentful of the fact that they were required to leave the panel meeting after 'having their say', so that the meeting could consider what activities might be most appropriate for the offender.[46] Crawford and Newburn (2003: 205) also express concern that a majority (70 per cent) of those who did not stay for the entire meeting were not informed about the outcome even though they would like to have been. Moreover, they are rightly critical of the fact that by raising victims' expectations by inviting them to participate only to dash them again by requiring them to leave and neglecting to keep them informed of the outcome, victims are once more reminded of their subordinate status (Crawford and Newburn 2003: 228).

A small sample of victims who did not attend panel meetings was also interviewed, over two-fifths of whom (43 per cent)[47] had not been offered a realistic opportunity to attend a meeting. Almost half of these indicated that they would have attended given the chance (Crawford and Newburn, 2003: 194). Only just under one-quarter (23 per cent) of the sample did not wish to have any involvement in the process. The remaining one-third cited other reasons precluding their attendance, and most of these (80 per cent) indicated that they would otherwise have liked to attend. Where victims do not attend meetings in person, the responsibility for ensuring that a victim perspective is provided falls to the panel itself. The pilot evaluation found that panel members did discharge this responsibility in 56 per cent of the panel meetings they observed, but that no mention of a victim perspective was made in one-fifth (21 per cent) of panels (Crawford and Newburn, 2003: 127).[48]

Contextual factors

The introduction of the referral order confirms that it is possible for conferencing type processes to be introduced as mainstream responses for a wide variety of offences, at least with regard to young offenders, while avoiding many of the difficulties experienced by stand-alone initiatives. Yet Crawford and Newburn (2003: 239) are right to emphasize that the findings of their evaluation were undoubtedly influenced by the context in which the new initiative was introduced. One of the most important contextual factors was the seemingly unending raft of reforms associated with the ongoing transformation of the youth justice system, including the institutional changes associated with the creation of youth offending teams and Youth Justice Board and a plethora of new sentences. The introduction of the radically different referral order and youth panel system so soon after these other changes carried a high risk of 'initiative fatigue', and yet the pilot evaluation found that they were well received and enthusiastically embraced. Crawford and Newburn (2003: 238) attribute this positive response largely to the restorative justice ideals and values underpinning the new initiative, which appeared to be welcomed by magistrates and youth justice practitioners alike as an opportunity for 'something different' to be tried.

Nevertheless, it is possible that the scale and pace of change within the English youth justice system could help to explain, at least in part, the disappointing level of victim participation within the pilot youth offending panels. Crawford and Newburn (2003: 187) attribute this partly to implementational failure, stemming from a lack of familiarity with the most effective ways of involving victims in restorative justice procedures. They also draw attention to the variable levels of victim participation across the pilot areas. The areas that were most successful at involving victims in panel meetings tended to be those prepared to dedicate the resources, personnel and time required. One of the more successful high volume pilot sites, for example, was Nottingham City, which had helped to pioneer the development and use of dedicated 'victim liaison officers' who are responsible for managing victim contact arrangements. It is also interesting to note that two of the most successful areas of all (Hammersmith and Fulham and Westminster with victim attendance rates of 41 per cent and 37.5 per cent respectively) had also piloted the earlier youth offending team reforms. This supports the suggestion that the low victim participation rates may in part have been the result of inexperience and inadequate or unrealistic preparation time, though the evidence is far from conclusive given the very small numbers of victims in both of these latter areas. Moreover, Crawford and Newburn (2003: 238) were undoubtedly correct in emphasizing the fundamental challenge that working with victims presents to the culture and organizational practice of all agencies involved in youth justice work.[49]

Another contextual factor, pointing this time to the possibility of a more systemic failing on the part of the youth offender panel process, is the tension that undoubtedly exists between the community involvement and victim participation elements of the process.[50] Crawford and Newburn (2003: 241) shrewdly warn that the involvement of community representatives could serve to dilute the central importance of the victim, particularly if the community is thought capable of injecting a victim perspective by virtue of its own status and role as indirect or secondary victim of a crime. In a context of limited resources and a degree of cultural and philosophical resistance towards working with victims on the part of some youth justice agencies and practitioners, there is a danger that community involvement could both inhibit and 'be used as an excuse for victim non-attendance'.[51] This is not an inevitable outcome, however, and the pilot evaluation also showed that those community panel members who had experience of panels attended by victims were in general favourably impressed by the positive impact their presence had on the dynamics of the process (Crawford and Newburn, 2003: 148).

Finally, there is another potential systemic weakness with the youth offender panel system, at least when introduced in the context of a youth justice system that is uncertain about the role and status of victims, and often coercive and punitive in its attitudes towards offenders. This relates to the risk that the outcomes which emerge from the panel process may take the form of 'routinized', standardized penalties that are not unlike those imposed by courts, instead of being related to the harm that has been caused or the preferences of the participants. Once again this risk is likely to be increased when victims are not seen as central to the process. But even when present, the pilot evaluation showed that victims were responsible for suggesting only 14 per cent of the elements considered for inclusion in youth offender contracts (Crawford and Newburn, 2003: 129).[52] Even so, this was substantially higher than the proportion of elements proposed by young offenders themselves (5 per cent) or their supporters (2 per cent). Such findings are also disappointing since the accompanying Guidance advised that 'contracts should be negotiated with offenders, not imposed on them' (para. 8.16).[53]

Although reparation was the most prevalent element in youth offender panel contracts (featuring in 76 per cent of contracts where there had been an initial panel meeting) this usually took the form of community reparation (42 per cent; Crawford and Newburn, 2003: 136). Moreover, the evaluation reported an increasing tendency for pilot areas repeatedly to utilize the same limited range of reparative activities, prompting concerns that the measure could come to resemble other reparative penalties such as those associated with action plan orders, reparation orders or even community service.[54] Another element that is liable to be routinized and emptied of relevance is the written apology, which featured in 38 per cent of contracts. The problem here is that offenders may be required to write such letters even though they are not always delivered, and sometimes even regardless of victims' expressed wishes on the subject. In marked contrast, direct reparation to victims including compensation featured much less frequently (in only 7 per cent of contracts).[55] Similar concerns over the use of ritualized and token reparative measures have been raised in relation to other reparative initiatives (Dignan, 2000: 24; Holdaway et al., 2001: 91ff). Clearly, one of the biggest challenges confronting mainstream restorative measures is the need to foster creative and responsive forms of reparation that are more likely to be seen as meaningful and relevant by both victims and offenders. On the evidence reviewed in this chapter, it may be easier to meet this challenge where victims are centrally involved in the deliberative process, and more difficult where a higher emphasis is placed on community involvement at the expense of direct victim participation.

Healing and sentencing circle initiatives: an evaluative overview

In contrast to the other restorative justice approaches featured in this chapter, circle-based initiatives have largely been confined to indigenous communities in North America.[56] Since they have not as yet been nearly so extensively evaluated either, they will be dealt with much more briefly in this chapter. Circles are intended to meet the needs of victims, offenders and communities in a holistic and reintegrative manner, and may involve separate healing circles for victims and offenders before the sentencing circle itself is convened (Schiff, 2003: 322). However, the attempt to accommodate all these interests can be problematic from a victim perspective. One source of tension relates to the potential conflict between the needs and wishes of victims and those of the wider community, whose active participation is also a high priority (LaPrairie, 1995). Another source of tension relates to the potential conflict between the desire to deal with even serious offenders in the community and the concern for victim safety, particularly in small-scale, isolated communities where victims lack anonymity and may be extremely vulnerable (Crnkovich, 1993; cited in Lilles, 2001: 171). Both sets of tensions can be exacerbated by the fact that indigenous communities are often characterized by acute power imbalances encompassing generational, gender and kinship factors (Griffiths and Hamilton, 1996). In the absence of reliable research evidence, it is almost impossible to ascertain victim participation rates, though there are anecdotal estimates that in some areas such as the Yukon the rate is upwards of 50 per cent (Lilles, 2001: 172). From the mostly qualitative research that has so far been undertaken it appears that, in common with other restorative justice approaches, victims largely attest to the fairness of the circle process (Coates et al., 2000). Victims and offenders both appreciate the experience of 'connecting with people in the circle', and victims particularly appreciate the opportunity to tell their story and listen to others. The main drawback, in the eyes of both victims and offenders, relates to the time-consuming nature of the process.[57] There is no reliable evidence as yet relating to recidivism rates for circle-based initiatives.

Conclusions

Mara Schiff (2003: 330) has suggested that many restorative justice initiatives are, at best, fledgling efforts to devise new ways of preventing and responding to crime, and the same could also be said of attempts to evaluate them. Consequently, the current evidence base is limited and incomplete, and we need to be extremely cautious about the conclusions we draw from the research findings to date. From the evidence reviewed in this chapter, it would be fair to say that most restorative justice approaches have been positively evaluated with regard to *process* issues, and that victims tend to feel they have been fairly treated. The findings relating to *outcomes* on the other hand are much more equivocal, whether in respect of recidivism rates or in relation to various victim restoration measures. However, neither set of findings provides a definitive answer to the question whether or not there is merit in extending a restorative justice approach either within the criminal justice system or beyond.

With regard to the process findings, positive as they are, it has to be acknowledged that many (though by no means all)[58] are based on 'demonstration' projects or pilot initiatives, and there are grounds for supposing that such projects may generate better results than mainstream follow-ups (Raynor, 2004). For example, it seems probable that demonstration projects are more likely to be run by enthusiastic, committed and, in some instances, charismatic and evangelical practitioners. As such, they are more likely to be well informed about the theory and values underlying a given initiative, reflective about their own practice and keen to adapt and develop 'best practice' methods for themselves and others. The same cannot always be said of less committed or experienced practitioners who may be called upon to implement a new approach once the decision has been taken to adopt it as a regular response.[59] Herein lies a major challenge for those who would seek to 'mainstream' restorative justice initiatives within a criminal justice environment that may be less sympathetic towards and less cognizant of the underlying values and principles than those early pioneers who helped to formulate them.

With regard to the outcome findings, equivocal as many of these undoubtedly are, they fail to demonstrate any systemic shortcomings with regard to restorative justice, which at worst is generally shown to perform no worse than conventional approaches, for example with regard to recidivism rates. They do confirm the immense challenges faced by those seeking to develop 'alternative' approaches within the context of an established and often defensive criminal justice system. They also affirm that, particularly when they are not properly conducted, restorative processes can disappoint, disempower and even revictimize key stakeholders.[60] But it would be wrong to conclude from the somewhat indifferent outcome findings that restorative justice is *incapable* of delivering on its promised benefits since in most instances it is impossible to divorce the findings themselves from the extremely problematic implementational context in which they were generated.

The problem with regard to both sets of findings is compounded by the fact that much empirical research in the field of restorative justice is itself still at the fledgling (or even pre-fledgling) stage. Much of it has suffered from two principal 'infantile disorders': the first relating to a variety of methodological shortcomings, as indicated above; the second to a lack of appropriate and serviceable effectiveness measures. Even if these methodological problems were to be resolved, however, most restorative justice research suffers from a third major shortcoming, which is that much of it is incredibly narrowly focused. Most restorative justice evaluation to date has taken the form of 'programme evaluations' that set out to measure the extent to which they achieve certain specific aims relating to the delivery of a limited number of beneficial consequences with regard to offenders, victims or in some instances the wider community.

Much of the research has focused on the possible impact that restorative justice might have on offender reconviction rates, with far less emphasis on its ability to alleviate the adverse impact of criminal victimization and particularly the durability of any such alleviation. To some extent this narrow offender-oriented focus is understandable, since much of it has been conceived and developed in the context of the 'what works' tradition,[61] with its emphasis on empirical efficacy. Policymakers, who have the power to pronounce on the fate and prospects of any proposal, have likewise consistently proclaimed[62] the virtues of an 'evidence-led approach'.

However, it is highly questionable whether the future of restorative justice could or should ever be reducible to a purely *empirical* question, since its appeal in the eyes of its proponents has always had as much to do with values as verdicts, and has been inspired as much by issues of principle as evidence of its performance. Indeed, much of restorative justice's initial appeal was founded on its 'transformative potential'. By this is meant not only its capacity to alter our attitudes towards victims, offenders and, to some extent, the concept of crime itself; but also its potential to contribute to a more radical reform of the way we respond to crime in general. Although some early restorative justice advocates were justifiably criticized for their heady and often excessively utopian talk of impending 'paradigm shifts'[63] more modest and realistic calls for reform have been associated with many reparative and restorative justice advocates from the days of Margery Fry onwards (see Chapter 1). Indeed, this 'aspirational agenda' – to alter the terms of the criminal justice debate about the most appropriate way of dealing with offenders and their victims – has always formed an important part of what might be termed the 'restorative justice project'. Consequently, this dimension also needs to be addressed in assessing both the actual and potential impact of restorative justice on the wider criminal justice system and beyond.

This is something that cannot be done simply by evaluating the effectiveness of particular forms of restorative justice practice in reducing offender reconviction rates, or meeting the needs of victims, however methodologically sound and rigorous the methods by which this is attempted. It calls instead for a more nuanced and qualitative approach. An important set of questions that any such approach must be capable of addressing were identified in the first chapter of this book. These questions provide us with a broader alternative victim-focused agenda against which to assess the potential and, where evidence is available, the actual performance of various kinds of restorative justice approaches. This agenda will form the basis of the concluding chapter of the book, to which we now turn.

Notes

1 As Pawson and Tilley (1994: 298) have noted, 'A particular programme will only "work" if the contextual conditions into which it is inserted are conducive to its operation, as it is implemented.'

2 For example, in ideal circumstances with the aid of inspired and dedicated practitioners.

3 For other general overviews see Braithwaite (1999), Dignan with Lowey (2000), Miers (2001), Kurki (2003); and, more specifically with regard to victims of juvenile offenders, see Immarigeon (1999); Strang (2001).

4 Home Office research has shown that one of the main reasons sentencers gave for not awarding compensation was that the offender lacked the means to pay, and some felt reluctant to make an award where the amount that could be afforded might appear too derisory (Flood-Page and Mackie, 1998: 62, 111).

5 However, they are also obliged to take the offender's means into account, both when determining the amount of any award, and in setting the size and frequency of payment. Consequently, victims frequently receive payments intermittently and in small amounts, often over a considerable period of time.

6 The position is different in some other jurisdictions that allow prosecutors to make any diversion conditional on the offender agreeing to make amends to the victim. Examples include Austria, France, Germany and the Netherlands (Miers, 2001; see also Cavadino and Dignan, 2005, forthcoming).

7 Moreover, it is a requirement laid down in National Standards that group placements should be 'demanding in the sense of being physically, emotionally or intellectually taxing' (Home Office et al., 1995).

8 Certain of the pilot areas managed to circumvent the restriction by persuading their local courts to be less prescriptive in determining the content of a reparation order where there had not yet been time for victims to be adequately

consulted. Instead, courts would authorize reparation workers to facilitate either an appropriate form of direct reparation (which could also include mediation) provided the victim was agreeable, or an appropriate form of community reparation where no such consent was forthcoming (Holdaway et al., 2001: 88; Dignan, 2002b: 79).

9 A third model (referred to as the 'mixed economy model') operated on a hybrid basis by seconding an employee from a specialist voluntary or not-for-profit organization to work within the YOT on matters relating to reparative work. This often included assessment and, sometimes, delivery of interventions, though the latter function might also be contracted out to external sources.

10 The precise aims of a given programme may depend in part on its principal sources of funding and referrals, and also its relationship with other formal criminal justice agencies.

11 In US programmes, 23 per cent indicated that they were afraid of revictimization before mediation, but only 10 per cent did so after mediation (Umbreit and Coates, 1993). In the Canadian programmes 11 per cent of victims feared revictimization after mediation compared with 31 per cent of the comparison sample, and in the English programmes the respective figures were 16 per cent and 33 per cent.

12 Although chiefly of interest to policymakers, victims also very often express the hope that something can be done to reduce the likelihood that 'their' offender will victimize someone else in the future. Because of space constraints, only a brief summary of such findings will be provided in this chapter, though references will also be provided to the extensive literature on the subject.

13 See Kurki (2003) for a fuller review of the reconviction study findings.

14 The only scheme to show a statistically significant reduction in reoffending levels was the West Yorkshire Victim Offender Unit, 44 per cent of whose offenders were reconvicted within two years compared with 56 per cent for the control group. Moreover, the experimental group also had fewer reconvictions per offender and for less serious offences. None of the other six schemes evaluated had statistically significant reductions in reoffending rates, though two schemes had not been operative long enough to allow for a reconviction study.

15 The position is very different in continental Europe (see Miers, 2001).

16 This philosophy and its consequences for the English juvenile justice system during the 1980s are described more fully in Bottoms and Dignan (2004).

17 Including the requirement to prioritize new duties in connection with the Victim's Charter (see Chapter 3, n. 61, above).

18 However it was also noted that, unlike victim–offender mediation, victims are required to absent themselves during a period known as 'family time' in which the young person and other family members formulate the recommendations they feel are appropriate. To this extent at least, family group conferencing could be thought to be potentially less 'empowering' for victims.

19 Apart from these large-scale evaluations, there have also been a number of smaller scale evaluations of family group conferencing in other jurisdictions, where it has mainly been introduced experimentally on a 'stand-alone' basis. In England and Wales the best known studies are by Gilroy (1998), Jackson (1998), and Crow and Marsh (2000).

20 The Children, Young Persons and their Families Act 1989 was amended in 1995 to ensure better consultation with victims over the timing and venue of conferences. There have been more recent reports of variable rates of victim

attendance in different parts of the country – 50 per cent in South Auckland and 70–80 per cent in Wellington (JUSTICE, 2000: 32).

21 Maxwell and Morris (1993: 116) rightly draw attention to a lack of precision and clarification surrounding the term 'satisfaction' and Daly (2001: 71) usefully notes that 'outcome satisfaction' is likely to relate in part at least to initial expectations.

22 The sample selected cases on the basis of their offence category and included violent offences (44 per cent of the sample) and property offences (56 per cent) but excluded shoplifting, drugs and public order cases.

23 South Australia Office of Crime Statistics (1999: 131, cited in Daly, 2003a: 222). As Daly points out, however, if victimless offences were excluded from the figures, the victim participation rate would be higher. She suggests that it might increase by as much as 8 to 10 percentage points.

24 Though one-fifth (21 per cent) of victims reported that when they left the conference they were upset by what the offender or the offender's supporters had said (Daly, 2003a: 225).

25 Almost 40 per cent of victims had been frightened of the offender before the conference, but this fell to 25 per cent after the conference and 18 per cent one year later. Over 75 per cent of victims had felt angry towards the offender before the conference, but this fell to 44 per cent afterwards and to 39 per cent one year later (Daly, 2003a: 230).

26 Moreover, a substantial minority of victims (approximately one-third) felt that the person who had committed the offence was intrinsically bad ('a bad person') not just that the thing they did was bad (Daly, 2001: 77).

27 Of those victims whose offender had completed an agreement, approximately half felt that it had helped repair the harm at least to some extent and a similar proportion felt it had helped them to put the offence behind them (Daly, 2003a: 229).

28 As in the RISE project in Canberra (see Strang, 2002: 65, 75).

29 As in the Thames Valley restorative cautioning initiative (see Hoyle et al., 2002: 76).

30 Police-led conferencing has also been evaluated in Bethlehem, Pennsylvania (see McCold and Wachtel, 1998).

31 Sometimes referred to as the 'gold standard' of evaluation (Pocock, 1983, as cited in Strang, 2002: 63). See also note 61.

32 See Strang (2002: ch. 4) for a much more detailed account of the RISE research design and methodology, including its strengths and weaknesses.

33 This category also included shop theft cases where the offender was apprehended by shop staff or managers. Shoplifting offences involving offenders who were apprehended by security personnel were assigned to a separate category. A fourth category consisted of drink driving offences involving offenders of all ages. Neither of the latter two categories was included in Strang's (2002) analysis of the impact of police-led conferencing on victims, however.

34 But see Young (2001: 210) for a detailed discussion of the strengths and weaknesses of the different methods that have been used to evaluate procedural fairness in relation to police conferencing in Bethlehem, Canberra and Thames Valley.

35 $p < 0.001$. Strang (2002: 133). Conversely, a greater proportion of victims whose cases had gone to court expressed anger at the way their case had been

dealt with than was the case with victims whose case had been assigned to conferencing (32 per cent and 18 per cent respectively).

36 Just over one-third (37 per cent) of conference victims indicated that they wanted financial compensation compared with just under half (47 per cent) of court victims ($p < 0.05$) (Strang, 2002: 93).

37 Interestingly, however, when asked what factors had influenced their decision to take part in a conference, wanting an apology did not feature among those mentioned (see Strang, 2002: 122, figure 5.4).

38 For victims of violence, as many as 45 per cent of 'court' victims admitted that they would do some harm to their offender if they had the chance, compared with just 9 per cent of conference victims ($p < 0.01$) (Strang, 2002: 138).

39 There was no significant effect either way on shoplifters or drink drivers.

40 According to the terminology adopted by the evaluators, cautioning sessions that are attended by victims are termed 'restorative conferences'; those that are not attended by victims are termed 'restorative cautions' (Hoyle et al., 2002: 9).

41 However, non-participating victims who received a written apology were less likely to appreciate this reparative gesture, particularly where they were expecting to receive compensation (Hoyle et al., 2002: 45).

42 Amounting to 11 per cent of potentially eligible violent offenders and 12 per cent of potentially eligible property offenders (Strang, 2002: 69).

43 But see Karp and Walther (2001).

44 Two interim reports were circulated within youth offending teams during the course of the evaluation, both of which were subsequently published and are available on the Home Office Research, Development and Statistics website (Newburn et al., 2001a, 2001b). See also the final report (Newburn et al., 2002).

45 In each case the figures relate to the proportion of victims saying that the factor was 'somewhat' or 'very' important to them. See Crawford and Newburn (2003: Table 11.5) for a more detailed breakdown.

46 Over half the victims (57 per cent) left before the meeting had ended, and four-fifths of these did so because they were required to either by the YOT or community panel members (Crawford and Newburn, 2003: 205). Presumably, this might help to account for the fact that even with regard to panels attended by victims, only 14 per cent of the elements considered for inclusion in youth offender contracts were proposed by victims (Crawford and Newburn, 2003: 129).

47 Crawford and Newburn (2003: 194) cite a figure of 53 per cent, but this is not in accordance with the figures provided in the accompanying Table 11.4.

48 Victims or their representatives provided this perspective in the remaining cases.

49 See also Holdaway et al. (2001: 87), who also drew attention to the resistance shown within some occupational cultures towards the idea of working with victims.

50 Mirroring the philosophical tension between the 'communitarian' and 'civilization' tendencies referred to in Chapter 4.

51 N.B. There was also evidence that youth offender panels were significantly less inclusive in certain other respects – including young offenders' family members and supporters – than family group conferences (Crawford and Newburn, 2003: 122).

52 Moreover the few elements that were proposed by victims were the most likely

to be rejected by panels, usually because they were considered impracticable or disproportionate (Crawford and Newburn, 2003: 130).

53 A tendency to impose terms on offenders rather than negotiating with them is likewise associated with the Vermont Community Reparative Boards (Karp, 2002: 76).

54 Or 'community punishment order' as it was officially renamed in the Criminal Justice and Court Services Act 2000.

55 Of reparative elements 10 per cent were said to take the form of 'indirect reparation' (Crawford and Newburn, 2003: 136), but it is not clear from either the text or the accompanying table (8.3) what kind of reparative activity this term might encompass.

56 At least in a criminal justice setting. Elsewhere, circle-based processes tend to be used much more widely in school settings where they are often, though not invariably, used in conjunction with restorative justice approaches.

57 A series of circles may be held for offenders, victims and community, each of which can take as long as four months to prepare (Canada, 1997; cited in Roberts and Roach, 2003: 241).

58 For example, family group conferencing in New Zealand and victim-offender mediation in some European countries such as Austria, Belgium, Finland and Germany (see Miers, 2001: 81).

59 See also, in a rather different context, Raynor and Vanstone (2001).

60 See also Barton (2000: 69ff).

61 One of the principal exponents of this approach is Larry Sherman, who has also helped to develop the use of randomized controlled trials as a technique for evaluating restorative justice, both in the RISE evaluation in Canberra and also two of the adult-based restorative justice initiatives that are being evaluated by Sheffield University (see Sherman et al. 1997, 2002; see also Shapland et al., 2002).

62 Rhetorically at least, if not always in practice. Enthusiasm for an evidence-led approach to policymaking did not begin with, but certainly reached a zenith under, the New Labour government that was elected in 1997. Its influence can be discerned in a raft of initiatives that were intended to reform the criminal justice and youth justice systems, including the introduction of various measures inspired by restorative justice precepts (see also Holdaway et al., 2001).

63 See, for example Cantor (1976), Barnett (1977), Zehr (1990) and Fattah (1998). Such talk of a 'paradigm shift' has been criticized for assuming that this would happen automatically and for its failure to articulate a 'transitional strategy' by which this might be achieved (see, for example, Dignan, 1994).

Further reading

Braithwaite, J. (1999) Restorative justice: assessing optimistic and pessimistic accounts, *Crime and Justice: A Review of Research*, 25: 1–127.

Crawford, A. and Newburn, T. (2003) *Youth Offending and Restorative Justice: Implementing Reform in Youth Justice*. Cullompton: Willan.

Daly, K. (2002a) Restorative justice: the real story, *Punishment and Society*, 4: 55–79.

Holdaway, S., Davidson, N., Dignan, et al., (2001) *New Strategies to Address Youth Offending: The National Evaluation of the Pilot Youth Offending Teams*. RDS Occasional Paper no. 69. London: Home Office. Also available online at: www.homeoffice.gov.uk/rds/index.html

Hoyle, C., Young, R. and Hill, R. (2002) *Proceed with Caution: An Evaluation of the Thames Valley Police Initiative in Restorative Cautioning*. York: Joseph Rowntree Foundation.

Kurki, L. (2003) Evaluating restorative justice practices, in A. von Hirsch, J. Roberts, A.E. Bottoms, K. Roach and M. Schiff (eds) *Restorative Justice and Penal Justice: Competing or Reconcilable Paradigms?* Oxford: Hart.

Morris, A.M., Maxwell, G. and Robertson, J. (1993) Giving victims a voice: a New Zealand experiment, *Howard Journal of Criminal Justice*, 32: 304–21.

Strang, H. (2001) Justice for victims of young offenders: the centrality of emotional harm and restoration, in A.M. Morris and G. Maxwell (eds) *Restorative Justice for Juveniles: Conferencing, Mediation and Circles*. Oxford: Hart.

Strang, H. (2002) *Repair or Revenge: Victims and Restorative Justice*. Oxford: Clarendon Press.

K

Assessing restorative justice: the broader picture

Acknowledging the limits of restorative justice
Assessing restorative justice with regard to the 'ideal victim'
   stereotype
Striking the right balance or lacking checks and balances?
Summary and final remarks
Notes
Further reading

In this final chapter I will reflect upon three remaining sets of questions. These are questions that cannot be answered solely with reference to research findings, however conclusive these might ultimately turn out to be with regard to the effectiveness of restorative justice either in meeting the needs of victims or in reducing the likelihood of reoffending. They are, however, of considerable importance to the future prospects of restorative justice and the form it is likely to assume.

The first set of questions relates to the limits to which restorative justice may be subject in its capacity to assist the victims of crime, however positive the research findings relating to its overall effectiveness. These limits also have an important bearing on the relationship between restorative justice initiatives and the other victim-oriented measures that we have examined in earlier chapters.

The second set of questions picks up on an issue that was raised in Chapter 1 concerning the 'ideal victim' stereotype. This stereotype, as we saw, has been hugely influential in shaping the debate about social and criminal justice policy towards victims, directing the activities of criminal justice agencies and influencing the media's reporting of crime and victim-related issues. Yet it is confounded, as we have seen, by much of the empirical evidence relating to victims and their attributes, which reveals a far more complex and highly nuanced picture. Since part of restorative justice's appeal rests on its claim to offer a more constructive way of dealing with crime and its consequences, it is pertinent to ask whether it too shares the same set of fallacious assumptions with regard to victims, their attributes and also the process of victimization. Or whether it might form the basis of a less myopic and more realistic approach that more accurately reflects the complex social realities of crime and its consequences.

The third and final set of questions focuses on the credibility of claims that restorative justice processes strike an appropriate balance between the interests of victims and those of the other principal stakeholders and asks what additional safeguards might be needed to ensure that such a balance is maintained.

Acknowledging the limits of restorative justice

In assessing their capacity to improve the way in which victims of crime are dealt with, it is important to acknowledge at the outset that restorative justice initiatives are subject to exactly the same operational constraints as all other forms of criminal justice interventions. The most debilitating constraint is that the vast majority of offences do not result in an offender being apprehended, convicted and dealt with, which is when most such interventions come into play (Dignan, 2001: 341).[1] Indeed, the scale of the 'attrition rate'[2] within the criminal justice system is such that only approximately 3 per cent of offences committed result in either a caution or a conviction.[3] Whatever potential benefits a restorative justice approach might be capable of delivering for victims, therefore, they are unlikely to offer any assistance to the great majority of victims whose offenders are never apprehended or convicted. Consequently, restorative justice by itself will never be capable of providing an adequate substitute for other victim-focused reforms of the kind we examined in Chapter 2, such as better victim support facilities or criminal injuries compensation schemes that are not dependent upon the apprehension of an offender.

For victims whose offenders are caught and convicted, however, those who participate in restorative justice processes are more likely to find them fair and satisfying than those who are dealt with by means of conventional criminal trial procedures, as we saw in Chapter 5. Indeed, the findings referred to in Chapter 5 have been buttressed by a recent meta analysis[4] of 13 studies that incorporated an experimental research design (Latimer et al., 2001: 910). This confirmed that victims who participated in restorative justice processes had significantly higher satisfaction ratings than those who experienced the conventional criminal justice process.[5] The experimental methodology used by the studies included in the analysis renders them much less vulnerable to charges that they incorporate a 'self-selection bias',[6] which is a complaint levelled against many evaluations. These latest findings provide additional support for restorative justice's claim to offer more to victims than the conventional criminal process. Moreover, they are also consistent with the findings of social psychologists that active participation in decision-making processes is positively correlated with perceptions of fairness, which in turn are associated with increased levels of satisfaction towards and acceptability of resulting outcomes (Lind and Tyler, 1988; Tyler, 1990).[7]

Nevertheless, it has to be conceded that victim satisfaction with the process of restorative justice provides an imperfect measure of its ability to secure substantive restoration, echoing the doubts raised by Daly (2001, 2003a) that were referred to in Chapter 5. More specifically, there is relatively little robust evidence as yet regarding the ability of restorative justice to routinely (as opposed to sometimes) restore victims in terms of many of the known consequences of victimization as outlined in Chapter 1.

With regard to material reparation, we know from the conventional criminal justice system that most offenders, and particularly young offenders, are unlikely to be capable of making redress in full. This may not matter provided that victims are prepared to accept symbolic reparation rather than insisting on obtaining their 'pound of flesh'. There is evidence from a number of studies that for many victims this is indeed the case (Marshall and Merry, 1990; Umbreit et al., 1994). Thus, Shapland et al. (1985: 123) found that many victims were satisfied with relatively small amounts of compensation, which they appeared to welcome for their symbolic value even though the value of the redress may be limited. Such findings suggest that, even though restorative justice approaches do not provide a substitute for state-funded compensation schemes, they may be capable of providing a kind of additional solace for some victims at least that state-funded compensation and other forms of victim assistance cannot, though they are unlikely to satisfy or meet the needs of all victims. In the RISE experiments, for example, just under a third of victims reported that the recovery of material reparation was for them an important reason for attending a conference (Strang, 2001: 185). Moreover, others have argued strongly that the weight of empirical evidence does *not* support the view that material restitution is unimportant for victims (see e.g. Davis, 1992: 171).

When it comes to emotional restoration, it is usually assumed by restorative justice writers that this is achieved by means of an apology. There is certainly evidence that some forms of restorative justice such as conferencing are much more likely to result in victims receiving an apology than are court victims (see, for example, Strang, 2001: 190; see also Chapter 5). Much is also made in the theoretical literature, as we saw in Chapter 4, of the 'near miraculous qualities' of a satisfying apology (Tavuchis, 1991: 6; Retzinger and Scheff, 1996: 316). However, sociologically informed commentators such as Tony Bottoms (2003: 98) have pointed out that the context in which the 'ideal-typical apology' occurs assumes that victim and offender are part of the same moral/social community, and that this is not necessarily the case in contemporary urban societies. Bottoms also draws attention to anthropological evidence suggesting that when disputes arise between people who do not form part of the same moral/social community then indigenous procedures (which are akin in many respects to restorative justice processes) 'are cumbersome and not altogether efficient' (Gulliver, 1963: 263). Bottoms's observations raise doubts as to whether an apology by itself is sufficient to bring about successful reconciliation, at least in a context where the social mechanisms on which restorative justice appears to depend for its effectiveness (namely 'thick social relationships') are absent. As he points out, these doubts are confirmed by empirical evidence showing that apologies are not invariably perceived by victims to be sincere and that there are limits on the extent to which victims view offenders in a positive light after the conference (Daly, 2001, 2003a; see also Chapter 5). In general, however, the empirical evaluations of restorative justice are of limited assistance in shedding light on the issues raised by Bottoms. Very few studies have included in their analysis specifically victim-centred characteristics including relationship (if any) to the offender, and those that have sought to do so tend to lack empirical depth (Kurki, 2000). Much more research is needed, therefore, on the circumstances in which restorative justice processes are likely to result in successful emotional restoration including reconciliation.

Turning next to the restoration of physical or psychological harm resulting from an offence, there are obvious limits to the ability of any criminal justice based intervention to 'restore' *physical injury*, and restorative justice is no exception. Its capacity to restore victims who have suffered *psychological* harm has also suffered in the past from a paucity of robust empirical evidence, though this is partly due to the tendency for most restorative justice initiatives to be confined to cases involving juvenile offenders and relatively minor offences. There has been some anecdotal evidence that victims of even the most serious offences can find it helpful to meet up with their offenders.[8] However, most empirical research investigating the use of restorative justice approaches in respect of serious offences has involved very small samples of cases (see for example Flaten, 1996; Umbreit et al., 1999; O'Connell, 2001). Although the findings are often encouraging they are also vulnerable to the critique that Kathy Daly refers to as the 'Nirvana story' of restorative justice (see also Chapter 5) since they indicate what it may be possible for it to achieve rather than providing conclusive evidence of what is practicable on a routine basis. Once again there is a lack of robust empirical evidence to support the often exaggerated claims that are advanced by some restorative justice advocates, particularly with regard to the durability of any positive behavioural or attitudinal changes on the part of victims (Miers, 2001: 85).

The research position is changing rapidly, however, and research that is already underway could provide further evidence of restorative justice's capacity to help victims in the aftermath of an offence. One example relates to the recent introduction in parts of England and Wales of pilot restorative justice initiatives in cases involving adult offenders who have committed much more serious offences, which is part of a large-scale study commissioned by the Home Office.[9] Preliminary and as yet unverified results of a separate small-scale study that is being conducted on the back of this main evaluation exercise appear to show that victims who are randomly assigned to take part in restorative justice conferences exhibit lower levels of post-traumatic stress disorder than those who do not (Sherman and Strang, 2004: 19). In the meantime, however, a note of caution may be warranted since there is also evidence from research on family group conferencing in New Zealand that victims whose offences had the greatest psychological and emotional impact on them were *more* likely to be adversely affected by attending a conference (Morris et al., 1993: 312–14).

One final constraint that has to be acknowledged relates to the willingness of victims to take part in restorative justice processes. Prior to 1998 there was indirect evidence from questions put to victim respondents taking part in the 1984 British Crime Survey that just over half (51 per cent) would be willing to meet 'their' offender out of court in the presence of a third party with a view to negotiating reparation (Maguire and Corbett, 1987: 227–31).[10] In the 1998 survey a slightly smaller proportion (41 per cent) indicated that they would be willing to take part in such a meeting in order to ask their offender why they had committed the offence and to tell them how it had made them feel (Mattinson and Mirlees-Black, 2000: 40–4). When put to the test in the context of particular restorative justice initiatives of various kinds in England and Wales, however, the actual participation rates have invariably been very much lower, as we have seen, particularly in comparison with those recorded in other jurisdictions. Thus, the victim participation rates for the three main kinds of restorative justice interventions were around 14 per cent in the case of the Thames Valley police-led conferencing initiative, 13 per cent in the case of youth offender panels to which offenders are referred under the terms of a referral order at the point of first conviction and 9 per cent in respect of court-imposed reparation orders.[11]

Part of the reason for the disappointingly low victim participation rates almost certainly has to do with implementational problems, including very limited 'lead-in' times, ineffective victim consultation procedures, data protection problems and a degree of cultural resistance on the part of some of the agencies involved. Even when allowance is made for these factors, however, the fact remains that a fairly substantial proportion of victims at the present time appear to be unwilling to confront their offenders, at least in the context of current restorative justice initiatives.[12] One question this raises is whether it is possible for certain types of restorative justice processes, for example, those based on conferencing, to proceed in the absence of the direct victim, perhaps by involving secondary or indirect victims or by allowing victims to contribute to the process in other ways. A second question is what should happen in those cases where the victim does not wish to have anything to do with the proceedings even though the offender might be willing to make amends, particularly if the case is then dealt with by the conventional criminal justice system. These are questions to which we will return later in the chapter.

Assessing restorative justice with regard to the 'ideal victim' stereotype

One question that we need to address in this section is whether the work of restorative justice theorists, advocates and practitioners has been informed by the same kind of stereotypical assumptions that Nils Christie encapsulated in his construct of the 'ideal victim'. A second, closely related question is whether restorative justice processes are any more appropriate and effective than the conventional criminal justice system when it comes to dealing with cases involving 'non-standard' victims and offenders. Questions such as these rarely feature in the restorative justice literature,[13] much of which displays a surprising degree of myopia towards these broader victimological concerns.

When depicting the 'restorative justice paradigm', for example, there is a common tendency, in seeking to differentiate it from the conventional criminal justice paradigm, for crime to be redefined simply and exclusively as a violation 'of one individual by another'[14] rather than as an offence against the state. Richard Young (2000: 229) is one of the few commentators to have drawn attention to the rather simplistic way in which much of the restorative justice literature thus tends to conceptualize victims almost exclusively in terms of discrete, identifiable 'flesh-and-blood' individuals. Likewise, in much of the *research* on restorative justice victims are mostly presented in what Young (2002: 146) elsewhere describes as an undifferentiated homogenized mass of 'ageless, colourless, genderless, classless individuals'. So perhaps it is hardly surprising that in some restorative justice writing there is also a tendency to make rather sweeping and all-embracing claims about its beneficial impact on victims in general.[15] Yet as the work of some of the more rigorous restorative justice researchers makes clear, those individual victims who do take part in restorative justice processes are decidedly heterogeneous with regard to their personal attributes, the type and degree of harm they have experienced, and also their reactions to the process (Strang, 2002: 208; Daly, 2003b). One question which this insight raises is whether it is realistic to expect that participating in a restorative justice process could ever be *equally* beneficial for *all* victims regardless of their attributes, attitudes or experiences; and if not, whether more could be done to help victims decide for themselves[16] on a more informed basis whether or not they would be likely to benefit from participating in the process (and if so, what form this participation might assume).[17]

Turning now to the related question regarding the suitability of restorative justice in cases involving 'non-standard' victims and offenders, various such categories can be identified, though they have little in common apart from the fact that they are all potentially challenging from a restorative justice perspective. Many of them, it should be noted, are also equally challenging from a conventional criminal justice perspective. In this section I will consider the following six potentially problematic categories of cases:

1 Cases involving 'non-stranger' victims, an important subcategory of which are victims of domestic violence.
2 Cases involving what could be described as 'representative' or 'generic' victims (an important subcategory of which are victims of 'hate crimes' of various kinds), as opposed to those who are known to their offender or who are randomly targetted.[18]
3 Secondary or indirect victims.
4 Cases involving victims of 'non-standard' offenders, as in the case of corporate wrongdoing or wrongdoing by agents of the state.
5 Cases in which the status of the victim may be problematic or contested because they may also be culpable to some degree.
6 Cases involving impersonal victims, notably corporate victims.

In each case we need to consider whether they really do pose a challenge for restorative justice (or indeed for more conventional forms of criminal justice), and whether restorative justice is capable of rising to the challenge insofar as it is possible to determine this in the light of current knowledge.

'Non-stranger' victims including victims of domestic violence

On the face of it, it seems odd that cases involving victims who are known in some way to their offender should be thought to be in any way problematic from a restorative justice point of view. After all, in cases such as these there can be little doubt that victims and offenders do indeed form part of the same social/moral community that is generally assumed to provide the optimum setting in which social mechanisms (such as an apology) might work best. Moreover, there has been considerable discussion in the restorative justice literature about whether or not such mechanisms might be expected to work in contemporary urban contexts in which it is assumed that such settings are scarcer.

Somewhat surprisingly, however, the same level of interest in the topic has not generally been shown by those conducting research into the effectiveness of restorative justice. To echo a point made earlier, relatively few studies, for example, have attempted to compare the outcomes of restorative justice interventions in cases according to whether the parties did form part of the same moral community or not. One relatively small scale early study (Dignan, 1990: 21) did show that individual victims were more likely to agree to a face-to-face meeting where they knew their offender than when they did not (40 per cent and 30 per cent respectively). But by far the highest level of direct mediation (approximately 65 per cent) involved victims and offenders who were members of the same family (and thus engaged in the kind of 'thick' social relationships that Bottoms refers to). In marked contrast, those describing themselves as 'friends' or 'neighbours' were no more likely to agree to direct mediation than victims who were unknown to their offenders. Unfortunately, the number of victims in each category was too small to enable comparisons to be made in terms of types of outcome including the making of apologies and degrees of reconciliation. However, Kathy Daly (2003b: 29), in one of the few other studies to include victim–offender relationships among the variables studied, found that whether victims and offenders were known to each other or not did *not* appear to be associated with the 'restorativeness' or otherwise of a conference.[19] This finding also needs to be interpreted with caution though, since the variable simply differentiated between those who did not know one another at all and those who knew each other in any capacity, including simply by sight. Clearly, much more research is needed before we are able to say whether the prospects of reaching a restorative outcome really are affected by such 'relational' factors.

One important subcategory of 'non-stranger' victims comprises victims of domestic violence, most of whom presumably are, or have been, involved in exceedingly close personal relationships with their offenders, and some of whom may wish to restore them. On the face of it both parties also appear to form part of the same social/moral community, thus satisfying several of the requirements presumed in the literature to afford a conducive context in which to pursue restorative justice processes. Moreover, the conventional criminal justice system is widely perceived to have failed such victims,[20] at least in the past. Thus, critics have complained that the police and prosecuting authorities do not take such offences sufficiently seriously, either by declining to prosecute or by facilitating plea bargains that enable offenders to get off more lightly by pleading guilty to less serious charges (see, for example, Dobash and Dobash, 1979, 1992; Edwards, 1989; Buzawa and Buzawa, 1990; Hoyle, 1998; Mirlees-Black, 1999). Conversely, it is claimed that even when the authorities are prepared to act, victims may feel reluctant to precipitate a complaint[21] which could result in their partner being imprisoned, and that many who do persevere may experience secondary victimization at the hands of the criminal justice process.

However, it is by no means universally accepted that restorative justice provides an adequate, or even acceptable, alternative to the conventional criminal justice response in such cases, particularly in the wake of recent reforms to the criminal justice system. Those who oppose the use of restorative justice in this context (see, for example, Martin, 1996; Stubbs, 1997; Cayley, 1998: ch. 1) are apt to complain that by effectively 'privatizing' the response to domestic violence it trivializes a particularly serious form of crime which merits unconditional community condemnation. Concerns have also been raised regarding the acute power imbalance – fuelled by resource constraints and relationships based on economic and emotional dependency – that exists in many family settings, where it both reflects and is entrenched by wider structural inequalities (see, for example, Busch, 2002; Coker, 2002; Daly, 2002b; Stubbs, 2002). For critics of restorative justice, such concerns call into question many of the assumptions – relating to autonomy, choice and safety – that underpin a restorative justice approach. Moreover, a degree of caution tinged with scepticism extends also to many of those who are otherwise supportive of restorative justice in other settings, including a number of practitioners, policymakers and even some otherwise sympathetic researchers (see Daly, 2002b). Thus, for example, domestic violence cases involving partners are frequently excluded from the eligibility criteria of restorative justice schemes and pilot initiatives, two notable examples being the adult restorative justice pilots that are currently taking place in England and Wales and also New Zealand. This is not invariably the case, however. In the Thames Valley police-led conferencing project, for example, such cases are not categorically excluded, though Young and Hoyle (2003: 280) report that officers are 'wary' of using restorative justice in cases involving domestic violence and sexual assaults.

Within other parts of the restorative justice movement one response has been to try to rebut such criticisms, largely on the basis of philosophical and normative considerations (see, for example, Morris and Gelsthorpe, 2000; Morris, 2002). Thus, it is emphasized that restorative justice processes such as conferencing do not seek to displace criminal procedures but rather to supplement them by exploiting the potential for the offender's family and friends to act as powerful denunciatory agents. The potentially empowering opportunity for the victim to present her own story in a form that the offender will find it difficult to ignore, and to have it validated by others present at the conference, is also stressed. Braithwaite and Daly (1994), in an early contribution to the debate, suggested how a restorative justice approach might be integrated within the conventional criminal justice system whereby formal criminal justice measures would only be brought into play when restorative justice measures had failed to have the desired effect. Although various attempts have been made to put restorative justice principles into practice within a domestic violence context, robust and reliable empirical evidence is still a relatively rare commodity amid the welter of claims and counterclaims. So it is difficult to reach any firm conclusions in the current state of knowledge. In the meantime, Pennell and Burford's study of a family group decision-making project in Newfoundland and Labrador is one of the few evaluations to offer some reasonably sound, though still limited, empirical support for the claims advanced by proponents (Pennell and Burford, 1997, 2000, 2002). They found that in cases involving an FGCtype response to domestic violence there was a 33 per cent *decrease* in the level of demand made by families on support from police and social services, compared with a 43 *increase* in demand in the control group using a normal police response.[22]

'Generic' or 'representative' victims

A second category of vulnerable victims that is potentially problematic within a restorative justice context consists of those who are victimized not because they are known to the offender, or randomly and for opportunistic reasons, but because they belong to or represent groups towards whom the offender harbours feelings of resentment and hatred. So-called 'hate' crimes of this kind may consist of a variety of offences. They range from the most serious forms of violence to the issuing of threats, vandalism or the daubing of offensive graffiti directed against particular groups in the community, whether defined on the basis of race, gender, age, religion or sexual predilection. As such, they often involve harm that is directed against a specific individual, but may also involve (and be intended to involve) what Young (2000: 234) refers to as 'second-order harm' against other members of that particular grouping by deliberately undermining their sense of security.[23] Hate crimes have proved problematic within a conventional criminal justice context, in part because of a reluctance or inability on the part of the police even to acknowledge or record such incidents, much less successfully prosecute the perpetrators (Knight and Chouhan, 2002).

It is unusual for hate crimes to be specifically referred to in restorative justice writing, but Barbara Hudson (2003: 183; see also Kelly, 2002), who is one of the few to do so, points out that 'with racial as well as with gendered crime, conferencing or similar procedures can force the offender to see the victim as a "real" person, with qualities, commitments and emotion other than those attributed to him by the offender through stereotype or fantasy'. This may well be the case, but we cannot be sure that they will have this effect, particularly if the procedure involves some form of conferencing to which the offender is entitled to bring along family or supporters. For there is an obvious risk that they may share the same stereotypes or fantasies with regard to the victim. Indeed, it is not difficult to imagine that for some forms of hate crime – for example, violence directed at those suspected of being paedophiles – the same stereotypes or fantasies might be prevalent or even overwhelmingly predominant within particular local communities. The significance of this example is that it calls into question an assumption commonly made by restorative justice advocates regarding the existence of 'a powerful consensus in modern industrial societies over the rightness of criminal laws which protect our persons and properties' (Braithwaite, 1989: 13). Thus, it cannot simply be assumed that the kind of benign, tolerant, 'republican virtues' that Braithwaite favours (Braithwaite and Pettit, 1990) will necessarily be supported or respected within the real-life communities in which restorative justice processes may come to be introduced.[24] While this remains the case, hate crimes are potentially likely to prove no less problematic for restorative justice approaches – particularly those involving conferencing – than for conventional criminal justice approaches. If such procedures were to be adopted with regard to hate crimes it would be particularly important to retain some form of judicial oversight combined with the power to review outcomes that could be seen as excessively lenient from the perspective of the hate crime victim.[25]

Secondary and indirect victims

Secondary or indirect victims are not very well catered for in general by the conventional criminal justice system, as we saw in Chapter 3. If acknowledged as victims at all, their only involvement in a case is likely to be if they are summoned to act as witnesses. Certain forms of restorative justice, including victim–offender mediation, would appear to be equally incapable of accommodating the interests of secondary victims (see Braithwaite and Daly, 1994: 206; Dignan and Cavadino, 1996: 169). In the case of family group conferencing participation is restricted, as we have seen, to the victims' and offenders' communities of care. This makes it possible to address some of the 'collateral harm'[26] that may have been caused by an offence, but only where the harm is sustained by those who fall within the respective communities of care (Young, 2000: 237).

With other restorative justice processes, however, there is – at least in principle – greater scope for certain forms of indirect or second-order harm to be acknowledged and addressed. In the case of police-led conferencing, for example, Young correctly points out that there is no reason in principle why facilitators should not identify and involve[27] other victims who do not stand in such 'caring' relationships with the primary victim (or offender). Indeed, he suggests that only by adopting such a 'multi-victim perspective' will the cautioning process have the potential to be restorative and reintegrative in all cases, including those in which there may not be a primary individual victim, or there is such a victim but the latter does not wish to participate. The evaluation of the Thames Valley restorative cautioning initiative suggested that facilitators did routinely refer to the kind of second-order harm associated with more indirect forms of victimization; but that this was more likely to happen in cases that did not involve an identifiable victim (Young, 2000: 238). The inclusion of a multi-victim perspective does of course raise a number of difficult questions, as Young himself acknowledges. They include the extent of the offender's responsibility to provide reparation, the entitlement (if any) of secondary victims to such reparation, and also the prioritization of victims' claims for reparation where different categories of victim are involved. These are questions to which we will return in the final section of this chapter.

Victims of corporate and state wrongdoing

It is sometimes suggested[28] that restorative justice 'is not readily suited' to certain types of crime including, for example, regulatory offences or other forms of corporate wrongdoing.[29] This is far from being the case, however, since, as Bottoms (2003: 108) has also noted, John Braithwaite has done more than any other restorative justice writer to highlight the potential value of restorative justice mechanisms in dealing with such offences in contemporary societies (see, for example, Braithwaite, 1985, 1999, 2002, 2003; see also Ayres and Braithwaite, 1992; Fisse and Braithwaite, 1993).

Braithwaite (2003: 161) himself has observed that in his experience 'some of the most moving and effective restorative justice conferences ... have been business regulatory conferences, especially following nursing home inspections in the US and Australia'. Moreover, this is one aspect of restorative justice practice that is supported by sound empirical evidence, much of it obtained in a variety of regulatory settings by Braithwaite and others working with him. Contexts in which restorative justice mechanisms – including the use of reintegrative shaming techniques – have been shown to work effectively include the enforcement of trade practices in the interests of consumer protection and also with regard to diverse sets of regulatory regimes. They include those governing nursing homes, the coal industry, insurance industry and even the nuclear industry (Rees, 1994).

As always, such findings need to be interpreted with caution, particularly from within a victim perspective since not all the restorative justice mechanisms referred to in the literature systematically seek to involve victims and address their needs, though some do.[30] It is also possible that some of them may be vulnerable to Daly's 'Nirvana story' critique, particularly where they rely heavily on qualitative data and case study illustrations as opposed to more rigorous experimental methods that set out systematically to compare 'restorative' and 'non-restorative' approaches from a specifically victim-centred approach. Nevertheless, one very strong argument in support of restorative justice in this particular context is that it potentially offers a more constructive and socially inclusive way of dealing with a group of victims whose interests have in the past been grievously neglected by the conventional criminal justice system (see Chapter 1). Indeed, if the same socially inclusive approach were to be made more widely available for the victims of *both* predatory *and* regulatory offences, this would help to address the concerns of critics who have long argued that their differential treatment is both illogical and indefensible (see, for example, Sanders and Young 2000: 364–77; Sanders, 2002).

With regard to state-sponsored wrongdoing, the challenges facing both restorative justice and conventional criminal justice approaches are infinitely more taxing. Nevertheless, there is evidence from the post-apartheid experience in South Africa that, at least in some circumstances, restorative justice mechanisms such as the Truth and Reconciliation Commission can form the basis of a socially inclusive approach that offers a constructive way of responding to even deep-seated intercommunal conflict.[31]

'Culpable' victims

According to the 'ideal victim' stereotype that we examined in Chapter 1, victims are generally seen as utterly blameless and offenders as entirely culpable. The reason for this is that the criminal justice system is predicated on a highly dichotomous view of the world and is reluctant to investigate too closely the process of social construction giving rise to these categories.[32] This sharply polarized perspective often fails to reflect the much more nuanced morality of many victim–offender encounters in the real world, where it is often a matter of chance who is charged as 'the assailant', and whose testimony will be sought as 'the victim'. This is particularly true, as we saw in Chapter 1, of violent offences involving young men, especially where drink is involved.

On the face of it, restorative justice processes would appear to provide a far more nuanced approach in such cases. They are likely to be less hamstrung, for example, by concepts of 'legal relevance', which may act as a filter on the admissibility of any evidence that does not have a direct bearing on the issue of whether or not the defendant is guilty as charged. Thus, one apparent advantage is that such processes potentially 'leave open multiple interpretations of responsibility while refusing to allow the offender to deny personal responsibility entirely' (Braithwaite and Mugford, 1994: 146). In practice, however, the scope for adopting a more nuanced approach may be somewhat limited, particularly with regard to restorative justice processes that are closely tied to the criminal justice system.

Richard Young (2000: 244) provides a good example of both the potential advantages and the practical limitations of a restorative justice approach in the context of an offence that was dealt with by the Thames Valley police-led cautioning initiative. The episode that gave rise to the offence, which involved an assault by a 50-year-old man on his neighbour, clearly called into question the very labels 'victim' and 'offender' and the appositeness of their application with regard to this particular case. The offence took place after the 'victim', who had a violent disposition and was in the habit of driving dangerously on the narrow roads of the estate where he lived, had forced off the road a car driven by the offender's son. The 'offender' had gone to the victim's house to remonstrate with him and was punched three times before returning a blow and, after a brief struggle, walking away. The offender's wife at that point shouted out that the trouble had arisen because of the victim's dangerous driving, only to be told that she should stand in the road next time 'so I can kill you'. This so enraged the offender that he chased the victim and landed two more punches before being pulled away by his wife, who was also assaulted by the victim in the process. The offender then called the police and confessed to having 'just slapped a neighbour', while 'the victim' lost consciousness for over an hour and required hospital treatment.

Young describes how the offender and his wife were the only ones to attend the cautioning session. When asked who had been harmed by the incident, both refused to accept that the victim, whom they maintained had instigated the matter, had been harmed in any way. Young also speaks approvingly of the way the facilitator dealt with the matter. Instead of challenging the offender's view that only he and his wife had been harmed by the incident, he suggested that the offender might have reacted inappropriately by lowering himself to the victim's level in punching him rather than telephoning the police after the initial assault. This was a suggestion to which the offender readily assented. Young cites this example as a good illustration of the way in which the facilitating officers, when faced with a 'messy' case of this kind were able, in effect, to adopt 'a multi-victim perspective' while not condoning a serious transgression on the part of the offender. There is much merit in this assessment. At the same time, however, the offender was clearly left with a (justifiable)[33] sense of injustice inasmuch as 'the victim', who was not present at the cautioning session, had escaped all formal censure. What was missing, arguably, was a 'multi-offender' perspective since it might have been better if the ostensible victim had also been summoned to the cautioning session and himself cautioned for his part in the incident.[34] Only by involving both parties in this way would it be possible for 'sanctions [to be] directed against those deserving sanctions' (Christie, 1986: 29).

More generally, it has to be acknowledged that not all restorative justice advocates consistently distance themselves from the 'ideal victim' stereo-type. There is a tendency in much restorative justice writing to assume without question that victims and offenders belong to entirely separate categories, and these assumptions are also frequently built into accounts of the way the restorative justice process operates and its presumed impact on those involved. Scheff (1998: 105), for example, in spelling out the requirements of a successful conference suggests that it involves ensuring 'that all of the shame connected with the crime is accepted by the offender ... acknowledging his or her complete responsibility for the crime'. Incidents of the kind described by Young suggest that this may not always be appropriate. Restorative justice practitioners may also be limited in the extent to which they are free to adopt a more nuanced approach, particularly where they accept referrals from criminal justice agencies. For these will normally arrive after 'responsibility' for the offence has already been assigned to, and accepted by, just one of the parties. Likewise, for their part, those who have studied restorative justice processes have rarely sought to examine the reality that lies behind the labels 'victim' and 'offender' when interviewing those who have participated in them. Moreover, we know very little about how many 'offenders' may themselves have been victimized in the past, nor how many 'victims' may have offended. Nor do we know whether such factors might have any bearing on their willingness to take part in restorative justice processes and, if they do, on the nature of their involvement.

Corporate victims

Most corporate victims clearly fall outside the conventional ideal victim stereotype since they lack many of the attributes associated with individual victims, including susceptibility to physical injury, hurt feelings and fear. There is no doubt, however, that they are both extremely numerous[35] and form a significant part of the conventional criminal justice system's case-load.[36] What is less clear is whether such cases also lend themselves to a restorative justice approach. Corporate victims are potentially problematic from a restorative justice perspective, as we shall see, and this may be one reason why they have been largely ignored in much of the restorative justice literature.

Richard Young (2002), who is one of the few people to address the issue, has suggested a number of possible reasons for this reticence.[37] First, as we have seen, there is a tendency in some restorative justice writing to conceptualize victims in terms of a conventional 'ideal victim' by representing crime as being 'primarily a violation of one individual against another' (see, for example, Wundersitz and Hetzel, 1996: 113). Second, there is an emphasis in much of the literature on the psychological or emotional benefits of restorative justice processes, particularly with regard to their 'healing' potential for victims. This may also appear to limit their applicability to more conventional forms of victimization that are directed against individual victims (Young, 2002: 135). Third, the context within which any encounter between victim and offender takes place is likely to be very different when 'the victim' is a large corporation or institution that is represented by someone appearing in an official capacity.[38] Not only are they less likely to form part of the same social/moral community,[39] but the institutional representative in such cases is also arguably more likely to be perceived as an impersonal authority figure, in much the same way as judges and magistrates. Consequently, there may well be doubts as to whether such encounters are likely to be as 'meaningful' for offenders (Blagg, 1985; Dignan, 1994: 235). It is also doubtful whether their 'reintegrative shaming' potential is as great as might be expected when personal victims are involved. Partly for that reason, one very early researcher and commentator differentiated between a 'personal reparative model' and what he called an 'institutional reparative model', which he suggested called for much more sensitive handling (Blagg, 1985: 267). Fourth, Young (2002: 149) has suggested that for some within the restorative justice movement corporate victims may often appear to be 'ideologically uncongenial', particularly where they are large and powerful and the offender is poor and weak.[40] Fifth, and finally, difficulties can also arise in determining who is best suited to represent a corporate victim in any restorative justice process, and to whom any reparation ought to be directed (see also Wasik, 1999: 470; Young, 2002: 167).

Whatever the reasons might be, corporate victims have been neglected by many restorative justice practitioners and researchers. Some restorative justice schemes have simply excluded corporate victims as a matter of policy, particularly in the past.[41] Even where they are included, it is relatively unusual within restorative justice research for the findings to differentiate between the experiences and perceptions of individual and corporate victims.[42] Although challenging and potentially problematic from a restorative justice perspective, this neglect of corporate victims is questionable for a number of reasons.

First, as Young (2002: 135) has argued, if it is conceded that restorative justice processes are *not* applicable to cases involving corporate victims, this would place a significant restriction on their scope and relevance. Second, there is no reason to suppose that restorative justice is unsuited in principle to cases involving corporate victims. After all, many of the benefits that restorative justice advocates proclaim on behalf of individual victims might also be of interest to corporate victims. They include the possibility of receiving reparation, having the opportunity to hear from the offender about how and why the offence was committed and the chance to explain the harm they may have sustained as a result. They might also be keen to participate in a process that, if it succeeds in shaming offenders reintegratively, could reduce the likelihood of future victimization, at least at the hands of this particular offender. Moreover, some corporate victims do experience vicariously, through the effects on their staff, many of the personal and emotional effects reported by individual victims, particularly in offences involving burglary or extensive property damage (Redshaw and Mawby, 1996). There is also some empirical evidence supporting the view that restorative justice may indeed be applicable to corporate victims, at least in some instances. Thus, it appears that corporate victims may be just as willing to participate in victim–offender mediation initiatives as individual victims and, if anything, may be even more willing to take part in face-to-face mediation meetings (Marshall and Merry, 1990: 108–15; Dignan, 1992: 459). In some studies they also appear to have been more satisfied with the experience than individual victims (Dignan, 1992: 461).

At the same time the involvement of corporate victims does pose some very significant challenges for restorative justice. In the context of the Thames Valley Restorative Cautioning initiative, for example, Young (2002: 154) has raised concerns regarding the motives of some corporate victims, and also the manner in which they participate in those sessions they do attend. Thus, if all they are interested in is the recovery of compensation to which they consider they are entitled, such attitudes are not consistent with the principles of restorative justice. Likewise, if they see the conference as a way of securing the permanent exclusion of offenders from their premises, they are likely to subvert rather than facilitate the practice of reintegrative shaming. Unfortunately, there is evidence that the approach of some corporate victims is indeed characterized by an 'exclusionary logic' and that this may on occasions be pursued with the active connivance of the conference facilitator (as in a case study recounted by Young, 2002: 157). Concerns were also expressed that where 'repeat' victims agree to participate in conferences, their contributions are likely to become 'increasingly formulaic and routinized', making them much less meaningful for offenders. On the other hand, there was no evidence of corporate victims seeking to use the conference as a substitute small claims court, as has happened in the Bethlehem police-led conferencing initiative in the United States (McCold and Wachtel, 1998: 37). Moreover, Young (2002: 163) also found evidence that some corporate victims did participate in conferences in ways that furthered the goal of social inclusion,[43] suggesting that the involvement of corporate victims is not intrinsically incompatible with the pursuit of restorative justice ideals. It appears that corporate victims, no less than individual victims, vary greatly with regard to their experiences when victimized, and also the responses they deem to be appropriate. So while they do undeniably pose a challenge for restorative justice, there is some evidence at least that the hurdle may not be insurmountable.

In this section we have sought to evaluate restorative justice with regard to Christie's 'ideal victim' stereotype and, as might have been anticipated, the resulting 'balance sheet' shows both debits and credits. On the debit side, we have seen that not all of those who belong to the restorative justice movement are entirely immune from the kind of assumptions that are associated with the stereotype. On the credit side, however, we have seen that some forms of restorative justice appear to provide a constructive way of addressing the interests of particular groups of victims that have been particularly badly neglected in the past: notably indirect or secondary victims and those who are victimized by corporate or state offenders. We have also noted that there are a number of 'missing entries' in the ledger, where we currently lack sufficiently reliable empirical evidence that would enable us to conclude whether restorative justice really is capable of providing an effective way of dealing with certain groups of 'non-standard' victims. This is particularly true of victims of domestic violence; but the same could also be said of other categories including 'generic' victims, victims who may share a degree of culpability and also corporate victims.[44] On balance, however, while accepting that restorative justice approaches are by no means problem-free, they do in principle appear to be broadly compatible with a way of reconceptualizing victims that is more in line with complex social realities than the thoroughly discredited ideal victim stereotype.

Striking the right balance or lacking checks and balances?

In this final section we will consider one remaining contention, which relates to restorative justice's ambitious claim that it is capable of providing an appropriate balance between the various sets of interests that are in play in the aftermath of various forms of culpable wrongdoing. As we saw in the previous section, one of the merits of a restorative justice approach is that it can be consistent with a radical broadening of the category of 'victims' whose interests need to be addressed. Broadening the concept of victims in this way could in turn help to eliminate some of the arbitrary divisions that have been insisted upon in the past, according to which only certain narrowly defined categories of victims are officially recognized and deemed worthy of assistance in various ways. At the same time, it has to be conceded that the adoption of a restorative justice approach, whatever form this may take, could undoubtedly give rise to a number of difficult conflicts of interest, and it is to these that we must now turn. In this section we will focus mainly on the following three potentially conflicting sets of interests: those of victims and of offenders; those of victims (or offenders) as opposed to those of the wider community; those of the state as opposed to the interests of 'civil society'.

Competing interests: victims and offenders

One of the principal attractions of restorative justice is its claim to be capable of delivering a more even-handed form of justice, in which an appropriate balance is struck between the competing interests of victims and offenders (Dignan, 1992: 456, 1994: 235). However, it is important to acknowledge that these interests are likely to be in contention in most cases, and thus it is essential for restorative justice advocates to be able to show how the tension between them might be resolved. The three main sets of issues around which the interests of victims and offenders are likely to come into conflict relate to the criteria for selection and referral to restorative justice processes; the type and intensity of any response to an offence; and what should happen in cases that are not dealt with by means of a restorative justice approach. Regrettably, however, such matters have rarely been given the attention they deserve within the restorative justice literature.

Elsewhere Michael Cavadino and I have argued that all these issues are capable of being resolved in a principled way by applying a rights-based approach that acknowledges the rights of both victims and offenders and, more importantly, specifies what should happen in cases where their rights are in conflict (Cavadino and Dignan, 1996; see also Dignan, 2003).[45] One of the strongest arguments in favour of such an approach is that it is capable of striking a fairer balance between the interests of victims, offenders and ordinary members of the community – who are also potential victims – than is currently achieved under the conventional model of criminal justice.

Michael Cavadino and I have argued that one of the most important human rights is the equal right of individuals to maximum 'positive freedom',[46] by which we mean their ability to make effective choices about their lives (Cavadino and Dignan, 1996: 245). Rights theory allows for a person's rights (including even the right to positive freedom) to be restricted in certain circumstances, but only where the restriction is justified on the basis of another person's 'competing rights' (Dworkin, 1978).

This provides a prima facie moral justification for two different types of response to a given offence. First, if the offence has resulted in harm to a victim, that person is likely to have experienced some reduction in positive freedom to function free from physical or psychological pain or disability, or to choose how to use or dispose of their resources. It is this 'special harm' that entitles victims to reparation at the hands of their offenders, even though *their* positive freedom may be diminished thereby.[47]

Rights theory thus provides a principled justification for restorative justice processes that provide an appropriate forum in which victims[48] and offenders may deliberate about the offence and its consequences, including the type and amount of reparation to which a victim may be entitled. Moreover, if victims are to be treated with *equal* concern and respect, which is also in line with a rights-based approach (Dworkin, 1978), then their entitlement to seek and receive reparation from an offender should apply irrespective of the type or seriousness of the offence in question. Thus, under an even-handed model of restorative justice victim concerns should be given as much weight as offender concerns. Consequently, cases should be selected for referral whenever it appears likely that victims might benefit from such an approach, rather than when they happen to fit a predetermined schedule of 'appropriate' offences (see also Dignan, 1994: 235). It follows that there is no reason in principle why *any* offence (including, for example, domestic violence, or those associated with hate crimes) should be excluded from eligibility *provided* that victims feel they would benefit from such an approach.

One of the most effective ways of restoring the victim's sense of autonomy – of *re-empowering* the victim – is by inviting him or her to participate in determining ways in which the upset and any material loss might be made good. Indeed, under the competing rights principle, the victim's entitlement to reparation should prevail even if a convicted offender is unwilling to participate in a restorative justice process or to acknowledge the victim's entitlement to reasonable reparation.[49] This does not mean, however, that whatever the victim says or desires goes; for offenders also have rights, as explained below. In particular, the assertion of a right for victims to participate in the offence resolution process does not entitle the victim to have any special say in matters that go beyond the question of reparation.[50] Consequently, practices such as victim allocution or victim impact statements that go beyond the provision of basic factual information about the effects of an offence (see Chapter 3) would not be justified under a rights-based approach.

So far we have been considering the first of two types of response to any given offence that can be justified on the basis of rights theory; one that is specifically victim focused since it is restricted to the issue of reparation. Now we must turn to the second type of response, which is also relevant from a restorative justice perspective, though it is one in respect of which victims do not have a 'competing right' that entitles them to special consideration. Where it can plausibly be argued that restricting the positive rights of an offender may reduce the likelihood of reoffending, which could thereby prevent the diminution of other people's positive freedom in the future, this may provide a second independent justification for taking such action. As we have seen, certain types of restorative justice processes such as conferencing and community reparation boards provide a forum in which those with a legitimate interest can agree to constructive action that may help to integrate or reintegrate the offender back into the community of law-abiding citizens rather than excluding them.[51]

Under an even-handed approach, however, none of the parties whose interests are represented in restorative justice processes should be allowed to ride roughshod over the interests of offenders, since they also have rights that need to be protected. Consequently, both the pursuit of appropriate reparation and the pursuit of constructive reintegrative action to be taken by the offender need to be subjected to appropriate safeguards. Thus, although offenders are liable to forfeit certain of their rights because they have infringed the rights of others, they should not be subjected to disproportionately harsh outcomes, and safeguards are required to ensure that this is the case. Under a rights-based approach such as the one that Michael Cavadino and I have advocated, the overall response to an offence (taking into account both reparation for the victim and any additional reintegrative action) should take into account the moral gravity of an offence. The latter prescribes an upper limit[52] for the response to an offence, taken as a whole. Where that upper limit should be set is another issue that restorative justice advocates need to be able to respond to, though few have attempted to do so.[53] But this also raises an equally important question about what should happen in cases that are not dealt with by means of a restorative justice approach, and whether the same limiting principles should be applied in respect of both restorative and conventional criminal justice processes. There is a strong case for saying that they should, since offenders as well as victims are entitled to be treated with equal concern and respect.

On what basis, then, should the upper limits be determined? If the punishment practices associated with our conventional criminal justice system are assessed from a rights-based standpoint, then offenders have a right not to have their freedom gratuitously diminished to a greater degree than is required in order to reduce levels of reoffending. Judged against this standard, it is difficult to resist the conclusion that current punishment levels (particularly with regard to the use of imprisonment) are scandalously excessive (Cavadino and Dignan, 2002: 57). Thus, if these levels were to be adopted when determining where the limits on excessive outcomes should be set for both restorative justice and criminal justice processes, it is clear that they would not provide an adequate safeguard for offenders, however they are dealt with. Moreover a further problem arises if restorative justice processes are authorized in respect of certain types of cases[54] but not others. For this would result in offenders (and victims) being dealt with in one of two fundamentally different ways: the first based on a participatory procedure that is designed to facilitate constructive inclusionary outcomes; the second based on a non-participatory procedure that is likely to result in the imposition of exclusionary and excessively punitive outcomes.

Consequently, if offenders are to be afforded adequate safeguards against excessive levels of intervention regardless of the way their case is dealt with, this is unlikely to happen if the punishment practices of the conventional criminal justice system are adopted as the yardstick (see also Ashworth, 2002: 589). An alternative strategy, which would be much more consistent with the rights-based approach I have outlined above, would be to recalibrate the upper limits or gravity scales in accordance with restorative rather than retributive precepts and to apply these across the board, whether a case is dealt with according to restorative justice or criminal justice processes.[55]

Under such a system, the victim's entitlement to appropriate reparation from the offender, if desired, would need to be acknowledged in all cases, and whatever procedure is adopted. Moreover, victims and offenders should be offered an opportunity to participate in a restorative justice process that would enable them to determine what form this reparation should take, irrespective of the nature of the case and regardless of its seriousness. Provided this is done voluntarily and on a fully informed basis, the restorative justice goal of empowering the parties to participate actively in the offence resolution process is not compatible with the principle of strict proportionality (Cavadino and Dignan, 1996: 247). Consequently, parties should normally be free to determine for themselves what is appropriate, taking into account the offender's culpability,[56] the financial circumstances of the offender,[57] and subject to the need to avoid disproportionately harsh outcomes.

Offenders who take part in restorative justice processes may also agree to take part in some form of constructive intervention which is designed to reduce the likelihood of reoffending in a way that is inclusionary rather than exclusionary. Where this is the case, however, it is likely to entail a restriction on the offender's positive freedom that goes beyond the provision of reparation to which a victim is entitled under the competing rights principle. Accordingly, there is a greater need in such cases to ensure that any obligations that are undertaken by an offender do not constitute a disproportionate response taking into account the seriousness of the initial offence. Even where cases are diverted from the criminal justice system, therefore, it is desirable for the final say to rest with either the prosecutor or the court, in order to safeguard the interests of the parties themselves and also the wider public interest.

What about cases that cannot be satisfactorily dealt with solely on the basis of a restorative justice approach?[58] Under an even-handed approach it would be appropriate to require courts, wherever possible, to impose restorative interventions, both in order to satisfy the victim's entitlement to reparation (where desired) and also to promote greater consistency in the way offenders are dealt with. Indeed, in the overwhelming majority of cases where the offender does not pose a threat to the personal safety of others there is a strong case for restricting the sentencing powers of the court to reparative measures or to constructive community-based measures that are designed to prevent reoffending.[59] It would also be important to require courts, when imposing such restorative interventions, to take into account and make due allowance for any reparation or amends that an offender might already have undertaken or agreed to undertake in connection with a prior restorative justice process. Under such a system the use of custody would be strictly reserved for offenders who pose a serious and continuing threat to the personal safety of others (Dignan, 2003: 151).[60]

Even in cases such as these there could still be scope for restorative justice processes to be invoked, either at the behest of a victim if they felt it could be beneficial, or more routinely as part of the resettlement process prior to release. Conferencing, for example, could be used as a means of building or reforging links between an offender and families, friends or associates in the community to which they are likely to be released.[61]

One of the strongest arguments in support of a restorative justice approach is that it seeks to address the legitimate interests of victims without, at the same time, fuelling the demand for ever more repressive and exclusionary measures to be applied to offenders. This is a worthwhile short-term goal in its own right. As I have tried to show, however, it might also be possible for restorative justice to furnish the kind of 'replacement discourse' concerning the purpose and practice of punishment that some penal reformers have called for (see, for example, Ashworth, 1997), but which has so far proved all too elusive. If so, restorative justice could have the potential to contribute to a longer term reformation of the existing criminal justice and penal systems – in the interests of both victims and offenders – that many advocates of penal reform would consider desirable irrespective of its capacity to reduce levels of reoffending.

Competing interests: victims, offenders and 'the community'

The need to strike an appropriate balance between the interests of victims and offenders is not the only challenge that restorative justice advocates need to address. Indeed, those forms of restorative justice (such as victim–offender mediation) that concentrate exclusively on achieving such a balance have been criticized for failing to acknowledge that most serious offences have broader social consequences which transcend the personal harm or loss experienced by the direct victim (see, for example, Dignan and Cavadino, 1996: 160). Most other forms of restorative justice that we have been examining do acknowledge the need to address a wider set of interests, including those of 'the community'. Beyond that, as we have seen, there is no unanimity with regard to the way 'community' is defined or the role that is accorded to it in restorative justice processes. But once it is accepted that restorative justice processes should also address the interests of 'the community', this introduces two new potential sets of tensions. The first arises where the interests of victims and those of the community come into conflict; the second arises where the interests of offenders may come into conflict with those of the community.

Even where the term 'community' is defined in its most restrictive sense by limiting it to the 'offence community' or 'communities of care',[62] there may be tension between the views of the primary victim and those of the victim's carers and supporter(s) as to how a given offence should be resolved. Where the term is defined more broadly as encompassing the interests of secondary, indirect or even generic victims,[63] it raises the additional possibility of competing claims involving different categories of victims. Given the limited means of most offenders, it poses difficult questions about the basis on which they should be ranked and the 'weight' that should be assigned to them. It is also possible for the term to be conceptualized more broadly still, by including members of a geographical locality who have no direct interest in either the offence or its principal protagonists. Where this is the case it can also give rise to tensions between the priority that is accorded to victim participation as opposed to community involvement (as we saw in Chapter 5). Finally, in cases where 'the community' itself is conceptualized as the primary victim,[64] this raises additional questions relating to the type and amount of any reparation that might be appropriate.

If restorative justice is to make good its claim to strike an appropriate balance between the various sets of interests that are in play in the aftermath of an offence, it has to be capable of resolving – both in principle and in practice – the tensions outlined above; and also those that arise when the interests of offenders come into conflict with those of 'the community'.

The first set of tensions results from the introduction of a 'multi-victim perspective' as part of a restorative justice process. In principle at least, the rights-based approach outlined in the previous section should be capable of resolving many of the more obvious tensions. Where there are different categories of victims, for example, Richard Young (2000: 238) has argued that the claims of any primary victim(s)[65] should take precedence over all other claims, and this would certainly be consistent with a rights-based approach. For their rights alone are likely to have been directly infringed, resulting in personal harm or loss of a kind that is not experienced by other types of victims (Watson et al., 1989: 219). Consequently, only the primary victim(s) should be entitled to material reparation (if desired) from an offender, though all victims[66] might have an interest in symbolic reparation. The latter might include an acknowledgement of the hurt, alarm or offence that an offender has caused, possibly in combination with an apology or an undertaking to take appropriate steps to reduce the likelihood of any further offence in the future. By restricting the claims of non-primary victims to symbolic reparation in this way, the risk of imposing disproportionately harsh outcomes on offenders should also be reduced. In practice, very few restorative justice researchers have attempted to investigate the way in which the potentially conflicting interests of different categories of victims have been handled by the restorative justice processes they have studied. One of the few to have done so is Richard Young (2000) himself, as part of the Thames Valley Restorative Cautioning evaluation project. While acknowledging the risk that the adoption of a multi-victim perspective could result in a diminution of the primary victim's 'special status', there was no evidence that this had happened in the cautioning sessions he observed. Conversely, however, there was a tendency for the more indirect forms of victimization (those extending beyond the victims' and offenders' 'communities of care') to be overlooked in offences that involved a primary victim (Young, 2000: 238).

The second set of tensions that needs to be addressed relates to the potential for conflict between the interests of victims (of whatever category) and those of 'the community'. The potential for such conflict has already been noted. For, as we saw in Chapter 5, there is a risk that certain forms of restorative justice processes – notably those that seek to involve 'ordinary' members of the community in the decision-making process – may prioritize this goal over that of encouraging participation by victims themselves. Community reparation boards and citizen panels are particularly vulnerable to such charges, and concerns have been raised in connection with both the Vermont Reparation Board and English Youth Offender Panels that the interests of victims are liable in practice to be subordinated beneath the goal of community empowerment. This is likely to be a particular problem where restorative justice reforms which are intended to benefit victims are introduced on a piecemeal basis in the context of a criminal justice system that is reluctant to embrace them wholeheartedly. Recent reforms in England and Wales, for example, have had to compete with potentially conflicting objectives such as speeding up the criminal justice process. Moreover, the goal of promoting restorative justice approaches has been subordinated to the overriding aim of reducing offending behaviour. So it is perhaps not surprising that their beneficial impact on victims has for the most part been somewhat marginal. This is not an inevitable outcome, but it does call for vigilance on the part of those who support restorative justice as a means of empowering victims.

The third set of tensions that needs to be addressed relates to the potential for conflict between the interests of the 'wider community' and those of offenders. The need for effective legal safeguards to protect offenders from possible abuse by community-based restorative justice processes has already been mentioned in the discussion on hate crimes above. Another potential source of conflict arises where the only (or main) direct victim is 'the community' itself. Should the community be entitled to reparation from the offender and, if so, what form should this take and to what proportionality limits if any should it be subject? At first glance it might seem inappropriate to equate the 'loss' to the community with that suffered by an individual offender. But although any such loss might seem more affordable, it could still 'hurt' and upset any users of the facilities that are damaged, and may deprive them of their ability to use and enjoy them. In principle, therefore, an even-handed, rights-based approach would acknowledge the community's entitlement to reparation from an offender in such cases. This could be either symbolic (in the form of an acknowledgement of the wrongfulness of the act, or an apology) or material in the form of community reparation or community service. Any material reparation would need to be subject to upper limits (taking into account the financial circumstances of the offender and also the seriousness of the offence), as in the case of individual victims (see previous section). There may also be a case for scaling back the upper limits where the community is the victim in recognition of the fact that the material loss will almost certainly be more sustainable. But, as in the case of individual victims, the goal of empowering the parties to determine for themselves within these parameters[67] the type and amount of reparation that is appropriate is not compatible with the principle of strict proportionality that is favoured by just deserts theorists (see, for example, Ashworth, 2002: 583).

The potential for conflict between the interests of offenders and those of the wider community may go beyond the issue of reparation, however. Where restorative justice processes are used for more serious offences, for example, many within the restorative justice movement would acknowledge that there is also a need to address the wider community interest, and not just that of the victim. This could involve the imposition of coercive measures upon offenders to prevent further offending and, as Ashworth (2000: 196) has argued, this does oblige restorative justice advocates to give principled consideration to the need for limits on the ensuing burdens. I have set out the basis on which this might be done[68] in the previous section and will not, therefore, rehearse those arguments again here.

Competing interests: state and civil society

As Adam Crawford (2000: 304) has observed, implicit in much restorative justice writing is a call for a re-evaluation of the responsibilities that are attributed to government, communities and individuals when it comes to responding to victimization and the harms caused by crime. Much of the restorative justice literature, as we have seen, also reflects a pronounced anti-statist ethos, and this raises important questions about the 'balance' that needs to be struck between the responsibilities of the state and those of individuals, communities and 'civil society' at large. There would clearly be dangers in pressing the 'anti-statist' argument too far, particularly if it resulted in a 'privatization of criminal justice' whereby the state was permitted to abdicate its responsibilities towards victims (and also towards vulnerable offenders) by shifting the entire burden onto individuals and communities instead. It is especially important to remember the limits of restorative justice with regard to victims that were outlined earlier in this chapter and to acknowledge the importance of and continuing need for other (state-sponsored) victim-focused reforms such as criminal injuries compensation and victim support.

At the same time it is also important to appreciate the limits of the criminal justice system as a means of combating crime and promoting security whether this is attempted by means of conventional 'retributive' responses or those associated with restorative justice approaches. This is partly because so few offences result in a criminal conviction, but also because criminal justice interventions of whatever kind, and however holistic or restorative they may be, are unlikely to be able to address the complex social, economic and cultural factors that chiefly influence crime rates (Roach, 2000; Dignan, 2001: 344). One of the main attractions of a restorative justice approach, however, as I argued in an earlier section, is that it could help to mobilize support for a more modest and realistic criminal justice agenda: one that rescues victims from neglect without turning them into instruments of vengeance.

In arguing that restorative justice could have the potential to bring about a longer term transformative effect on the criminal justice system by helping to promote inclusionary reforms and counter exclusionary tendencies, it is important not to overstate the consequences of such a shift. Although it could have a profound effect in countering some of the worst excesses of the criminal justice system, this would not in itself have any transformative effect on civil society at large, which would continue to be wracked by much injustice that could in turn have direct criminogenic consequences (see Braithwaite, 1991a, 1991b; Dignan, 2001). Just as restorative justice could provide a catalyst for a more progressive criminal justice reform programme, however, many of the insights that are associated with such an approach could also help to inform a more progressive and proactive social policy agenda founded on principles of social *inclusion* rather than *exclusion*. If such an agenda were to be vigorously pursued within the spheres of child care, economic, educational, employment, housing, regulatory, social and welfare policies, this could arguably form the basis of a far more effective crime prevention strategy than one that is founded on a reactive criminal justice approach. If such a strategy were to be adopted it would be unrealistic in the extreme to imagine that it would bring about a society that was free of crime. But it is more plausible to suppose that such an approach could help significantly to reduce the amount of collateral damage that is currently caused to offenders, society at large and, above all, victims by responding to crime in an inappropriate, frequently inhumane and all too often counter-productive manner.

Summary and final remarks

In conclusion, this book has traced various strands relating to both the 'victims' movement' and the 'restorative justice movement' in an attempt to shed new light on two complementary sets of discourses that until now have frequently failed adequately to 'engage with' one another. One key aim, set out in the Introduction, has been to articulate an analytical framework that, in the absence of a consensually acceptable definition, will hopefully bring some much needed conceptual clarity to the relationship between the various sets of recent restorative justice initiatives and a parallel series of longer established victim focused reforms that draw upon quite different philosophical foundations.

Chapter 1 sketched the growing prominence that has been accorded to victim-related issues on the part of policymakers and others, and suggested some of the reasons that lie behind this development. The concept of 'the victim' was examined in the light of the idealized imagery that is often deployed in this context, and also in terms of the available empirical data. The chapter posed a number of questions about the adequacy of conventional conceptions of crime victims, and drew attention to the challenges such questions may pose for exponents of all three victim-focused approaches that are featured in the book. The chapter also examined the process of victimization and summarized some of the main debates within the field of victimology.

It was shown in Chapter 2 that there are other ways of seeking to put right the harm caused by an offence that have little or nothing to do with the emergence of restorative justice values and practices. They include the provision of financial compensation from the state, and the tendering of information and emotional support by voluntary organizations such as Victim Support.[69] Each of these victim-focused responses shares the same 'harm redressing' goal as restorative justice and to that extent they are *compatible* with restorative justice ideals. But none of these victim assistance measures should be confused with the concept of restorative justice itself, since they lack the latter's focus on the offender's personal accountability to those who have been harmed and do not involve an inclusive decision-making process, which is why they are assigned to a separate 'welfare model' within the main analytical framework.

In Chapter 3 the spotlight was turned on the very extensive litany of victim-focused reforms that have been incorporated in recent years within the regular criminal justice process – a point often overlooked in the restorative justice literature – but at the same time the restricted nature of this 'partial enfranchisement' of victims was also emphasized. Likewise in the policy sphere, attention was drawn to the selective and frequently stereotypical assumptions that have underpinned many of the policy reforms outlined in this chapter.

Turning to the restorative justice model, one of the key aims in Chapter 4 has been to dispel the illusion that there is a single restorative justice approach with an identical set of goals, values and operating principles. This aim has been pursued in part by spelling out the different intellectual and philosophical foundations that have contributed to the various strands of the 'restorative justice movement'. Given such disparate origins, it is not surprising to find that the restorative justice model itself comprises a number of discrete practice variants, which are also compared in this chapter. Another important observation relates to the profound ambivalence with regard to victims that has characterized each of the main intellectual traditions which have contributed to the development of a reasonably coherent body of restorative justice thinking and practice. This is a point that needs to be borne in mind when assessing the research evidence relating to the various restorative justice initiatives.

Chapter 5 examines the research base for each of the main restorative justice variants from a predominantly – but not exclusively – victim-focused standpoint. The main conclusion, echoing that of other restorative justice studies, is that restorative justice approaches tend to be positively evaluated with regard to *process* issues, but with regard to *restorative outcomes* the findings are rather more equivocal. The chapter also reflects on the current state of empirical research in this field and, in particular, its somewhat narrow focus. It concludes by asking whether the kind of empirical research that has been undertaken so far is capable of satisfactorily resolving key policy questions relating to the scope for and merits of further restorative justice reforms.

Finally, Chapter 6 attempts to sketch out the parameters in terms of which a broader, more qualitative assessment of restorative justice and its strengths and weaknesses might be undertaken. Three neglected sets of issues are flagged up for consideration. The first is a plea for greater realism and openness in acknowledging the limits of restorative justice and what it might be capable of achieving for victims, however positive the empirical evidence might ultimately turn out to be. This is linked to the observation that it is equally important to acknowledge the gaps in our current research agenda, and to set about rectifying them.

The second issue takes the form of an alternative set of criteria against which the performance of restorative justice initiatives might be assessed. The key questions here relate to the way victims are conceptualized within specific restorative justice initiatives, and the relative performance of such initiatives compared with more conventional approaches when dealing with particular categories of 'non-standard' victims. With only one or two exceptions, such questions have been neglected in most contemporary evaluations of restorative justice initiatives, despite their obvious relevance from a victim-focused standpoint.

The third and final issue relates to yet another set of criteria for assessing the merits of a restorative justice approach, this time focusing on its claim to strike an appropriate balance between the various sets of interests that are in play in the aftermath of various forms of criminal wrongdoing. Questions of this kind cannot be resolved on the basis of empirical research alone, however rigorous it might profess to be in terms of its methodology, but call instead for judgements based on normative and ultimately wider political considerations. So while there is clearly a need for high quality empirical research in the field of restorative justice, it would be a mistake to assume that policy questions relating to future developments can be based solely on the answers to technocratic questions of this kind. It is just as important to address the much broader range of moral and penal policy questions without which it would be very difficult to form a balanced judgement on the overall merits or limitations of a restorative justice approach. Once again there has been a tendency for such questions to be neglected in much of the restorative justice literature, and the final chapter of this book represents an attempt to begin making good this omission.

Notes

1 Though it is worth noting that some forms of restorative justice such as community mediation or peer mediation may provide an alternative forum for dealing with 'quasi-criminal disputes' that may be unlikely to be dealt with by criminal justice procedures.

2 Factors contributing to the attrition rate include the relatively small proportion of crimes that are reported to the police (less than 50 per cent); the fact that the police record only just over half of the offences reported to them; a detection rate of only around 25 per cent; and the fact that not all detected cases are prosecuted, and not all prosecutions result in a conviction (see Home Office, 1999a for the overall attrition rate; and see Simmons and Dodd, 2003: 109 for latest detection rate figures).

3 In recent years the government has tended to refer to the 'Justice Gap' – which is the difference between the number of crimes that are recorded by the police and the number which result in their perpetrator being brought to justice (see, for example, Home Office et al., 2002c). On this measure, which eliminates two key elements in the attrition rate (see note 2, above), the 'Justice Gap' in 2000 stood at 80.2 per cent as opposed to 97 per cent.

4 Meta-analysis is a technique for recording and analysing the aggregated statistical results from a collection of discrete empirical research studies.

5 Only one study, evaluating a programme that accepted referrals at the post-sentence stage of the process, reported contrary findings.

6 Since participation in restorative justice processes is meant to be voluntary for victims, the fact that very high satisfaction ratings are obtained could in part be due to the fact that participants were predisposed in favour of restorative justice from the outset. This is much less likely to be the case when cases are assigned at random though, as we noted in Chapter 5, cases are often allocated on the basis of offender-related criteria rather than those relating to the victim.

7 A similar point has also been made by Pavlakis (2002), whose analysis I have found helpful in drafting this section.

8 See, for example, Lesley Moreland's (2001) account of her meeting with the man who killed her daughter.

9 See above Chapter 5, note 61. The pilots cover interventions operating at almost every stage of the criminal justice process from pre-prosecution to post-sentence, including offenders who are serving substantial custodial sentences. The independent evaluation being conducted by Sheffield University is due to report in 2006.

10 An even higher proportion of victims (58 per cent) indicated that they would be willing to receive some form of reparation without meeting the offender.

11 These figures are taken from Dignan (2002c). But see also Chapter 5, which refers directly to the relevant research findings.

12 Of those victims who were contacted and consulted as part of the YOT evaluation (accounting for around two-thirds of relevant cases), just under one-third (31 per cent) agreed to accept some form of direct reparation for themselves. A further 18 per cent were willing for the offender to undertake direct reparation to the community. And half (50 per cent) were not willing to consent to either form of reparation (Holdaway et al., 2001: 86).

13 The work of Richard Young (2000, 2002) is a notable exception.

14 See, for example, Barnett (1977: 288), Zehr (1990: 182), Wundersitz and Hetzel, (1996: 113), Umbreit et al. (2003). But cf. Löschnig-Gspandl (2003: 145), who suggests that from a restorative justice point of view, crime is an act 'that results in injuries to individual or corporate victims, communities and also the offender him/herself'.

15 See, for example, the claim that '*only* restorative justice meets *all* the requirements of victims' (Pollard, 2001: 1, emphasis added). Similar sentiments have been expressed by Fattah (1998: 108), who argued that 'the punishment system, as detrimental as it is to the interests of victims, will have to give way to another system in which victim needs are met and victim wishes are respected'. Cf other restorative justice advocates who have warned against seeing restorative justice as a panacea for victims (e.g. Bazemore, 1999: 315; see also Strang, 2002: 210).

16 As opposed to this decision being taken paternalistically on their behalf, which is an allegation that has been levelled at some restorative justice initiatives. See Hagley (2003), referred to in Chapter 5.

17 As Hoyle (2002: 98) points out, it may be more constructive to think of participation in terms of a continuum rather than a dichotomous all-or-nothing choice.

18 This category derives from an important distinction drawn by Hudson (2003: 179) between victims who are targeted randomly, on the basis of something other than their personal characteristics; those who are targeted as specific individuals with whom the offender has an ongoing relationship of some kind; and those who may be targeted solely because of some personal attribute (such as their race, or their status as in the case of a convicted or suspected paedophile).

19 The 'restorativeness' measure sought to capture an observer's judgement about the extent to which the conference could be said to have 'ended on a high, a positive note of repair and good will' together with a rating reflecting procedural justice criteria and co-ordinator skill in handling the conference.

20 Although most victims of domestic violence are women, and most aggressors are men, Grady (2002) is right to warn of the risks of stereotyping in this context since male victimization does also undoubtedly occur, even though it is likely to be much less visible.

21 Morley and Mullender (1994), for example, estimated that on average a victim was assaulted 35 times before summoning the police.

22 This finding was also reported in the government's restorative justice strategy document (Home Office et al., 2003: 17), which noted that a similar initiative known as the Dove Project has been set up in Hampshire, where it is being evaluated by researchers at Portsmouth University.

23 Although conventional offences may also undermine the sense of security of others in the community, this wider effect is usually incidental rather than something that is intended by the offender.

24 See also Johnstone (2002: 57), who raises a similar objection in the context of domestic violence and sexual assaults. In some communities it is possible to imagine that other forms of violence – for example, violence directed against asylum seekers – might be far from universally condemned.

25 Or excessively punitive in respect of offenders who happen to belong to a group that is viewed with intolerance within a particular local community.

26 Braithwaite and Mugford (1994: 144–5) also make use of the term 'collateral damage'.

27 They could either be invited to attend in their own right, or to relay their views and concerns via the facilitator.

28 See, for example, Miers (2001: 87); also Pavlakis (2002: 50). Pavlakis has suggested that this is because the restorative justice paradigm is founded on the conception of crime as a conflict between individuals, so that in the absence of a single identifiable and culpable offender it is not possible to fully address the emotional and psychological needs of victims.

29 A category that includes crimes against persons that may result in injury or death, but also economic crimes including bribery, money laundering, price fixing, bankruptcy offences, production and sale of unsafe products, misrepresentations in advertising and also environmental offences (see Löschnig-Gspandl, 2003: 147).

30 For example with regard to nursing home regulation and also the enforcement of trade practices in the interests of consumer protection. Others appear to rely more heavily on didactic forms of compliance-based negotiation with offenders, in which victims may not be invited to participate.

31 See, for example, the final report of the Truth and Reconciliation Commission at www.gov.za/reports/2003/trc/ (see also Huyse, 1998; Tutu, 1999; Dignan with Lowey, 2000: 12).

32 The nearest it comes to this is by allowing 'defences' such as that of 'provocation' or 'self-defence', though the effect of such defences, if successfully established, is to exculpate the alleged 'offender' without, normally, incriminating 'the victim' or acknowledging the possibility that both parties may be culpable to some extent.

33 Since the offender's version of events appears from Young's account to have been largely corroborated by facts contained in the police file that were also available to the facilitator.

34 Involving both parties in this way would be more akin to the somewhat analogous 'community mediation' approach that was briefly described in Chapter 4. However, in cases such as these, the 'no-blame' approach that is a hallmark of community mediation – and also the assumption within both criminal and restorative justice processes that there is a single 'guilty' and a single 'innocent' party – would need to give way to an acknowledgement that there might well be 'multiple interpretations of responsibility'.

35 A Home Office survey showed that retail or manufacturing premises were six times more likely to be burgled than domestic premises and were much more likely to experience repeat victimization (Mirlees-Black and Ross, 1995: Table 6.1).

36 Official statistics do not generally differentiate between categories of victims, making it difficult to quantify the proportion of corporate victims among the caseloads of the police and courts. However, the Thames Valley restorative cautioning evaluation showed that for the kind of offences that were likely to be cautioned the proportions of corporate and individual victims were almost identical, 37 per cent in each case (Young, 2002: 143).

37 This next section draws on and develops some of the ideas contained in his very useful account.

38 There may be much less of a difference in other instances; for example where the corporate or institutional victim is a 'corner shop', and is represented by the individual proprietor whose livelihood may be more directly threatened by store thefts, etc.

39 See discussion in Chapter 4.

40 Many within the restorative justice movement are sensitive to concerns about possible power imbalances in other contexts (such as domestic violence) so this sounds plausible. Equally, there could also be a perception that some corporate victims may have contributed to their own victimization, for example, by failing to take adequate steps to prevent shop theft.

41 See Davis (1992: 29, 69). Some schemes that do so appear to have been influenced by Blagg's reasoning (see above; ibid. at pp. 29, 137).

42 Though there are exceptions. See Dignan (1990) and Marshall and Merry (1990). The RISE research did include corporate victims among those victimized by personal property offences, though the findings do not differentiate between different categories of victim.

43 See the case study recounted by Young (2002: 163). Evidence of a socially inclusionary approach was particularly notable in the contributions made the representative of a local library, which is an institution that might be expected to be more 'publicly minded'. However, similar attitudes were also reported in respect of more commercially minded organizations including, in one case, the operators of a privately owned shopping mall (Young, 2002: 162).

44 In respect of the latter category the evidence is mixed rather than absent.

45 Others have attempted to develop a similar approach in terms of a 'freedom model' (see in particular Sanders and Young, 2000; Sanders, 2002). There is much common ground between the two approaches, but when it comes to resolving competing interests, it is difficult to see how this can be satisfactorily accomplished except on the basis of the rights of the respective parties. It is interesting to note that much of the discussion in Sanders and Young's 'freedom model' is indeed also couched in the language of 'rights'.

46 This has some affinity with John Braithwaite's concept of freedom as 'non-domination', but is arguably more content specific, and therefore more capable of generating limiting principles by which it is possible to evaluate outcomes as either just or unjust. See Braithwaite and Pettit (1990).

47 Thus, to this limited extent it is justifiable, under an even-handed approach, for the victim's rights to be prioritized over the offender's because of the special harm that has been sustained by the victim with regard to this particular offence. The fact that victims and offenders in general may form overlapping rather than discrete categories does not affect this proposition, as some have argued (see, e.g. Sanders and Young, 2000: 56, ch. 12; Sanders, 2002: 210). However, the position might well be different in a specific case in which the ostensible 'victim' may also be culpable, as in the case discussed on page 174 above. Here, both parties appeared to be guilty of infringing the other party's right to positive freedom.

48 Defined broadly as all those whose entitlement to 'positive freedom' may have been diminished by an offence, so including 'generic' and other indirect or secondary victims.

49 However, the kind of reparation that an offender might be obliged to make in such a case would almost certainly be quite different from the kind of reparation that might be expected to emanate from a consensual restorative justice process. Apologies, for example, would be ruled out since a coerced apology is likely to be worth less in the eyes of a victim.

50 Ashworth's (2002: 586) objection that restorative justice approaches which allow victims to determine the outcome might infringe an offender's right to a

fair hearing by an independent and impartial tribunal has much less force where the victim's input is restricted to matters relating to reparation.

51 Once the issue of reparation has been satisfactorily addressed however, the 'competing rights' argument would not justify giving victims a determinative role in such a process any more than it would support a right of 'victim allocution'.

52 This principle is referred to in the philosophy of punishment literature as the 'retributive maximum' (see Morris, 1974: 75; Morris and Tonry, 1990).

53 Some (e.g. Wright, 1991: 15, 1996: 27; Walgrave, 1999: 146) appear to deny the need to specify limits on the grounds that restorative measures do not constitute punishment. Others have challenged this reasoning on the ground that it is philosophically untenable (see, for example, Dignan, 2003: 139).

54 Whether eligibility is determined according to type of offence, offender-related characteristics (such as age), willingness of the parties to participate, or stage in the criminal justice procedure at which the process is intended to operate.

55 Such a strategy would also address many of the concerns raised by proportionality theorists in respect of the 'default' settings that are favoured by some restorative justice writers. Braithwaite (1999: 61ff), for example, has advocated the use (or at least the threatened use) of conventional deterrent or incapacitative strategies in respect of offenders who do not respond to restorative justice processes.

56 The degree of harm that is sustained by a victim may be the same whether an offender is fully competent, drugged, drunk or insane, though an even-handed approach would require that any mitigating factors should also be taken into account.

57 Walgrave and Geudens (1997) have also proposed that the degree of restorative effort required of the offender should also be taken into account in assessing the proportionality of a response.

58 Including those where the offence is too serious, where the offender has unreasonably refused to make adequate amends, or where the offender represents a serious and continuing threat to the personal safety of others.

59 Elsewhere I have described how existing non-custodial penalties including the fine, probation, community service and even electronic monitoring could be modified in order to promote restorative outcomes wherever possible (see Dignan, 2002a: 183).

60 There may also be a case for using imprisonment as a 'default sanction', in order to secure compliance with a restorative intervention imposed by means of a non-custodial order. However, it would be important for this to be restricted to cases in which the offence itself was sufficiently serious and all appropriate non-custodial options had been tried and failed.

61 See, for example, the work of the International Centre for Prison Studies' Restorative Prison Project: www.kcl.ac.uk/depsta/rel/icps/restorative_prison.html.

62 As Morris and Maxwell (2000: 215) have argued it should be.

63 As is the case with some police-led forms of conferencing; see for example Richard Young's discussion of the scope for integrating a 'multi-victim perspective' within the context of the Thames Valley restorative cautioning initiative (Young, 2000: 238).

64 For example, in cases involving the destruction of or damage to community amenities such as public parks, buildings or recreational facilities.

65 Where there is more than one primary victim, there could still b[...]
between their respective wishes and demands, and this could be more[...]
to reconcile in practice, although in principle each should have an equal r[...]
some appropriate form of reparation from the offender.

66 Including any secondary, indirect or even 'generic' victim of an offence ([...]
above).

67 Subject also to the need for safeguards to ensure that the stronger party is not[...]
able to derive an unfair advantage from the 'power imbalance' that is likely to
prevail in such cases.

68 Using a scale that is calibrated in accordance with restorative justice precepts
rather than the predominantly retributive principles that are favoured by
proportionality theorists.

69 This is not an exhaustive list. It might also include the provision of NHS-funded
healthcare to those who have been injured by an offender.

Further reading

Cavadino, M. and Dignan, J. (1996) Reparation, retribution and rights, *International Review of Victimology*, 4: 233–53.

Crawford, A. (2000) Salient themes and the limitations of restorative justice, in A. Crawford and J. Goodey (eds) *Integrating a Victim Perspective within Criminal Justice*. Aldershot: Ashgate Dartmouth.

Hudson, B. (2004) Balancing the rights of victims and offenders, in E. Capes *Reconciling Rights in Criminal Justice: Analysing the Tension between Victims and Defendants*. London: Legal Action.

Young, R. (2000) Integrating a multi-victim perspective into criminal justice through restorative justice conferences, in A. Crawford and J. Goodey (eds) *Integrating a Victim Perspective within Criminal Justice*. Aldershot: Ashgate Dartmouth.

Young, R. (2002) Testing the limits of restorative justice: the case of corporate victims, in C. Hoyle and R. Young (eds) *New Visions of Crime Victims*. Oxford: Hart.

abolitionism. A penal reform movement that seeks to abolish all or part of the penal system, particularly its most coercive practices such as the use of capital punishment and imprisonment.

caution. A formal disposal of a criminal case, consisting of a warning that is administered to an offender in person by a senior police officer in uniform, usually in a police station. The measure is an alternative to further criminal proceedings and therefore does not involve either prosecution or the courts. Since 1998 the old-style caution system has now been replaced for offenders who are under the age of 18 by a statutory régime comprising a single reprimand, followed by a (final) warning and then a prosecution. *See also* **restorative caution** and **restorative conference.**

communitarianism. A philosophy that can be seen as a third way between extreme collectivism and extreme individualism, based on the presupposition that humans are 'social beings' who can only thrive within human communities. While they might have rights owed to them by society and the state, they in turn owe social obligations and responsibilities to uphold the common good and not merely pursue their own selfish interests. Different variants of communitarian thought range along a continuum from more liberal, individual-centred versions to more repressive authoritarian versions that favour the interests and claims of the community above, and almost to the exclusion of, those of its individual members.

communities of care. A term used by some restorative justice advocates as a means of identifying those who might be invited to participate in **restorative conferencing** processes. Communities of care have been defined as the 'group of people who are committed to care for, protect, support and encourage an individual' (Van Ness and Crocker, 2003), and are often referred to as supporters of either the victim or the offender.

compensation. Financial redress provided for victims of crime. In the UK, compensation is paid by the state-funded **Criminal Injuries Compensation Scheme** (CICS) to victims of violent crime, irrespective of whether an offender has been convicted or even detected. Alternatively, offenders who are convicted by the criminal courts may be ordered to pay compensation to their victim(s) provided they have the means to do so, irrespective of the type of offence they may have committed.

conferencing. Name given to an informal process bringing together those who have been affected in some way by an offence and who have an interest in the way it is resolved (often referred to as **stakeholders**). Several variants of conferencing can be found, the most important of which are referred to in this book as family group conferencing and police-led conferencing. The term conferencing itself is not used with any great consistency, however, even within the restorative justice literature, where it is occasionally used as a synonym for 'restorative justice' in general, thus encompassing other processes including victim–offender mediation, reparative boards, circle sentencing, etc.

controlled experiment. Research that is designed to try to hold constant conditions other than those the experiment is intended to investigate, for example, by using a process of random allocation to assign cases either to an experimental intervention or a control group. For example, offenders might be randomly assigned either to a restorative justice process or the normal criminal justice process.

corporate crime. A violation of a criminal statute by a corporate entity or, more accurately, by executives, employees or agents acting for or on behalf of the corporation, firm or other business enterprise.

Criminal Injuries Compensation Scheme (CICS). A state-funded scheme providing financial **compensation** for victims of crime that results in physical injury provided they meet the relevant eligibility criteria.

Criminal justice system. A collective term encompassing the various agencies responsible for maintaining law and order and the administration of justice, including the police, prosecuting authorities, the criminal courts and correctional agencies such as the probation service and prison system.

final warning. An alternative to prosecution for young offenders (aged 10–17), also known as a 'warning'. The final warning forms the second phase of a 'three strikes and you're out' approach, whereby young offenders may expect to receive a 'reprimand' for an initial offence followed by a single 'final warning' if they offend again. The final warning is normally accompanied by a 'rehabilitation' or 'change' programme, the content of which is determined by the local **Youth Offending Team**. It could include some form of reparation or a police-led conference. Any subsequent offence, however minor, is likely to result in a criminal charge followed by court proceedings. Where a first (or second) offence is deemed too serious for a reprimand or warning, it could result in an immediate charge.

justice model / just deserts. Doctrine and movement advocating that the *amount* of punishment imposed on an offender should be *proportionate* to the seriousness of the offence that has been committed.

mediation. An informal dispute resolution process involving the parties who are directly involved and an independent mediator who facilitates the process. Mediation is used in both civil and criminal cases and can either take the form of a direct meeting between the parties or an indirect exchange of views and opinions in which the mediator acts as a 'go-between'. The former is sometimes referred to as 'face-to-face' mediation, while the latter is also known as 'indirect mediation' or 'shuttle diplomacy'. Mediation differs from other dispute resolution processes inasmuch as the mediator has no authority to impose or recommend a solution, but merely facilitates a dialogue between the parties.

meta analysis. A technique for recording and analysing the aggregated statistical results from a collection of discrete empirical research studies.

paradigm. A general framework of knowledge comprising a coherent set of shared assumptions and understandings relating to a given natural or social phenomenon. A paradigm shift is said to occur when a fundamental change takes place with regard to the 'world view' that is encompassed by the paradigm. An example that is relevant to the subject matter of this book relates to two diametrically different 'understandings' of the concept of crime. The first sees crime as first and foremost an offence that is committed against the state, and which therefore needs to be dealt with in accordance with public interest considerations. The second sees crime as essentially a form of wrongdoing involving personal harm that is inflicted on an individual victim, who thus has an interest in how the matter is ultimately resolved.

positivism. A standpoint based on the assertion that crime, together with all other natural and social phenomena, is *caused by* factors and processes that can be discovered by means of scientific investigation involving techniques such as observation, experimentation, quantification, statistical analysis and prediction.

recidivism. The repetition of criminal behaviour, one (relatively imperfect) measure of which is the 'reconviction rate' based on the number of cautions or convictions an offender receives after a particular event or intervention.

Referral Order. A semi-mandatory penalty comprising an order that is imposed by a court on a young offender (aged 10–17) who pleads guilty and is convicted for the first time provided the offence is imprisonable and is not one for which the court considers the following disposals to be more suitable: absolute discharge, custody or a hospital order. The order consists of a referral to a **Youth Offender Panel.**

reintegrative shaming. A term coined by John Braithwaite and used to describe a process whereby an offender is shamed in the company of victims and significant others for what they have done, while treating the offender with concern and respect, the aim being to strengthen the moral bonds between the offender, the offender's family and the wider community.

reparation. A term that refers to any action that is undertaken by an offender to help put right or 'repair' the wrong they have done, thereby acknowledging the wrongfulness of their actions. Reparation can take many forms, though the two principal variants consist of 'material' and 'symbolic' reparation. 'Material reparation' can take the form of compensating the victim of the offence, or doing something else for, or on behalf of, a victim. It can also take the form of community reparation (sometimes referred to as 'payback'); for example where 'community assets' (such as a school or playing field) have been damaged, or where the victim expresses a preference for this. 'Symbolic reparation' is a term that is often used to refer to an apology or other manifestations of regret or contrition by the offender to the victim, one possible consequence of which could be to alleviate the emotional harm that the latter may have experienced.

Reparation Order. One of a number of youth justice penalties that are intended to embody restorative elements. The Reparation Order was introduced by the Crime and Disorder Act 1998 as an 'entry level' penalty for relatively minor offenders, though offenders who are convicted for the first time will now normally receive a **Referral Order**. Reparation Orders are administered by local **Youth Offending Teams** who are supposed to elicit the views of victims when advising the court regarding the possible content of a Reparation Order. Reparation may also form part of other youth justice penalties including Action Plan Orders and Supervision Orders.

restitution. Sometimes used as a synonym for compensation or reparation, but perhaps best thought of as a more specific remedy involving the return of stolen property or reimbursement of stolen money.

restorative caution. A term adopted by the police-led Thames Valley restorative justice initiative, where it is specifically applied to conferences that do not involve victims as participants (including those in which there is no identifiable victim).

restorative conference. A term adopted by the police-led Thames Valley restorative justice initiative, where it is specifically applied to conferences at which one or more victims are present.

restorative justice. A collective term that is commonly used to refer to a wide range of informal processes that seek to resolve offences by bringing together those who are considered to be the key **stakeholders**. They include victim–offender mediation, various forms of conferencing, community reparative boards and circle sentencing. There is an ongoing debate regarding the extent to which restorative justice could or should be 'mainstreamed' within the criminal justice system, either by the introduction of 'hybrid' reparative measures such as the **Reparation Order,** or by reforming the criminal justice itself in accordance with restorative justice precepts and with a view to promoting restorative outcomes.

RISE. An acronym that stands for Reintegrative Shaming Experiments that involve the use of controlled experimental techniques to investigate the effects of conferencing on different types of criminal offences in the context of a police-led conferencing scheme in Canberra.

secondary vicitimization. A term encompassing the various additional adverse material and emotional consequences that a victim may experience at the hands of all those responsible for responding to an offence.

sentencing circles. A community-based restorative justice process originating in Canada that seeks to involve and address the concerns of a wide variety of interested parties including victim(s), offender(s), their supporters, plus members of the wider community and also criminal justice officials including police, prosecutor, defence counsel, judge and court personnel. The process, which often involves ceremonial aspects, aims to produce a consensual sentencing plan that is put before the sentencing judge.

stakeholder. A term used to describe those who are considered to have a sufficiently close interest in an offence or its outcome to justify their inclusion among those who are invited to participate in the various forms of restorative justice processes that are referred to above.

stereotype. A schematic portrayal of a type of person based on a limited range of assumed attributes that may be at odds with the empirical reality.

stigmatic shaming. The shaming of an offender in a public, indelible and open-ended fashion that results in them being stigmatized as a 'bad person' and makes it harder for them to be accepted back into the community following an offence.

victim allocution. A particular form of **victim impact statement** that enables the victim at the time of sentence to express an opinion orally on what they think should happen to an offender.

victim impact statement. A written document describing the harm, loss or suffering that has been experienced by a victim as the result of an offence.

victim survey. An alternative method of measuring the volume of crime that avoids some of the known defects associated with more traditional methods based on police records and other official sources, though it can also be used to shed light on the attributes and perceptions of those victims who are targeted by the survey.

victim–offender mediation. A specific application of the general technique of **mediation** in a criminal justice context. Here, the independent mediator facilitates a dialogue or exchange of information between victim(s) and offender(s). It aims to promote a better mutual understanding by the parties of one another, and also of the offence and its consequences, to encourage offenders to assume responsibility for the harm they have caused, and to help the victim come to terms with the offence and move on.

victimology. A field of study focusing on the victims of crime, the latter's consequences for victims and the way they and others respond to it.

Victim Support. A 'not-for-profit' charitable organization that offers advice and practice assistance for crime victims to help them cope with the effects of crime, and which also seeks to influence government policy by promoting and advancing the rights and interests of victims and witnesses.

VORP. An acronym that stands for Victim Offender Reconciliation Project. These were among the earliest reparative justice initiatives, originating among the Mennonite communities in North America during the 1970s and 1980s. The goal of reconciliation, which involved bringing offenders and victims together to achieve a better mutual understanding, was pursued regardless of whether the parties knew one another at the time of the offence.

Youth Justice Board. The Youth Justice Board is a 'non-departmental public body' with strategic responsibility for the youth justice system as a whole, including extensive grant-making powers to promote the development and evaluation of new and innovative practice initiatives.

Youth Offender Panel. A forum to which offenders in receipt of a **Referral Order** are referred, comprising two trained volunteers and an advisor from the **Youth Offending Team**. The panel convenes one or more meetings, the purpose of which is to agree a programme involving **reparation** and action to tackle the causes that are thought to have caused the young person's offending behaviour.

Youth Offending Teams. Multi-agency teams (with input from police, social services, probation, local education and health authorities) that are responsible for delivering community-based interventions and supervision for young offenders.

References and Bibliography

Abel, C.F. and Marsh, F.A. (1984) *Punishment and Restitution: A Restitutionary Approach to Crime and the Criminal*. Westport VA: Greenwood Press.

Abel, R.L. (ed.) (1982) *The Politics of Informal Justice* (2 vols). New York: Academic Press.

Adler, Z. (1987) *Rape On Trial*. London: Routledge and Kegan Paul.

Ashworth, A. (1986) Punishment and compensation: victims, offenders and the state, *Oxford Journal of Legal Studies*, 6: 86–122.

Ashworth A. (1993) Victim impact statements and sentencing, [1993] *Criminal Law Review*: 498–509.

Ashworth A. (1994) *The Criminal Process: An Evaluative Study*. Oxford: Clarendon Press.

Ashworth, A. (1997) Sentenced by the media, *Criminal Justice Matters*, 29: 14–15.

Ashworth, A. (1998) *The Criminal Process: An Evaluative Study*, 2nd edn. Oxford: Oxford University Press.

Ashworth, A. (2000) Victims' rights, defendants' rights and criminal procedure, in A. Crawford and J. Goodey (eds) *Integrating a Victim Perspective within Criminal Justice*. Aldershot: Ashgate Dartmouth.

Ashworth, A. (2002) Responsibilities, rights and restorative justice, *British Journal of Criminology*, 42: 578–94.

Assembly of Manitoba Chiefs (1989) *Final Submission to the Aboriginal Justice Enquiry*. Manitoba: Department of Justice.

Association of Chief Probation Officers (ACOP) (1993) *Victim's Charter: Probation Service Responsibility for Ensuring Victim's Interests are Considered when Formulating Release Plans for Life Sentence Prisoners*. Wakefield: ACOP.

Association of Chief Probation Officers (ACOP) (1994) *Victim's Charter*. Wakefield: ACOP.

Association of Chief Probation Officers (ACOP) and Victim Support (1996) *The Release of Prisoners: Informing, Consulting and Supporting Victims*. London: ACOP.

Atiyah, P.S. (1970) *Accidents, Compensation and the Law*. London: Weidenfeld and Nicolson.

Auld, Lord Justice (2001) *Review of the Criminal Courts of England and Wales*. London: HMSO. Also available online at: www.criminal-courts-review.org.uk/auldconts.html

Ayres, I. and Braithwaite, J. (1992) *Responsive Regulation: Transcending the Deregulation Debate*. New York: Oxford University Press.

Barclay, G. (1995) *Criminal Justice System in England and Wales*, 3rd edn. London: Home Office.

Barclay, G.C., Tavares, C. and Prout, A. (1995) *Digest: Information on the Criminal Justice System in England and Wales 3*. London: Home Office Research and Statistics Department.

Barnett, R.E. (1977) 'Restitution: a new paradigm of criminal justice', *Ethics*, 87: 279–301.

Barnett, R.E. (1980) The justice of restitution, *American Journal of Jurisprudence*, 25: 117–32.

Barnett, R.E. and Hagel, J. (1977) *Assessing the Criminal: Restitution, Retribution and the Criminal Process*. Cambridge MA: Ballinger.

Barton, C. (2000) Empowerment and retribution in restorative justice, in H. Strang and J. Braithwaite (eds) *Restorative Justice: Philosophy to Practice*. Dartmouth: Ashgate.

Bazemore, G. (ed.) (1999) *Restorative Juvenile Justice: Repairing the Harm of Youth Crime*. Monsey NY: Criminal Justice Press.

Bazemore, G. and Umbreit, U. (2001) *A Comparison of Four Restorative Conferencing Models*. Available online at: www.ncjrs.org/html/ojjdp/2001 (accessed 11 Nov. 2003).

Bazemore, G. and Walgrave, L. (1999) *Restorative Juvenile Justice: Repairing the Harm of Youth Crime*. Monsey NY: Criminal Justice Press.

Beveridge, Sir W. (1942) *Social Insurance and Allied Services*, Cmd. 6404. London: HMSO.

Bianchi, H. (1994) *Justice as Sanctuary: Toward a New System of Crime Control*. Bloomington IN: Indiana University Press.

Bianchi, H. and van Swaaningen, R. (eds) (1986) *Abolitionism: Towards a Non-Repressive Approach to Crime*. Amsterdam: Free University Press.

Birch, D. (2000) The Youth Justice and Criminal Evidence Act 1999. A better deal for vulnerable witnesses? [2000] *Criminal Law Review*, 223–49.

Blagg, H. (1985) Reparation and justice for juveniles: the Corby experience, *British Journal of Criminology*, 25: 267–79.

Bottoms, A.E. (2003) Some sociological reflections on restorative justice, in A. von Hirsch, J. Roberts, A.E. Bottoms, K. Roach and M. Schiff (eds) *Restorative Justice and Penal Justice: Competing or Reconcilable Paradigms?* Oxford: Hart.

Bottoms, A.E. and Costello, A. (2001) Offenders as victims of property crimes in a deindustrialised city. Paper presented to the Annual Meeting of the European Society of Criminology, Lausanne, Switzerland.

Bottoms, A.E. and Dignan, J. (2004) Youth justice in Great Britain, in M. Tonry and A. N. Doob (eds) *Youth Crime and Youth Justice: Comparative and Cross-National Perspectives. Crime and Justice: A Review of Research, Vol. 31*. Chicago and London: University of Chicago Press.

Box, S. (1983) *Power, Crime and Mystification*. London: Routledge.

Boyack, J. (2004) Adult restorative justice in New Zealand/Aotearoa. Paper presented to the Second International Restorative Justice Conference, Winchester, 24–25 March.

Braithwaite, J. (1985) *To Punish or Persuade: Enforcement of Coal Mine Safety*. Albany: State University of New York Press.

Braithwaite, J. (1989) *Crime, Shame and Reintegration*. Cambridge: Cambridge University Press.

Braithwaite, J. (1991a) The political agenda of republican criminology. Paper presented to the British Criminology Society Conference, York, 27 July.

Braithwaite, J. (1991b) Power, poverty, white collar crime and the paradoxes of criminological theory, *Australian and New Zealand Journal of Criminology*, 24: 40–58.

Braithwaite, J. (1992) Juvenile offending: new theory and practice. Address to the National Conference on Juvenile Justice, Adelaide, Institute of Criminology, September.

Braithwaite, J. (1999) Restorative justice: Assessing optimistic and pessimistic accounts, *Crime and Justice: A Review of Research*, 25: 1–127.

Braithwaite, J. (2000) Survey article: repentance rituals and restorative justice, *Journal of Political Philosophy*, 8: 115–31.

Braithwaite, J. (2002) *Restorative Justice and Responsive Regulation*. Oxford: Oxford University Press.

Braithwaite, J. (2003) Responsive justice and corporate regulation, in E.G.M. Weitekamp and H.-J. Kerner (eds) *Restorative Justice in Context: International Practice and Directions*. Cullompton: Willan.

Braithwaite, J. and Daly, K. (1994) Masculinities, violence and communitarian control, in T. Newburn and B. Stanko (eds) *Just Boys Doing Business: Men, Masculinity and Crime*. London: Routledge.

Braithwaite, J. and Mugford, S. (1994) Conditions of successful reintegration ceremonies: dealing with juvenile offenders, *British Journal of Criminology*, 34: 139–71.

Braithwaite J. and Parker, C. (1999) Restorative justice is republican justice, in G. Bazemore and L. Walgrave (eds) *Restorative Juvenile Justice: Repairing the Harm of Youth Crime*. Monsey NY: Criminal Justice Press.

Braithwaite, J. and Pettit, P. (1990) *Not Just Deserts: A Republican Theory of Criminal Justice*. Oxford: Oxford University Press.

Braithwaite, J. and Roche, D. (2001) Responsibility and restorative justice, in G. Bazemore and M. Schiff (eds) *Restorative Community Justice: Repairing Harm and Transforming Communities*. Cincinnati OH: Anderson.

Brienen, M. and Hoegen, E. (2000) *Victims of Crime in Twenty-Two European Criminal Justice Systems*. Nijmegen: Wolf Legal Productions.

Briere, J. (1984) The long term effects of child sexual abuse: defining a post-sexual abuse syndrome. Paper presented to the Annual Meeting of the American Psychological Association, Los Angeles.

Bucke, T. (1995) *Policing and the Public: Findings from the 1994 British Crime Survey*. Home Office Research Findings no. 28. London: Home Office.

Burgess, A. (1975) Family reactions to homicide, *American Journal of Ortho-Psychiatry*, 45(3): 391–8.

Burgess, A. and Holmstrom, I. (1974a) Rape trauma syndrome, *American Journal of Psychiatry*, 131: 981–6.

Burgess, A. and Holmstrom, I. (1974b) *Rape: Victims of Crisis*. Bowie MD: Brady.

Burgess, A. and Holmstrom, I. (1976) Coping behavior of the rape victim, *American Journal of Orthopsychiatry* 46(2): 413–17.

Burt, M. and Katz, B. (1985) Rape, burglary and robbery: responses to actual and feared victimization, with special focus on women and the elderly, *Victimology*, 10: 325–58.

Busch, R. (2002) Domestic violence and restorative justice initiatives: who pays if we get it wrong?, in H. Strang and J. Braithwaite (eds) *Restorative Justice and Family Violence*. Cambridge: Cambridge University Press.

Buzawa, E. and Buzawa, C. (1990) *Domestic Violence*. Newbury Park CA: Sage.

Canada (1997) *The Four Circles of Hollow Water*. Ottawa: Solicitor General Aboriginal Correctional Policy Unit.

Cantor, G.M. (1976) An end to crime and punishment, *The Shingle (Philadelphia Bar Association)*, 39(4): 99–114.

Capes, E. (2004a) Victims' rights and defendants' rights, *Legal Action*, April: 6.

Capes, E. (2004b) *Reconciling Rights in Criminal Justice: Analysing the Tension between Victims and Defendants*. London: Legal Action.

Cavadino, M. and Dignan, J. (1992) *The Penal System: An Introduction*. London: Sage.

Cavadino, M. and Dignan, J. (1996) Reparation, retribution and rights, *International Review of Victimology*, 4: 233–53.

Cavadino, M. and Dignan, J. (2002) *The Penal System: An Introduction*, 3rd edn. London: Sage.

Cavadino, M., Crow, I. and Dignan, J. (1999) *Criminal Justice 2000: Strategies for a New Century*. Winchester: Waterside Press.

Cavadino, M. and Dignan, J. (with others) (2005 forthcoming) *Penal Systems: A Comparative Approach*. London: Sage.

Cayley, D. (1998) *The Expanding Prison: The Crisis in Crime and Punishment and the Search for Alternatives*. Cleveland OH: Pilgrim Press.

Challiner, V., Brown, L. and Lupton, C. (2000) *A Survey of Family Group Conference Use across England and Wales*. Portsmouth and Bath: University of Portsmouth Social Services Research and Information Unit and University of Bath Department of Social and Policy Sciences.

Christie, N. (1977) Conflicts as property, *British Journal of Criminology*, 17: 1–15 (originally published as N. Christie (1976) *Conflicts as Property*. Sheffield: University of Sheffield).

Christie, N. (1982) *Limits to Pain*. Oxford: Martin Robertson.

Christie, N. (1986) The ideal victim, in E. Fattah (ed.) *From Crime Policy to Victim Policy*. Basingstoke: Macmillan.

Classen, R. (1996) Measuring restorative justice. Paper available electronically from the Centre for Peacemaking and Conflict Studies at Fresno Pacific College: www.fresno.edu/pacs/docs/jscale.html

Classen, R. and Zehr, H. (1989) *VORP Organizing: A Foundation in the Church*. Elkhart IN: Mennonite Central Committee, US, Office of Criminal Justice.

Coates, R.B., Umbreit, M. and Vos, B. (2000) *Restorative Justice Circles in South Saint Paul, Minnesota*. St Paul MN: Centre for Restorative Justice and Peacemaking, University of Minnesota.

Cohen, S. (2001) *States of Denial*. Cambridge: Polity Press.

Coker, D. (2002) Transformative justice: anti-subordination processes in cases of domestic violence, in H. Strang and J. Braithwaite (eds) *Restorative Justice and Family Violence*. Cambridge: Cambridge University Press.

Crawford, A. (1997) *The Local Governance of Crime: Appeals to Community and Partnerships*. Oxford: Clarendon Press.

Crawford, A. (2000) Salient themes and the limitations of restorative justice, in A. Crawford and J. Goodey (eds) *Integrating a Victim Perspective within Criminal Justice*. Aldershot: Ashgate Dartmouth.

Crawford, A. and Clear, T. (2001) Community justice: transforming communities through restorative justice?, in G. Bazemore and M. Schiff (eds) *Restorative Community Justice: Repairing the Harm and Transforming Communities*. Cincinnati OH: Anderson.

Crawford, A. and Enterkin, J. (1999) *Victim Contact Work and the Probation Service: A Study of Service Delivery and Impact*. Leeds: CCJS Press.

Crawford, A. and Enterkin, J. (2001) Victim contact work in the probation service: paradigm shift or Pandora's box, *British Journal of Criminology*, 41: 707–25.

Crawford, A. and Newburn, T. (2003) *Youth Offending and Restorative Justice: Implementing Reform in Youth Justice*. Cullompton: Willan.

Criminal Injuries Compensation Authority (2001) *A Guide to the Criminal Injuries Compensation Scheme*. Glasgow: Criminal Injuries Compensation Authority. Also available online at: www.cica.gov.uk/

Criminal Justice Review Commission (2000) *Review of the Criminal Justice System in Northern Ireland*. Belfast: The Stationery Office.

Crnkovich, M. (1993) *Report on the Sentencing Circle in Kangiqsujuaq*. Ottawa: Justice Canada.

Crow, G. and Marsh, P. (2000) *Family Group Conferences in Youth Justice: A Study of Early Work in Two Pilot Projects in Yorkshire*. Sheffield: Sheffield Children and Families Research Group, Dept. of Sociological Studies, University of Sheffield. Also available online at: www.shef.ac.uk~/~fwpg2000

Daly, K. (2001) Conferencing in Australia and New Zealand: variations, research findings and prospects, in A.M. Morris and G. Maxwell (eds) *Restorative Justice for Juveniles: Conferencing, Mediation and Circles*. Oxford: Hart.

Daly, K. (2002a) Restorative justice: the real story, *Punishment and Society*, 4: 55–79.

Daly, K. (2002b) Sexual assault and restorative justice, in H. Strang and J. Braithwaite (eds) *Restorative Justice and Family Violence*. Cambridge: Cambridge University Press.

Daly, K. (2003a) Mind the gap: restorative justice in theory and practice, in A. von Hirsch, J. Roberts, A.E. Bottoms, K. Roach and M. Schiff (eds) *Restorative Justice and Penal Justice: Competing or Reconcilable Paradigms?* Oxford: Hart.

Daly, K. (2003b) Making variation a virtue: evaluating the potential and limits of restorative justice, in E.G.M. Weitekamp and H.-J. Kerner (eds) *Restorative Justice in Context: International Practice and Directions*. Cullompton: Willan.

Davis, G. (1992) *Making Amends: Mediation and Reparation in Criminal Justice*. London: Routledge.

Davis, G., Boucherat, J. and Watson, D. (1988) Reparation in the service of diversion: the subordination of a good idea, *Howard Journal*, 27: 127–33.

Davis, G., Boucherat, J. and Watson, D. (1989) Pre-court decision-making in juvenile justice, *British Journal of Criminology*, 29: 219–35.

Davis, G., Messmer, H., Umbreit, M.S. and Coates, R.B. (1992) *Making Amends: Mediation and Reparation in Criminal Justice*. London and New York: Routledge.

Dignan, J. (1990) *Repairing the Damage: An Evaluation of an Experimental Adult Reparation Scheme in Kettering, Northamptonshire.* Sheffield: Centre for Criminological and Legal Research, University of Sheffield.

Dignan, J. (1992) Repairing the damage: can reparation be made to work in the service of diversion?, *British Journal of Criminology*, 32(4): 453–72.

Dignan, J. (1994) Reintegration through reparation: a way forward for restorative justice?, in A. Duff, S. Marshall, R.E. Dobash and R.P. Dobash (eds) *Penal Theory and Penal Practice: Tradition and Innovation in Criminal Justice.* Manchester: Manchester University Press.

Dignan, J. (1998) Evaluating community and neighbour mediation, in M. Liebmann (ed.) *Community and Neighbour Mediation.* London: Cavendish.

Dignan, J. (1999) The Crime and Disorder Act and the prospects for restorative justice, [1999] *Criminal Law Review*, 48–60.

Dignan, J. (2000) *Youth Justice Pilots Evaluation: Interim Report on Reparative Work and Youth Offending Teams.* London: Home Office Research, Development and Statistics Directorate.

Dignan, J. (2001) Restorative justice and crime reduction: are policy-makers barking up the wrong tree?, in E. Fattah and S. Parmentier (eds) *Victim Policies and Criminal Justice on the Road to Restorative Justice: Essays in Honour of Tony Peters.* Leuven: Leuven University Press.

Dignan, J. (2002a) Restorative justice and the law: the case for an integrated, systemic approach, in L. Walgrave (ed.) *Restorative Justice and the Law.* Cullompton: Willan.

Dignan, J. (2002b) Reparation orders, in B. Williams (ed.) *Reparation and Victim-Focused Social Work.* London and Philadelphia. Jessica Kingsley.

Dignan, J. (2002c) Empirical research with regard to restorative justice in Europe: a preliminary study. England and Wales. Paper written under the auspices of the COST Action project but not published as yet.

Dignan, J. (2003) Towards a systemic model of restorative justice, in A. von Hirsch, J. Roberts, A.E. Bottoms, K. Roach and M. Schiff (eds) *Restorative Justice and Penal Justice: Competing or Reconcilable Paradigms?* Oxford: Hart.

Dignan, J. and Cavadino, M. (1996) Towards a framework for conceptualising and evaluating models of criminal justice from a victim's perspective, *International Review of Victimology*, 4: 153–82.

Dignan, J. with Lowey, K. (2000) *Restorative Justice Options for Northern Ireland: A Comparative Review.* Review of the Criminal Justice System in Northern Ireland Research Report no. 10. Belfast: Criminal Justice Review Commission/ Northern Ireland Office.

Dignan, J. and Marsh, P. (2001) Restorative justice and family group conferencing in England, in A.M. Morris and G. Maxwell (eds) *Restorative Justice for Juveniles: Conferencing, Mediation and Circles.* Oxford: Hart.

Dignan, J., Sorsby, A. and Hibbert, J. (1996) *Neighbour Disputes: Comparing the Cost-effectiveness of Mediation and Alternative Approaches.* Sheffield: Centre for Criminological and Legal Research, University of Sheffield.

van Dijk, J. (2000) Implications of the international crime victims survey from a victim perspective, in A. Crawford and J. Goodey (eds) *Integrating a Victim Perspective within Criminal Justice.* Aldershot: Ashgate Dartmouth.

van Dijk, J.J.M. and Mayhew, P. (1992) *Criminal Victimization in the Industrialized World: Key Findings of the 1989 and 1992 International Crime Surveys.* The Hague: Directorate for Crime Prevention, Ministry of Justice.

Ditton, J. and Duffy, J. (1983) Bias in the newspaper reporting of crime news, *British Journal of Criminology*, 23(2): 159–65.

Doak, J. (2003) The victim and the criminal process: an analysis of recent trends in regional and international tribunals, *Legal Studies*, 23(1): 1–32.

Dobash, R.E. and Dobash, R.P. (1979) *Violence against Wives*. New York: Free Press.

Dobash, R.E. and Dobash, R.P. (1992) *Women, Violence and Social Change*. London: Routledge and Kegan Paul.

Dooley, M.J. (1995) *Reparative Probation Program*. Waterbury VT: Vermont Department of Corrections.

Dooley, M.J. (1996) *Restoring Hope through Community Partnerships: The Real Deal in Crime Control*. Lexington KY: American Probation and Parole Association.

Downes, D. (1983) *Law and Order: Theft of an Issue*. London: Blackrose Press.

Duff, P. (1987) Criminal injuries compensation and 'violent' crime, [1987] *Criminal Law Review*, 219–30.

Duff, P. (1988) The 'victim movement' and legal reform, in M. Maguire and J. Pointing (eds) *Victims of Crime: A New Deal?* Milton Keynes and Philadelphia: Open University Press.

Duff, P. (1998) Criminal injuries compensation, *Oxford Journal of Legal Studies*, 18: 105–42.

Duff, R.A. (1986) *Trials and Punishments*. Cambridge: Cambridge University Press.

Duff, R.A. (2001) *Punishment, Communication and Community*. Oxford: Oxford University Press.

Duff, R. A. (2002) Restorative punishment and punitive restoration, in L. Walgrave (ed.) *Restorative Justice and the Law*. Cullompton: Willan.

Duff, R. A. (2003) Restoration and retribution, in A. von Hirsch, J. Roberts, A.E. Bottoms, K. Roach and M. Schiff (eds) *Restorative Justice and Penal Justice: Competing or Reconcilable Paradigms?* Oxford: Hart.

Dworkin, R. (1978) *Taking Rights Seriously*. London: Duckworth.

Edgar, K., O'Donnell, I. and Martin, C. (2003) *Prison Violence: The Dynamics of Conflict, Fear and Power*. Cullompton: Willan.

Edwards, I. (2001) Victim participation in sentencing: the problem of incoherence, *Howard Journal*, 40(1): 39–54.

Edwards, S.M. (1981) *Female Sexuality and the Law*. Oxford: Robertson.

Edwards, S.M. (1989) *Policing Domestic Violence: Women, the Law and the State*. Newbury Park CA: Sage.

Eglash, A. (1977) Beyond restitution: creative restitution, in J. Hudson and B. Galaway (eds) *Restitution in Criminal Justice*. Lexington MA: D.C. Heath.

Eitinger, L. (1964) *Concentration Camp Survivors in Norway and Israel*. Oslo: Universities Press.

Eitinger, L. and Strom, A. (1973) *Morbidity and Mortality after Excessive Stress*. New York: Humanities Press.

Elias, R. (1985) Transcending our social reality of victimization: towards a new victimology of human rights, *Victimology*, 10: 6–25.

Elias, R. (1993) *Victims Still*. London: Sage.

Ellis, M., Atkeson, B. and Calhoun, K. (1981) An assessment of long-term reaction to rape, *Journal of Abnormal Psychiatry*, 90: 263–6.

Ellison, L. (2001) *The Adversarial Process and the Vulnerable Witness*. Oxford: Oxford University Press.

Ennis, P.H. (1967) *Criminal Victimization in the United States: A Report of a National Survey*. Washington DC: US Department of Justice.

Erez, E. (2000) Integrating a victim perspective through victim impact statements, in A. Crawford and J. Goodey (eds) *Integrating a Victim Perspective within Criminal Justice*. Aldershot: Ashgate Dartmouth.

Etzioni, A. (1995) *The Spirit of Community: Rights, Responsibilities and the Communitarian Agenda*. London: Fontana.

Eve, R. (1985) Empirical and theoretical findings concerning child and adolescent sexual abuse: implications for the next generation of studies, *Victimology*, 10: 97–109.

EU Council of Justice and Home Affairs Ministers (2001) *Standing of Victims in Criminal Proceedings*. Luxembourg: Office for Official Publications of the European Communities.

Falconer, Lord C. (2003) Parole Board annual lecture. Delivered on 8 April 2003.

Fattah, E. (1989) Victims and victimology: the facts and the rhetoric, *International Review of Victimology*, 1(1): 43–66.

Fattah, E. (1994) *The Interchangeable Roles of Victim and Victimizer*. Helsinki: European Institute for Crime Prevention and Control.

Fattah, E. (1995) Restorative and retributive justice models: a comparison, in H. Kuhne (ed.) *Festschrift für Koichi Miyazawa*. University of Trier, Germany: Nomos Verlagsgesellschaft.

Fattah, E. (1998) A critical assessment of two justice paradigms: contrasting the restorative and retributive models, in E. Fattah and T. Peters (eds) *Support for Crime Victims in Comparative Perspective: A Collection of Essays Dedicated to the Memory of Frederick McClintock*. Leuven: Leuven University Press.

Fenwick, H. (1995) Rights of victims in the criminal justice system: rhetoric or reality?, [1995] *Criminal Law Review*, 845–53.

Fisse, B. and Braithwaite, J. (1993) *Corporations, Crime and Accountability*. Cambridge: Cambridge University Press.

Flaten, C.L. (1996) Victim–offender mediation: application with serious offences committed by juveniles, in B. Galaway and J. Hudson (eds) *Restorative Justice: International Perspectives*. Monsey NY: Criminal Justice Press.

Fleming, J. (1979) *Stopping Wife Abuse*. New York: Doubleday.

Flood-Page, C. and Mackie, A. (1998) *Sentencing Practice: An Examination of Decisions in Magistrates' Courts and the Crown Courts in the mid-1990s*. Home Office Research Study no. 180. London: Home Office.

Foucault, M. (1977) *Discipline and Punish*. London: Penguin.

Foucault, M. (1980) Prison talk, in C. Gordon (ed.) *Michel Foucault: Power/ Knowledge, Selected Interviews and other Writings 1972–1977*. Brighton: Harvester Press.

Frieze, I. H., Hymer, S. and Greenberg, M. S. (1987) Describing the crime victim: psychological reactions to victimization, *Professional Psychology*, 18: 299–315.

Fry, M. (1951) *Arms of the Law*. London: Gollancz.

Fry, M. (1957) Victims of violence, *Observer*, 10 November. Reprinted as Justice for victims (1959) *Journal of Public Law*, 8: 191–4.

Fry, M. (1959) Justice for victims, *Journal of Public Law*, 8: 191–4.

Gampell, L. (1999) Prisoners' families – the forgotten years, *Criminal Justice Matters*, 35: 28–9.

Garland, D. (2001) *The Culture of Control: Crime and Social Order in Contemporary Society*. Oxford: Oxford University Press.

Gay, M., Holtom, C. and Thomas, M. (1975) Helping the victims, *International Journal of Offender Therapy and Comparative Criminology*, 19(3): 263–9.

Genn, H. (1988) Multiple victimization, in M. Maguire and J. Pointing (eds) *Victims of Crime: A New Deal?* Milton Keynes and Philadelphia: Open University Press.

Gilroy, P. (1998) The role of restoration, mediation and family group conferencing in the youth justice system. Paper presented to a Home Office Special Conference, 18–20 February.

Glidewell, I. (1998) *The Review of the Crown Prosecution Service: A Report*. Cmnd. 3960. London: HMSO.

Goggins, P. (2004) Witnessing the power of restorative justice, *Policy Review*, March: 10–11.

Goldson, B. (ed.) (2000) *The New Youth Justice*. Lyme Regis: Russell House.

Goodwin, J. (ed.) (1982) *Incest Victims and their Families*. Boston: John Wright.

Grace, S. (1995) *Policing Domestic Violence in the 1990s*. London: HMSO.

Grady, A. (2002) Female-on-male domestic abuse: uncommon or ignored, in C. Hoyle and R. Young (eds) *New Visions of Crime Victims*. Oxford: Hart.

Griffiths, T. and Hamilton, R. (1996) Sanctioning and healing: restorative justice in Canadian Aboriginal communities, in B. Galaway and J. Hudson (eds) *The Practice of Restorative Justice*. Monsey: Criminal Justice Press.

Gulliver, P.H. (1963) *Social Control in an African Society: A Study of the Arusha*. London: Routledge and Kegan Paul.

de Haan, W. (1990) *The Politics of Redress: Crime, Abolition and Penal Abolition*. London: Unwin Hyman.

Hagley, L. (2003) Disempowerment in victim-offender mediation. Unpublished PhD thesis.

Hamilton, J. and Wisniewski, M. (1996) *The Use of the Compensation Order in Scotland*. Edinburgh: Scottish Central Research Unit.

von Hentig, H. (1941) Remarks on the interaction of perpetrator and victim, *Journal of Criminal Law, Criminology and Police Science*, 31: 303–9.

von Hentig, H. (1948) *The Criminal and His Victim*. New Haven CT: Yale University Press.

Herman, J. (1981) *Father–Daughter Incest*. Cambridge MA: Harvard University Press.

Hill, R. (2002) Restorative justice and the absent victim: new data from the Thames Valley, *International Review of Victimology*, 9: 273–88.

HM Inspectorate of Probation (2000) *The Victim Perspective: Ensuring the Victim Matters*. London: Home Office.

Holdaway, S., Davidson, N., Dignan, J. et al. (2001) *New Strategies to Address Youth Offending: The National Evaluation of the Pilot Youth Offending Teams*. RDS Occasional Paper no. 69. London: Home Office. Also available online at: www.homeoffice.gov.uk/rds/index.html

Holtom, C. and Raynor, P. (1988) Origins of victims support and practice, in M. Maguire and J. Pointing (eds) *Victims of Crime: A New Deal?* Milton Keynes and Philadelphia: Open University Press.

Home Office (1986) *Violence Against Women. Treatment of Victims of Rape and Domestic Violence*. Home Office Circular 69/1986. London: Home Office.

Home Office (1988) *Victims of Crime*. Home Office Circular 20/1988. London: Home Office.

Home Office (1990) *Victim's Charter: A Statement of the Rights of Victims of Crime*. London: HMSO.

Home Office (1991) *The Victim's Charter: Life Sentence Prisoners*. CPO 41/91. London: Home Office.

Home Office (1994) *Cautioning of Offenders*. Home Office Circular 18/1994. London: Home Office.

Home Office (1995) *Probation Service Contact with Victims*. Probation Circular 61/1995. London: Home Office.

Home Office (1996) *The Victim's Charter: A Statement of Service Standards for Victims of Crime*. London: Home Office.

Home Office (1997) *No More Excuses – A New Approach to Tackling Youth Crime England and Wales*, Cmnd. 3809. London: Home Office.

Home Office (1999a) *Digest 4: Information on the Criminal Justice System in England and Wales*. London: Home Office Research, Development and Statistics Directorate.

Home Office (2000a) *Home Office Annual Report 1999/2000*. London: The Stationery Office.

Home Office (2000b) *Domestic Violence: Revised Circular to the Police*. Home Office Circular 19/2000. London: Home Office.

Home Office (2000c) *Circular Introducing the Final Warning Scheme: Revised Guidance*. London: Home Office. Also available online at: www.homeoffice. gov.uk/yousys/youth.htm

Home Office (2001a) *Criminal Justice: The Way Ahead*. Cmnd. 5074. London: The Stationery Office.

Home Office (2001b) *Review of the Victim's Charter*. London: Home Office.

Home Office (2001c) *Further Guidance on the National Probation Service's Work with Victims of Serious Crimes*. Probation Circular 61/2001. London: Home Office.

Home Office (2001d) *Criminal Statistics, England and Wales 2000*. Cmnd. 5312. London: The Stationery Office.

Home Office (2002) *Criminal Statistics, England and Wales 2001*. Cmnd. 5696. London: The Stationery Office.

Home Office (2004) *Compensation and support for victims of crime: a consultation paper on proposals to amend the Criminal Injuries Compensation Scheme and provide a wider range of support for victims of crime*. London: Home Office.

Home Office, Department of Health and Welsh Office (1995) *National Standards for the Supervision of Offenders in the Community*. London: Home Office.

Home Office, Lord Chancellor's Department and Attorney General (2002a) *Justice for All*. Cmnd. 5563. London: The Stationery Office.

Home Office, Lord Chancellor's Department and Attorney General (2002b) *A Better Deal for Victims and Witnesses*. London: Home Office Communications Directorate.

Home Office, Lord Chancellor's Department Attorney General and President of the Association of Chief Police Officers (2002c) *Narrowing the Justice Gap*. London: Home Office Communications Directorate.

Home Office, Lord Chancellor's Department and Youth Justice Board (2002d) *Referral Orders and Youth Offender Panels. Guidance for Courts, Youth*

Offending Teams and Youth Offender Panels. Available at: www.courtservice.gov.uk/cms/media/referral_orders_and_yop.pdf

Home Office, Department for Constitutional Affairs and Attorney General (2003) *A New Deal for Victims and Witnesses: National Strategy to Deliver Improved Services.* London: Home Office Communications Directorate.

Home Office Management Advisory Services (1991) *Abstracts from the Report of the Management Review of the Criminal Injuries Compensation Board.* London: Home Office.

Home Office and Youth Justice Board (2002) *The Final Warning Scheme Guidance for the Police and Youth Offending Teams.* London: Home Office.

Hough, J.M. (1986) Victims of violent crime: findings from the first British crime survey, in E. Fattah (ed.) *From Crime Policy to Victim Policy.* Basingstoke: Macmillan.

Howard League (1997) *Community Service: An Undervalued Sentence.* London: Howard League.

Hoyle, C. (1998) *Negotiating Domestic Violence: Police, Criminal Justice and Victims.* Oxford: Clarendon Press.

Hoyle, C. (2002) Securing restorative justice for the 'non-participating' victim, in C. Hoyle and R. Young (eds) *New Visions of Crime Victims.* Oxford: Hart.

Hoyle, C., Cape, E., Morgan, R. and Sanders, A. (1998) *Evaluation of the One Stop Shop and Victim Pilot Statement Projects.* London: Home Office.

Hoyle, C., Morgan, R. and Sanders, A. (1999) *The Victim's Charter: An Evaluation of Pilot Projects.* Home Office Research Findings no. 107. London: Home Office.

Hoyle, C. and Sanders, A. (2000) Police Response to Domestic Violence, *British Journal of Criminology,* 40: 14–36.

Hoyle, C., Young, R. and Hill, R. (2002) *Proceed with Caution: An Evaluation of the Thames Valley Police Initiative in Restorative Cautioning.* York: Joseph Rowntree Foundation.

Hudson, B. (2003) Victims and offenders, in A. von Hirsch, J. Roberts, A.E. Bottoms, K. Roach and M. Schiff (eds) *Restorative Justice and Penal Justice: Competing or Reconcilable Paradigms?* Oxford: Hart.

Hudson, B. (2004) Balancing the rights of victims and offenders, in E. Capes *Reconciling Rights in Criminal Justice: Analysing the Tension between Victims and Defendants.* London: Legal Action.

Hughes, G. (1996) Communitarianism and law and order, *Critical Social Policy,* 16: 17–41.

Hulsman, L.H.C. (1981) Penal reform in the Netherlands: Part I – Bringing the criminal justice system under control, *Howard Journal of Penology and Crime Prevention,* 20: 150–9.

Hulsman, L.H.C. (1982) Penal reform in the Netherlands: Part II – Reflections on a White Paper proposal, *Howard Journal of Penology and Crime Prevention,* 20: 35–47.

Hulsman, L.H.C. (1986) Critical criminology and the concept of crime, *Contemporary Crises,* 10: 63–80.

Hulsman, L.H.C. (1991) The abolitionist case: alternative crime policies, *Israel Law Review,* 25(3–4): 681–709.

Huyse, L. (1998) *Young Democracies and the Choice between Amnesty, Truth Commissions and Amnesty.* Leuven: Law and Society Institute, University of Leuven.

Immarigeon, R. (1999) Restorative justice, juvenile offenders and crime victims: a review of the literature, in G. Bazemore and L. Walgrave (eds) *Restorative Juvenile Justice: Repairing the Harm of Youth Crime*. Monsey NY: Criminal Justice Press.

Ingram, M. and Harkin, G. (2004) *Stakeknife: Britain's Secret Agents in Ireland*. Dublin: O'Brien Press.

Jackson, J. (2004) Putting victims at the heart of criminal justice: the gap between rhetoric and reality, in E. Capes *Reconciling Rights in Criminal Justice: Analysing the Tension between Victims and Defendants*. London: Legal Action.

Jackson, S. (1998) *Family Justice? An Evaluation of a Family Group Conference Project*. Southampton: Dept of Social Work Studies, University of Southampton.

Jefferson, T., Sim, J. and Walklate, S. (1991) Europe, the left and criminology in the 1990s: accountability, control and the social construction of the consumer. Paper presented to the British Criminology Conference, York, July.

Johnstone, G. (2002) *Restorative Justice: Ideas, Values and Debates*. Cullompton: Willan.

Jones, E.H. (1966) *Margery Fry: The Essential Amateur*. Oxford: Oxford University Press.

Jones, H. and Westmarland, N. (2004) Rape Crisis History: Remembering the past but looking to the future. Available online at: http://www.rapecrisis.org.uk/history.htm.

Jonker, J. (1986) *Victims of Violence*. London: Fontana/Collins.

Jordan, B. and Arnold, J. (1995) Democracy and criminal justice, *Critical Social Policy*, 15: 170–82.

Joutsen, M. (1994) Victim participation in proceedings and sentencing in Europe, *International Review of Victimology*, 3: 57–67.

JUSTICE (1998) *Victims in Criminal Justice: Report of the JUSTICE Committee on the Role of the Victim in Criminal Justice*. London: JUSTICE.

JUSTICE (2000) *Restoring Youth Justice: New Directions in Domestic and International Law and Practice*. London: JUSTICE.

Karmen, A. (1990) *Crime Victims: An Introduction to Victimology*, Pacific Grove CA: Brooks Cole.

Karp, D.R. (2002) The offender/community encounter: stakeholder involvement in the Vermont community reparative boards, in D.R. Karp and T.R. Clear (eds) *What is Community Justice?* Thousand Oaks CA: Sage.

Karp, D.R. and Walther, L. (2001) Community reparative boards: theory and practice, in G. Bazemore and M. Schiff (eds) *Restorative Community Justice: Cultivating Common Ground for Victims, Communities and Offenders*. Cincinnati OH: Anderson.

Katz, A. and Mazur, M. (1979) *Understanding the Rape Victim: A Synthesis of Research Findings*. New York: Wiley.

Kaufman, I. (1985) Child abuse – family victimology, *Victimology*, 10: 62–71.

Keller, S. (1968) *The Urban Neighbourhood: A Sociological Perspective*. New York: Random House.

Kelly, T. (2002) A critical review of issues in applying restorative justice principles and practices to cases of hate crime. Masters thesis, Portland State University.

Kershaw, C., Chivite-Matthews, N., Thomas, C. and Aust, R. (2001) *The*

2001 British Crime Survey: First Results, England and Wales. Home Office Statistical Bulletin 18/01. London: Home Office.

van Kesteren, J., Mayhew, P. and Nieuwbeerta, P. (2000) *Criminal Victimisation in Seventeen Industrialized Countries: Key Findings from the 2000 International Crime Victims Survey.* The Hague: Netherlands Institute for the Study of Criminality and Law Enforcement/WODC.

Knight, C. and Chouhan, K. (2002) Supporting victims of racist abuse and violence, in C. Hoyle and R. Young (eds) *New Visions of Crime Victims.* Oxford: Hart.

Kosh, M. and Williams, B. (1995) *The Probation Service and Victims of Crime: A Pilot Study.* Keele: Keele University Press.

Kurki, L. (2000) Restorative and community justice in the United States, in M. Tonry (ed.) *Crime and Justice: A Review of Research*, Vol. 26. Chicago IL: University of Chicago Press.

Kurki, L. (2003) Evaluating restorative justice practices, in A. von Hirsch, J. Roberts, A.E. Bottoms, K. Roach and M. Schiff (eds) *Restorative Justice and Penal Justice: Competing or Reconcilable Paradigms?* Oxford: Hart.

LaPrairie, C. (1995) Altering course: new directions in criminal justice: Sentencing circles and family group conferences, *Australian and New Zealand Journal of Criminology*, special issue: Crime, Criminology and Public Policy, December: 78–99.

Latimer, J., Dowden, C. and Muise, D. (2001) *The Effectiveness of Restorative Justice Practices: A Meta-Analysis.* Ottawa: Department of Justice.

Lea, J. and Young, J. (1984) *What is to be Done about Law and Order?* London: Penguin.

Levi, M. and Pithouse, A. (1992) The victims of fraud, in D. Downes (ed.) *Unravelling Criminal Justice.* London: Macmillan.

Levi, M. and Pithouse, A. (2005 forthcoming) *White Collar Crime and its Victims: The Social and Media Construction of Business Fraud.* Oxford: Oxford University Press.

Liebmann, M. (ed.) (1998) *Community and Neighbour Mediation.* London: Cavendish.

Lilles, H. (2001) Circle sentencing: part of the restorative justice continuum, in A.M. Morris and G. Maxwell (eds) *Restorative Justice for Juveniles: Conferencing, Mediation and Circles.* Oxford: Hart.

Lind, E.A. and Tyler, T. (1988) *The Social Psychology of Procedural Justice.* New York: Plenum Press.

Löschnig-Gspandl, M. (2003) Corporations, crime and restorative justice, in E.G.M. Weitekamp and H.-J. Kerner (eds) *Restorative Justice in Context: International Practice and Directions.* Cullompton: Willan.

McCold, P. (1996) Restorative justice and the role of community, in B. Galaway and J. Hudson (eds) *Restorative Justice: International Perspectives.* Monsey NY: Criminal Justice Press.

McCold, P. (2000) Towards a mid-range theory of restorative criminal justice: a reply to the maximalist model, *Contemporary Justice Review: Issues in Criminal, Social and Restorative Justice*, 4(3–4): 357–414.

McCold, P. and Wachtel, B. (1998) *Restorative Policing Experiment: The Bethlehem Pennsylvania Police Family Group Conferencing Project.* Pipersville PA: Community Service Foundation. Also available online at: www.realjustice.org

McCold, P. and Wachtel, B. (2002) Restorative justice theory validation, in E.G.M.

Weitekamp and H.-J. Kerner (eds) *Restorative Justice: Theoretical Foundations*. Cullompton: Willan.

McEvoy, K. and Mika, H. (2002) Restorative justice and the critique of informalism in Northern Ireland, *British Journal of Criminology*, 42: 534–62.

McEvoy, K., Mika, H. and Hudson, B. (2002) Practice, performance and prospects for restorative justice, *British Journal of Criminology*, 42: 469–75.

McIvor, G. (1992) *Sentenced to Serve*. Aldershot: Avebury.

Magee, D. (1983) *What Murder Leaves Behind*. New York: Dodd, Mead.

Maguire, M. (1980) The impact of burglary upon victims, *British Journal of Criminology*, 20(3): 261–75.

Maguire, M. (1985) Victims' needs and victim services: indications from research, *Victimology*, 10: 539–59.

Maguire, M. (1991) The needs and rights of victims of crime, in M. Tonry (ed.) *Crime and Justice: A Review of Research*, Vol. 14. Chicago: University of Chicago Press.

Maguire, M. with Bennett, T. (1982) *Burglary in a Dwelling: the Offence, the Offender and the Victim*. London: Heinemann.

Maguire, M. and Corbett, C. (1987) *The Effects of Crime and the Work of Victim Support Schemes*. Aldershot: Gower.

Maguire, M. and Kynch, J. (2000) *Public Perceptions and Victims' Experiences of Victim Support: Findings from the 1998 British Crime Survey*. London: Home Office Research, Development and Statistics Directorate.

Malmquist, C. (1986) Children who witness parental murder: post-traumatic aspects, *Journal of the American Academy of Child Psychiatry*, 25: 320–25.

Mansfield, M. (2002) Victims the law left out, *Guardian*, 20 November: 19.

Marshall, T.F. (1990) Results of research from British experiments in restorative justice, in B. Galaway and J. Hudson (eds) *Criminal Justice, Restitution and Reconciliation*. Monsey NY: Criminal Justice Press.

Marshall, T.F. (1994) Grassroots initiatives towards restorative justice: the new paradigm?, in A. Duff, S. Marshall, R.E. Dobash and R.P. Dobash (eds) *Penal Theory and Penal Practice: Tradition and Innovation in Criminal Justice*. Manchester: Manchester University Press.

Marshall, T.F. (1999) *Restorative Justice: An Overview*. London: Home Office Research and Development Statistics Directorate.

Marshall, T.F. and Merry, S. (1990) *Crime and Accountability: Victim/Offender Mediation in Practice*. London: HMSO.

Martin, P. (1996) Restorative justice – a family violence perspective, *Social Policy Journal of New Zealand*, 6: 56–68.

Masters, G. (2002) Family group conferencing: a victim perspective, in B. Williams (ed.) *Working with Victims of Crime: Policies, Politics and Practice*. London: Jessica Kingsley.

Mathiesen, T. (1974) *The Politics of Abolition: Essays in Political Action Theory*. Oxford: Martin Robinson.

Mathiesen, T. (1990) *Prison on Trial*. London: Sage.

Matthews, R. (1988) Reassessing informal justice, in R. Matthews (ed.) *Informal Justice*. London: Sage.

Mattinson, J. and Mirlees-Black, C. (2000) *Attitudes to Crime and Criminal Justice: Findings from the 1998 British Crime Survey*. Home Office Research Study no. 200. London: Home Office.

Mawby, R.I. and Gill, M.L. (1987) *Crime Victims: Needs, Services and the Voluntary Sector*. Tavistock: London and New York.

Mawby, R.I. and Walklate, S. (1994) *Critical Victimology*. London: Sage.

Maxwell, G. (1998) Crossing cultural boundaries: the experience of family group conferences. Paper presented to Conference Session on Implementing Restorative Justice in an International Context, Florida, November.

Maxwell, G. and Morris, A.M. (1993) *Family, Victims and Culture: Youth Justice in New Zealand*. Wellington: Social Policy Administration and Victoria University of Wellington.

Mayhew, P. (2000) Researching the state of crime: local, national and international victim surveys, in R.D. King and E. Whincup (eds) *Doing Research on Crime and Justice*. Oxford: Oxford University Press.

Mayhew, P. and van Dijk, J.J.M. (1997) *Criminal Victimisation in Eleven Industrialised Countries: Key Findings from the 1996 International Crime Victimisation Survey*. The Hague: Ministry of Justice, Dept of Crime Prevention.

Mendelsohn, B. (1956) Une nouvelle branche de la science psycho-sociale: la victimologie, *Revue Internationale de Criminologie et de Police Technique*, 10: 95–109.

Mendelsohn, B. (1974) The origin of the doctrine of victimology, in I. Drapkin and E. Viano (eds) *Victimology*. Lexington MA: Lexington Books.

Merry, S.E. (1982) The social organisation of mediation in nonindustrial societies: implications for informal community justice in America, in R.L. Abel (ed.) *The Politics of Informal Justice: Vol. 2, Comparative Studies*. New York: Academic Press.

Miers, D. (1978) *Responses to Victimisation*. Abingdon: Professional Books.

Miers, D. (1980) Victim compensation as a labelling process, *Victimology*, 5(1): 3–16.

Miers, D. (1989) Positivist victimology: a critique, *International Review of Victimology*, 1(1): 3–22.

Miers, D. (1990a) Positivist victimology: a Critique. Part 2: Critical victimology, *International Review of Victimology*, 1(3): 219–30.

Miers, D. (1990b) *Compensation for Criminal Injuries*. London: Butterworths.

Miers, D. (1992) The responsibilities and rights of victims of crime, *Modern Law Review*, 55: 482–505.

Miers, D. (1997) *State Compensation for Criminal Injuries*. London: Blackstone.

Miers, D. (2000) Taking the law into their own hands, in A. Crawford and J. Goodey (eds) *Integrating a Victim Perspective within Criminal Justice*. Aldershot: Ashgate Dartmouth.

Miers, D. (2001) *An International Review of Restorative Justice*. Crime Reduction Research Series Paper no. 10. London: Home Office.

Miers, D., Maguire, M., Goldie, S. et al. (2001) *An Exploratory Evaluation of Restorative Justice Schemes*. London: Home Office.

Ministerial Advisory Committee on a Maori Perspective for the Department of Social Welfare (1988) *Puao-Te-Ata-Tu (Daybreak) Report*. Wellington: New Zealand Department of Social Welfare.

Mirlees-Black, C. (1999) *Domestic Violence: Findings from a New British Crime Survey Self-completion Questionnaire*. Home Office Research Study no. 191. London: Home Office.

Mirlees-Black, C. and Ross, A. (1995) *Crime against Retail and Manufacturing*

Premises: Findings from the 1994 Commercial Victimisation Survey. Home Office Research and Planning Unit Paper no. 146. London: Home Office.

Moore, D.B. (1993) Evaluating family group conferences: some early findings from Wagga Wagga. Paper presented to the Australian Institute of Criminology Criminal Justice Planning and Co-ordinating Meeting, Canberra, April.

Moore, D.B. and O'Connell, T.A. (1993) Family conferencing in Wagga Wagga: a communitarian model of justice, in C. Alder and J. Wundersitz (eds) *Family Conferencing and Juvenile Justice: The Way Forward or Misplaced Optimism?* Canberra: Australian Institute of Criminology.

Moore, D.B. with Forsythe, L. (1995) *A New Approach to Juvenile Justice: An Evaluation of Family Conferencing at Wagga Wagga*. Wagga Wagga: Charles Sturt University.

Moreland, L. (2001) *An Ordinary Murder*. London: Aurum Press.

Morgan, R. and Sanders, A. (1999) *The Use of Victim Statements*. London: Home Office.

Morgan, J. and Zedner, L. (1992) *Child Victims: Crime, Impact and Criminal Justice*. Oxford: Oxford University Press.

Morley, R. and Mullender, A. (1994) Preventing domestic violence to women. Crime Prevention Unit Paper no. 48. London: Home Office.

Morris, A.M. (1999) Creative conferencing: revisiting principles, practice and potential, in A. Morris and G. Maxwell (eds) *Youth Justice in Focus: Proceedings of an Australasian Conference held on 27–30 October 1998 at the Michael Fowler Centre, Wellington*. Wellington: Institute of Criminology, Victoria University.

Morris, A.M. (2002) Critiquing the critics: a brief response to critics of restorative justice, *British Journal of Criminology*, 42(3): 596–615.

Morris, A.M. and Gelsthorpe, L. (2000) Revisioning men's violence against female partners, *Howard Journal of Criminal Justice*, 39(4): 412–28.

Morris, A.M. and Maxwell, G. (1998) Restorative justice in New Zealand: family group conferences as a case study, *Western Criminological Review*, 1(1). Available online at: www.wcr.sonoma.edu/v1n1/morris.html (accessed 1 Dec. 2003).

Morris, A.M. and Maxwell, G. (2000) The practice of family group conferencing, in A. Crawford and J. Goodey (eds) *Integrating a Victim Perspective within Criminal Justice*. Aldershot: Ashgate Dartmouth.

Morris, A.M. and Young, W. (2000) Reforming criminal justice: the potential of restorative justice, in H. Strang and J. Braithwaite (eds) *Restorative Justice: Philosophy to Practice*. Dartmouth: Ashgate.

Morris, A.M., Maxwell, G. and Robertson, J. (1993) Giving victims a voice: a New Zealand experiment, *Howard Journal of Criminal Justice*, 32: 304–21.

Morris, M. and Gould, M. (1963) *The Neglected–Battered Child Syndrome*. New York: Child Welfare League of America.

Morris, N. (1974) *The Future of Imprisonment*. Chicago: University of Chicago Press.

Morris, N. and Tonry, M. (1990) *Between Prison and Probation: Intermediate Punishments in a Rational Sentencing System*. New York: Oxford University Press.

Moxon, D., Corkery, J.M. and Hedderman, C. (1992) *Developments in the Use of Compensation Orders in Magistrates' Courts since October 1988*. Home Office Research Study no. 126. London: HMSO.

Myhill, A. and Allen, J. (2002) *Rape and Sexual Assult of Women: the nature and extent of the problem: findings from the British Crime Survey*. Home Office Research Study no. 237. London: HMSO.

NACRO (1997) *A New Three Rs for Young Offenders: Towards a New Strategy for Children who Offend*. London: NACRO.

Nathanson, D.L. (1992) *Shame and Pride: Affect, Sex and the Birth of the Self*. New York: Norton.

Newburn, T. (1993) *The Long-term Needs of Victims: A Review of the Literature*. Home Office Research and Planning Unit Paper no. 80. London: Home Office.

Newburn, T. and Merry, S. (1990) *Keeping in Touch: Police–Victim Communication in Two Areas*. Home Office Research Study no. 116. London: HMSO.

Newburn, T., Crawford, A., Earle, R. et al. (2001a) *The Introduction of Referral Orders into the Youth Justice System*. RDS Occasional Paper no. 70, London: Home Office. Also available online at: www.homeoffice.gov.uk/rds/index.html

Newburn, T., Crawford, A., Earle, R. et al. (2001b) *The Introduction of Referral Orders into the Youth Justice System: Second Interim Report*. RDS Occasional Paper no. 73, London: Home Office. Also available online at: http://www.homeoffice.gov.uk/rds/index.html

Newburn, T., Crawford, A., Earle, R. et al. (2002) *The Introduction of Referral Orders into the Youth Justice System*. Home Office Research Study 242, London: Home Office. Also available online at: http://www.homeoffice.gov.uk/rds/index.html

Norris, F.H., Kaniasty, K. and Thompson, M. P. (1997) The psychological consequences of crime findings from a longitudinal population-based study, in R.C. Davis, A.J. Lurigio and W.G. Skogan *Victims of Crime*, 2nd edn. London: Sage.

Northern Ireland Office (2001) Criminal Justice Review Implementation Plan. Belfast: Northern Ireland Office.

Nugent, W.R., Umbreit, M.S., Wiinamaki, L. and Paddock, J. (2001) Participation in victim–offender mediation and reoffense: successful replications?, *Research on Social Work Practice*, 11: 5–23.

O'Connell, T.A. (1992) Wagga Wagga juvenile cautioning programme: 'It may be the way to go!' Workshop address to the National Conference on Juvenile Justice, Adelaide, Australian Institute of Criminology, September.

O'Connell, T.A. (2001) Restorative justice for serious crimes. Paper presented to the Restorative and Community Justice: Inspiring the Future International Conference, The Guildhall, Winchester, 28–31 March.

O'Donnell, I. and Edgar, K. (1996) *Victimisation in Prisons*. Home Office Research Findings no. 37. London: Home Office Research and Statistics Directorate.

O'Donnell, I. and Edgar, K. (1998) Routine victimisation in prisons, *Howard Journal of Criminal Justice*, 37: 266–79.

Pavlakis, I. (2002) A Consumerist approach to restorative justice: victims' needs, wants and varying roles within restorative justice. Unpublished M.Phil in Criminological Research, University of Cambridge.

Pawson, R. and Tilley, N. (1994) What works in evaluation research?, *British Journal of Criminology*, 34(3): 291–306.

Peachey, D.E. (1989) The Kitchener experiment, in M. Wright and B. Galaway (eds) *Mediation and Criminal Justice: Victims, Offenders and Community*. London: Sage.

Pearce, F. (1976) *Crimes of the Powerful*. London: Pluto Press.

Pease, K. (1985) Community service orders, in N. Morris and M. Tonry (eds) *Criminal Justice: An Annual Review of Research*, Vol. 6. Chicago: University of Chicago Press.

Pease, K., Billingham, S. and Earnshaw, I. (1977) *Community Service Assessed in 1976*. Home Office Research Study no. 39. London: HMSO.

Pedersen, W. (2001) Adolescent victims of violence in a welfare state, *British Journal of Criminology*, 41(1): 1–21.

Peelo, M., Stewart, J., Stewart, G. and Prior, A. (1992) *A Sense of Justice: Offenders as Victims of Crime*. Wakefield: Association of Chief Officers of Probation.

Pennell, J. and Burford, G. (1997) *Family Group Decision Making: After the Conference – Progress in Resolving Violence and Promoting Well Being*. Vol. 1. St. John's, Newfoundland: Memorial University of Newfoundland.

Pennell, J. and Burford, G. (2000) Family group decision-making and family violence, in G. Burford and J. Hudson (eds) *Family Group Conferencing: New Directions in Community-Centred Child and Family Practice*. New York: Aldine de Gruyter.

Pennell, J. and Burford, G. (2002) Feminist praxis: making family group conferencing work, in H. Strang and J. Braithwaite (eds) *Restorative Justice and Family Violence*. Cambridge: Cambridge University Press.

Peters, J.J., Meyer, L.C. and Carroll, N.E. (1976) *The Philadelphia Assault Victims Study*. Washington DC: National Institute of Mental Health.

Pizzey, E. (1974) *Scream Quietly or the Neighbours Will Hear*. Harmondsworth: Penguin.

Platt, A. (1975) Prospects for a radical criminology in the USA, in I. Taylor, P. Walton and J. Young (eds) *Critical Criminology*. London: Routledge.

Pocock, S. (1983) *Clinical Trials: A Practical Approach*. Chichester: Wiley.

Pollard, C. (2000) Victims and the criminal justice system: a new vision, [2000] *Criminal Law Review*, 5–17.

Pollard, C. (2001) Restorative justice: justice for the future. Paper presented to the Restorative and Community Justice: Inspiring the Future International Conference, The Guildhall, Winchester, 28–31 March.

President's Commission on Law Enforcement and the Administration of Justice (1967) *The Challenge of Crime in a Free Society: A Report by the President's Commission on Law Enforcement and the Administration of Justice*. Washington DC: US Government Printing Office.

Priestley, P. (1970) *What about the victim?* Regional Information Paper no. 8. London: NACRO.

Priestley, P. (1974) The victim connection and penal reform. Speech to Margery Fry Centenary Proceedings, Bromsgrove, England. Unpublished.

Quinney, R. (1972) Who is the victim?, *Criminology*, November: 309–29.

Raynor, P. (2004, forthcoming) Rehabilitative and reintegrative approaches, in A.E. Bottoms, S. Rex and G. Robinson (eds) *Alternatives to Imprisonment* (provisional title). Cullompton: Willan.

Raynor, P. and Vanstone, M. (2001) Straight thinking on probation: evidence-based practice and the culture of curiosity, in G. Bernfield, P. Farrington and A. Leschied (eds) *Offender Rehabilitation in Practice*. Chichester: Wiley.

Redshaw, J. and Mawby, R. (1996) Commercial burglary: victims' views of the crime and the police response, *International Journal of Risk, Security and Crime Prevention*, 1(3): 185–93.

Rees, J.V. (1994) *Hostages of Each Other: The Transformation of Nuclear Safety after Three Mile Island*. Chicago: Chicago University Press.

Reiss, A. (1970) *The Police and the Public*. New Haven CO: Yale University Press.

Retzinger, S.M. and Scheff, T.J. (1996) Strategy for community conferences: emotions and social bonds, in B. Galaway and J. Hudson (eds) *Restorative Justice: International Perspectives*. Monsey NY: Criminal Justice Press.

Roach, K. (2000) Changing punishment at the turn of the century: restorative justice on the rise, *Canadian Journal of Criminology*, July: 249–80.

Roberts, J. and Roach, K. (2003) Restorative justice in Canada, in A. von Hirsch, J. Roberts, A.E. Bottoms, K. Roach and M. Schiff (eds) *Restorative Justice and Penal Justice: Competing or Reconcilable Paradigms?* Oxford: Hart.

Roberts, S. (1979) *Order and Dispute: An Introduction to Legal Anthropology*. Harmondsworth: Penguin.

Roche, D. (2001) The evolving definition of restorative justice, *Contemporary Justice Review: Issues in Criminal, Social and Restorative Justice*, 4(3–4): 341–53.

Rock, P. (1990) *Helping Victims of Crime: The Home Office and the Rise of Victim Support in England and Wales*. Oxford: Clarendon Press.

Rock, P. (1998) *After Homicide*. Oxford: Clarendon Press.

Rock, P. (2002a) On becoming a victim, in C. Hoyle and R. Young (eds) *New Visions of Crime Victims*. Oxford: Hart.

Rock, P. (2002b) Victims' rights in England and Wales at the beginning of the 21st century, in J. Ermisch, D. Galle and A. Heath (eds) *Social Challenges and Sociological Puzzles*. Oxford: Oxford University Press.

Ruggiero, V. (1999) Offences without offenders, *Criminal Justice Matters*, 35: 27–8.

Ryncarson, E. (1984) Bereavement after homicide: a descriptive study, *American Journal of Psychiatry*, 141: 1452–4.

Ryncarson, E. (1986) Psychological effects of unnatural dying on bereavement, *Psychiatric Annals*, 16: 272–4.

Sanders, A. (1999) *Taking Account of Victims in the Criminal Justice System: A Review of the Literature*. Edinburgh: Scottish Office.

Sanders, A. (2002) Victim participation in an exclusionary criminal justice system, in C. Hoyle and R. Young (eds) *New Visions of Crime Victims*. Oxford: Hart.

Sanders, A. and Young, R. (2000) *Criminal Justice*, 2nd edn. London: Butterworths.

Sanders, A., Hoyle, C., Morgan, R. and Cape, E. (2001) Victim impact statements: don't work; can't work, [2001] *Criminal Law Review*, 447–58.

Schafer, S. (1960) *Restitution to Victims of Crime*. London: Stevens.

Schafer, S. (1968) *Victimology: The Victim and his Criminal*. Reston VA: Reston.

Schafer, S. (1970) Compensation and Restitution to Victims of Crime. Montclair NJ: Patterson Smith.

Scheff, T. (1998) Community conferences: shame and anger in therapeutic jurisprudence, *Revista Juridica Universidad de Puerto Rico*, 67(1): 97.

Scheff, T.J. and Retzinger, S.M. (1991) *Emotions and Violence*. Lexington MA: Lexington Books.

Schiff, M. (2003) Models, challenges and the promise of restorative conferencing strategies, in A. von Hirsch, J. Roberts, A.E. Bottoms, K. Roach and M. Schiff (eds) *Restorative Justice and Penal Justice: Competing or Reconcilable Paradigms?* Oxford: Hart.

Schiff, M. and Bazemore, G. (2002) Restorative conferencing for juveniles in the United States, in E.G.M. Weitekamp and H.-J. Kerner (eds) *Restorative Justice: Theoretical Foundations*. Cullompton: Willan.

Schiff, M., Bazemore, G. and Erbe, C. (2001) Understanding restorative justice: a study of youth conferencing models in the United States. Updated paper presented to the Annual Meeting of the American Society of Criminology, San Francisco, November.

Schwendinger, H. and Schwendinger, J. (1975) Defenders of order or guardians of human rights, in I. Taylor, P. Walton and J. Young (eds) *Critical Criminology*. London: Routledge.

Shapland, J. (1981) Victims, the criminal justice system and compensation. Unpublished report to the Home Office, discussed at p.308 in P. Rock (1990) *Helping Victims of Crime: The Home Office and the Rise of Victim Support in England and Wales*. Oxford: Clarendon Press.

Shapland, J. (1988) Fiefs and peasants: accomplishing change for victims in the criminal justice system, in M. Maguire and J. Pointing (eds) *Victims of Crime: A New Deal?* Milton Keynes and Philadelphia: Open University Press.

Shapland, J. (2000) Victims and criminal justice: creating responsible criminal justice agencies, in A. Crawford and J. Goodey (eds) *Integrating a Victim Perspective within Criminal Justice*. Aldershot: Ashgate Dartmouth.

Shapland, J. (2003) Restorative justice and criminal justice: just responses to crime?, in A. von Hirsch, J. Roberts, A.E. Bottoms, K. Roach and M. Schiff (eds) *Restorative Justice and Penal Justice: Competing or Reconcilable Paradigms?* Oxford: Hart.

Shapland, J. and Bell, E. (1998) Victims in the magistrates' courts and Crown Court, [1998]*Criminal Law Review*, 537–46.

Shapland, J. and Cohen, D. (1987) 'Facilities for victims: the role of the police and the courts', [1987] *Criminal Law Review*, pp. 28–38.

Shapland, J. and Vagg, J. (1988) *Policing by the Public*. London and New York: Routledge.

Shapland, J., Willmore, J. and Duff, P. (1985) *Victims in the Criminal Justice System*. Aldershot: Gower.

Shapland, J., Hibbert, J., I'Anson, J., Sorsby, A. and Wild, R. (1995) *Milton Justice Criminal Justice Audit: Summary and Implications*. Sheffield: Institute for the Study of the Legal Profession on behalf of the Milton Keynes Youth Crime Strategy Group.

Shapland, J., Atkinson, A., Colledge, E. et al. (2002) Evaluating the fit: restorative justice and criminal justice. Paper presented to the Workshop on Restorative Justice, British Criminology Conference, Keele University, 16 July.

Shearing, C. (1994) Participatory policing: modalities for lay participation, *Imbizo*, 2: 5–10.

Sherman, L.W. and Strang, H. (2004) First, do no harm – then begin to heal, *Policy Review*, March: 18–19.

Sherman, L.W., Gottfredson, D., MacKenzie, D. et al. (1997) *Preventing Crime: What Works, What Doesn't, What's Promising*. Report to the US Congress. Washington DC: US Dept of Justice.

Sherman, L.W., Strang, H. and Woods, D.J. (2000) *Recidivism Patterns in the Canberra Reintegrative Shaming Experiments (RISE)*. Canberra: Centre for

Restorative Justice, Australian National University. Also available online at: www.aic.gov.au/rjustice/rise/recidivism/index.html

Sherman, L.W., MacKenzie, D.L. and Farrington, D.P. (2002) *Evidence-Based Crime Prevention*. London: Routledge and Kegan Paul.

Simmons, J. and Dodd, T. (2003) *Crime in England and Wales 2002/2003*. Home Office Statistical Bulletin no. 07/03. London: Home Office.

Simmons, J. et al. (2002) *Crime in England and Wales 2001/2002*. Home Office Statistical Bulletin no. 07/02. London: Home Office.

Sims, L. and Myhill, A. (2000) *Policing and the Public: Findings from the 2000 British Crime Survey*. Home Office Research Findings no. 136. London: Home Office.

Skogan, W. (1981) *Issues in the Measurement of Victimization*. Washington DC: US Department of Justice, Bureau of Justice Statistics.

Smart, C. (1977) *Women, Crime and Criminology*. London: Routledge and Kegan Paul.

Soothill, K. and Soothill, D. (1993) Prosecuting the victim? A study of the reporting of barristers' comments in rape cases, *Howard Journal of Criminal Justice*, 32(1): 12–24.

Soothill, K. and Walby, S. (1991) *Sex Crime in the News*. London and New York: Routledge.

South African Truth and Reconciliation Commission (1998) *The Report of the Truth and Reconciliation Commission*. Available online at: www.truth.org.za/final/execsum.html

South Australia Office of Crime Statistics (1999) *Crime and Justice in South Australia, 1998*. Adelaide: Attorney-General's Department.

Spalek, B. (2001) Regulation, white collar crime, and the Bank of Credit and Commerce International, *Howard Journal of Criminal Justice*, 40: 166–79.

Spalek, B. (2003) Victim work in the probation service: perpetuating notions of an 'ideal victim', in W.H. Chui and M. Nellis (eds) *Moving Probation Forward: Evidence, Arguments and Practice*. Harlow: Pearson Longman.

Sparks, R., Genn, H. and Dodd, D.I. (1977) *Surveying Victims*. Chichester: Wiley.

Stanko, E.A. (1988) Hidden violence against women, in M. Maguire and J. Pointing (eds) *Victims of Crime: A New Deal?* Milton Keynes and Philadelphia: Open University Press.

Stein, M.A. (1960) *The Eclipse of Community: An Interpretation of American Studies*. Princeton: Princeton University Press.

Strang, H., Barnes, G., Braithwaite, J. and Sherman, L. (1999) *Experiments in Restorative Policing: A Progress Report on the Canberra Reintegrative Shaming Experiments (RISE)*. Canberra: Australian National University.

Strang, H. (2001) Justice for victims of young offenders: the centrality of emotional harm and restoration, in A.M. Morris and G. Maxwell (eds) *Restorative Justice for Juveniles: Conferencing, Mediation and Circles*. Oxford: Hart.

Strang, H. (2002) *Repair or Revenge: Victims and Restorative Justice*. Oxford: Clarendon Press.

Stuart, B. (1996) Circle sentencing: turning swords into ploughshares, in B. Galaway and J. Hudson (eds) *Restorative Justice: International Perspectives*. Monsey NY: Criminal Justice Press.

Stubbs, J. (1997) Shame, defiance and violence against women, in S. Cook and J. Bessant (eds) *Women's Encounters with Violence: Australian Experiences*. London: Sage.

Stubbs, J. (2002) Domestic violence and women's safety: feminist challenges to restorative justice, in H. Strang and J. Braithwaite (eds) *Restorative Justice and Family Violence*. Cambridge: Cambridge University Press.

van Swaaningen, R. (1997) *Critical Criminology: Visions from Europe*. London: Sage.

Tarling, R., Dowds, L. and Budd, T. (2000) *Victim and Witness Intimidation: Key Findings from the British Crime Survey*. Home Office Research Findings no. 124. London: Home Office.

Tavuchis, N. (1991) *Mea Culpa: A Sociology of Apology and Reconciliation*. Stanford CA: Stanford University Press.

Taylor, I. Walton, P. and Young, J. (1973) *The New Criminology: For a Social Theory of Deviance*. London: Routledge and Kegan Paul.

Temkin, J. (1987) *Rape and the Legal Process*. London: Sweet and Maxwell.

Titus, R.M. (1999) The victimology of fraud. Paper presented to the Restoration for Victims of Crime: Contemporary Challenges, Australian Institute of Criminology and Victims Referral and Assistance Service Conference, Melbourne, 9–10 September.

Toews, B. and Zehr, H. (2001) Restorative justice and substance abuse: the path ahead, *Youth and Society*, 33(2): 314–28.

Tomkins, S. (1962) *Affect/Imagery/Consciousness*. New York: Springer.

Travis, A. (2003) Bill to help crime victims shelved in favour of legislation on begging, *Guardian*, 10 March.

Trickett, A., Ellingworth, D., Hope, T. and Pease, K. (1995) Crime victimization in the Eighties, *British Journal of Criminology*, 35(3): 343–59.

Tudor, B. (2002) Probation work with victims of crime, in B. Williams (ed.) *Working with Victims of Crime: Policies, Politics and Practice*. London: Jessica Kingsley.

Tutu, D. (1999) *No Future Without Forgiveness*. London: Rider.

Tyler, T.R. (1990) *Why People Obey the Law*. New Haven CT: Yale University Press.

Umbreit, M.S. (1994) *Victim Meets Offender: The Impact of Restorative Justice and Mediation*. Monsey NY: Criminal Justice Press.

Umbreit, M.S. (1996) Restorative justice through mediation: the impact of programs in four Canadian provinces, in B. Galaway and J. Hudson (eds) *Restorative Justice: International Perspectives*. Monsey NY: Criminal Justice Press.

Umbreit, M.S. (1997) Humanistic mediation: a transformation journey of peace-making, *Mediation Quarterly*, 14(3): 201–13.

Umbreit, M.S. and Coates, R.B. (1993) Cross-site analysis of victim-offender mediation in four states, *Crime and Delinquency*, 39: 565–85.

Umbreit, M.S. and Roberts, A. (1996) *Mediation of Criminal Conflict in England: An Assessment of Services in Coventry and Leeds*. St. Paul MN: Centre for Restorative Justice and Mediation, University of Minnesota.

Umbreit, M.S., Bradshaw, W. and Coates, R.B. (1999) Victims of severe violence meet the offender: restorative justice through dialogue, *International Review of Victimology*, 6: 321–43.

Umbreit, M.S., Coates, R. and Kalanj, B. (1994) *Victim Meets Offender: the Impact of Restorative Justice and Mediation*. Monsey NY: Criminal Justice Press.

Umbreit, M.S., Bradshaw, W. and Coates, R.B. (2003) Victims of severe violence in dialogue with the offender: key principles, practices, outcomes and implications, in E.G.M. Weitekamp and H.-J. Kerner (eds) *Restorative Justice in Context: International Practice and Directions*. Cullompton: Willan.

United Nations (1985) *Declaration of Basic Principles for Justice for Victims of Crime and Abuse of Power.* UN Doc A/40/53 (1985) United Nations: Geneva. Also available online at: www.unhcr.ch/

Van Ness, D. (1993) New wine and old wineskins: four challenges of restorative justice, *Criminal Law Forum*, 4(2): 251–76.

Van Ness, D. (1996) Restorative justice and international human rights, in B. Galaway and J. Hudson (eds) *Restorative Justice: International Perspectives.* Monsey NY: Criminal Justice Press.

Van Ness, D. and Crocker, C. (2003) Restorative justice: definition, principles, values and goals. Available online at: www.restorativejustice.org/rj3/RJ_City/01-03/rjcity_defetc.htm (accessed on 13 Oct. 2003).

Van Ness, D. and Strong, K.H. (1997) *Restoring Justice.* Cincinnati OH: Anderson.

Victim Support (1990) Rights and responsibilities, Editorial. *Victim Support*, September.

Victim Support (1995a) *The Rights of Victims of Crime.* London: Victim Support.

Victim Support (1995b) *Codes of Practice.* London: Victim Support.

Victim Support (2001) *Manifesto 2001.* London: Victim Support.

Victim Support (2002a) *Annual Report and Accounts 2002.* London: Victim Support. Also available online at: http://natiasso03.uuhost.uk.uu.net/annual_report/accounts_2002.pdf

Victim Support (2002b) *Criminal Neglect: No Justice Beyond Criminal Justice.* London: Victim Support. Also available online at: http://natiasso03.uuhost.uk.uu.net/neglect/criminal_neglect.htm

Victim Support (2003a) *Annual Report and Accounts 2002.* London: Victim Support. Also available online at: www.victimsupport.org/site_home.html

Victim Support (2003b) *Insult to Injury: How the criminal injuries compensation system is failing victims of crime.* London: Victim Support.

Walby, S. and Allen, J. (2004) *Domestic violence, sexual assault and stalking: findings from the British Crime Survey.* Home Office Research Study no. 276. London: HMSO.

Walgrave, L. (1999) Community service as a cornerstone of a systemic restorative response to (juvenile) crime, in G. Bazemore and L. Walgrave (eds) *Restorative Juvenile Justice: Repairing the Harm of Youth Crime.* Monsey NY: Criminal Justice Press.

Walgrave, L. (2000a) How pure can a maximilist approach to restorative justice remain? Or can a purist model of restorative justice become maximalist?, *Contemporary Justice Review*, 3(4): 415–32.

Walgrave, L. (2000b) Extending the victim perspective towards a systemic restorative justice alternative, in A. Crawford and J. Goodey (eds) *Integrating a Victim Perspective within Criminal Justice.* Aldershot: Ashgate Dartmouth.

Walgrave, L. and Aertsen, I. (1996) Reintegrative shaming and restorative justice: interchangeable, complementary or different?, *European Journal on Criminal Policy*, 4: 67–85.

Walgrave, L. and Geudens. H. (1997) The restorative proportionality of community service for juveniles, *European Journal of Crime, Criminal Law and Criminal Justice*, 4(4): 361–80.

Walker, I. (1979) *The Battered Woman*, New York: Harper and Row.

Walklate, S. (1999) Can there be a meaningful victimology?, *Criminal Justice Matters*, 39: 5–6.

Walklate, S. (2004) Justice for all in the 21st century: the political context of the policy focus on victims, in E. Capes *Reconciling Rights in Criminal Justice: Analysing the Tension between Victims and Defendants*. London: Legal Action.

Walklate, S. and Mawby, R. (1993) A victim oriented criminal justice system. Paper presented to the British Criminology Conference, Cardiff, July.

Wallis, E. (2003) Restorative justice: overview and challenges. Paper presented to the conference on Justice and Balance, Victim, Offender and Community Perspectives, Prague, 15–16 May.

Wasik, M. (1999) Reparation, sentencing and the victim, [1999] *Criminal Law Review*, 470–9.

Watson, D., Boucherat, J. and Davis, G. (1989) Reparation for retributivists, in M. Wright and B. Galaway (eds) *Mediation and Criminal Justice: Victims, Offenders and Community*. London: Sage.

Webber, M.M. (1970) Order in diversity: community without propinquity, in R. Gutman and D. Popenoe (eds) *Neighbourhood, City and Metropolis: An Integrated Reader in Urban Sociology*. New York: Random House.

Weitekamp, E.G.M. (1999) The history of restorative justice, in G. Bazemore and L. Walgrave (eds) *Restorative Juvenile Justice: Repairing the Harm of Youth Crime*. Monsey NY: Criminal Justice Press.

Whitehead, E. (2000) *Key Findings from the Witness Satisfaction Survey 2000*. Home Office Research Findings no. 133. London: Home Office.

Whittaker, Q. (2001) Victims, in K. Starmer, M. Strange and Q. Whittaker with A. Jennings and T. Owen (eds) *Criminal Justice, Police Powers and Human Rights*. London: Blackstone Press.

Widom, C.S. (1991) Childhood victimization: risk factor for delinquency, in M.E. Colton and S. Gore (eds) *Adolescent Stress: Causes and Consequences*. New York: Aldine de Gruyter.

Williams, B. (1996) *Counselling in Criminal Justice*. Buckingham: Open University Press.

Williams, B. (1999a) *Working with Victims of Crime: Policies, Politics and Practice*. London: Jessica Kingsley.

Williams, B. (1999b) The victim's charter: citizens as consumers of criminal justice services, *Howard Journal of Criminal Justice*, 38(4): 384–96.

Williams, D.B. (1972) *Criminal Injuries Compensation*, 2nd edn. London: Waterlow.

Williams, J. and Holmes, K. (1981) *The Second Assault: Rape and Public Attitudes*. Westport CO: Greenwood Press.

Wortman, C.B. (1983) Coping with victimisation: conclusions and implications for future research, *Journal of Social Issues*, 39(2): 195–221.

Wright, M. (1982) *Making Good*. London: Sage.

Wright, M. (1991) *Justice for Victims and Offenders*. Milton Keynes: Open University Press.

Wright, M. (1996) *Justice for Victims and Offenders: A Restorative Response to Crime*, 2nd edn. Winchester: Waterside Press.

Wundersitz, J. and Hetzel, S. (1996) Family conferencing for young offenders: the South Australia experience, in J. Hudson, A. Morris, G. Maxwell and B. Galaway (eds) *Family Group Conferences*. Annadale NSW: Federation Press.

Wykes, M. (2001) *News, Crime and Culture*. London: Pluto Press.

Wynne, J. (1996) Leeds mediation and reparation service: ten years experience of victim–offender mediation, in B. Galaway and J. Hudson (eds) *Restorative Justice: International Perspectives*. Monsey NY: Criminal Justice Press.

Young, J. (1986) The failure of criminology: the need for a radical realism, in R. Matthews and J. Young (eds) *Confronting Crime*. London: Sage.

Young, R. (2000) Integrating a multi-victim perspective into criminal justice through restorative justice conferences, in A. Crawford and J. Goodey (eds) *Integrating a Victim Perspective within Criminal Justice*. Aldershot: Ashgate Dartmouth.

Young, R. (2001) Just cops doing 'shameful' business? Police-led restorative justice and the lessons of research, in A.M. Morris and G. Maxwell (eds) *Restorative Justice for Juveniles: Conferencing, Mediation and Circles*. Oxford: Hart.

Young, R. (2002) Testing the limits of restorative justice: the case of corporate victims, in C. Hoyle and R. Young (eds) *New Visions of Crime Victims*. Oxford: Hart.

Young, R. and Hoyle, C. (2003) New, improved police-led restorative justice? Action research and the Thames Valley Police initiative, in A. von Hirsch, J. Roberts, A.E. Bottoms, K. Roach and M. Schiff (eds) *Restorative Justice and Penal Justice: Competing or Reconcilable Paradigms?* Oxford: Hart.

Young, W. and Morris, A. (1998) Reforming criminal justice: reflecting on the present and imagining the future. Inaugural lecture presented to the International Youth Conference, New Zealand, October.

Zedner, L. (1994) Reparation and retribution: are they reconcilable?, *Modern Law Review*, 57: 228–50.

Zedner, L. (2002) Victims, in M. Maguire, R. Morgan and R. Reiner (eds) *The Oxford Handbook of Criminology*. Oxford: Oxford University Press.

Zehr, H. (1985) *Retributive Justice: Restorative Justice*. Elkhart IN: Mennonite Central Committee, US Office of Criminal Justice.

Zehr, H. (1990) *Changing Lenses: A New Focus for Crime and Justice*. Scottdale PA: Herald Press.

Zehr, H. (2002) *The Little Book of Restorative Justice*. Intercourse PA: Good Books.

van Zyl Smit, D. (1999) Criminological ideas and the South African transition, *British Journal of Criminology*, 39(2): 198–215.

Index of authors

Subject index

N.B. an asterisk * after a page number refers to an entry in the glossary